A PRESENT FOR ALL TIME
A GRANDPARENT'S GIFT OF LOVE

GETTING PAID IN HUGS

JAKE was in the second grade when his parents told him they were throwing a surprise party for his grandpa who would be retiring. On the big day, Jake offered his special present to his grandpa. As Grandpa unwrapped the package, his cheeks grew moist with tears. Jake had given him official business cards with his new title: "Full-time Grandpa." There was no phone or fax number because now his time was his own. There was no business address because his new position didn't require one. Jake said, "Congratulations on your retirement. Now your full-time job is just being my grandpa!" Wiping his tears with his hand, Grandpa asked jokingly, "Well, how much do I get paid?" With his bright eyes expressing total devotion, Jake responded, "As many hugs as you want each day." Beaming with joy, Grandpa hugged Jake and buoyantly replied, "Well, I guess that means I'm a rich man."

❧

"There is a lifetime of wisdom and love compressed in each and every one of Edward Fays's treasured stories. Some of them will make you laugh. Some of them will make you cry. All of them will gently touch the deepest part of your heart."

    —Fr. Medard Laz, **author of** *Love Adds a Little Chocolate*

"Feeling jaded or cynical about the world? This lovely potpourri of heartwarming anecdotes and stories will bring a lump to the throat and a tear to the eye and make you feel good about human nature. Pick it up whenever you feel down."

    —Humphrey Taylor, **chairman, The Harris Poll**

ALSO BY EDWARD FAYS

The Grandparents' Treasure Chest

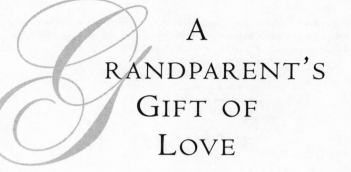

A Grandparent's Gift of Love

*True Stories of Comfort,
Hope, and Wisdom*

Edward Fays

WARNER BOOKS

An AOL Time Warner Company

Some of the individuals in the book have asked me
to respect their anonymity. Therefore, I have
modified their identities and certain
details about them.

Warner Books, Inc., 1271 Avenue of the Americas, New York, NY 10020

Visit our Web site at www.twbookmark.com.

 An AOL Time Warner Company

Printed in the United States of America

First Warner Books Printing: September 2002
10 9 8 7 6 5 4 3 2 1

Library of Congress Cataloging-in-Publication Data
Fays, Edward.
    A grandparent's gift of love: true stories of comfort, hope, and wisdom / Edward Fays.—
Warner Books ed.
      p. cm.
    ISBN 0-446-67857-0
    I. Grandparent and child. 2. Intergenerational relations. I. Title.

HQ759.9 .F394 2002
306.874'5—dc21   2002016823

Book design by Jo Anne Metsch
Cover design by Brigid Pearson
Cover photo by Kaz Mori / Image Bank

CONTENTS

CHAPTER 3 / COURAGE AND SACRIFICE 49
Admiring the strength of the human spirit that endures
tragedy and celebrates triumph

CHAPTER 4 / BELIEVING IN OURSELVES 79
Celebrating the gifts we possess, recognizing what
we are capable of accomplishing, and finding the
boldness to take action

CHAPTER 5 / HOPE AND SPIRIT 97
Finding the faith to guide us through life's darkest
moments

ACKNOWLEDGMENTS

I am deeply grateful and feel fortunate that this book found its way into the caring hands of my agent and friend Stacey Glick. Heartfelt thanks to Stacey and everyone at Jane Dystel Literary Management for nurturing this book and believing in me.

I am indebted to everyone at Warner Books. Thanks especially to my editor, John Aherne, for his passionate response and dedication to the stories in this book. Working with him has taught me that "The editor is always right." Thank you to Megan Rickman who inspired me with confidence, made me laugh when I needed it, and always offered great advice. And genuine appreciation to Amy Einhorn for her foresight and conviction—she turned this manuscript into a book. *Thank you.*

A book that reflects on the wisdom learned from a lifetime of living comes from many personal lessons. I would like to thank the many people from whom I've learned and who have inspired, encouraged, and made me laugh throughout the years: Gary and Linda Thomas, Nick Lombardi, Dan Flora, Martha Sullivan, Lori Baxter—and family, Pete Kressaty—and the whole clan, Craig D'Egidio, Tony Lamanna, Teresa Klein, Lisa Daniele, Steve Dioslaki, Joe Esposito, Schmitty, Danielle

D'Arecca, Gary Cichon, Andrew Duggan, and Mike, Rita, and Alla Ushakov.

To those people who have shared their feelings and inspired these stories. Allow me to share one thing with you . . .

What we share we keep, for it is in sharing that we are enriched. What we keep, we lose, for in keeping we are limited to ourselves. And when we die, all that we are is what we have shared . . .

Due to the unique circumstances with which the idea for this book came about, I'd like to thank the following people:

Jean Moore, for your love and support and for helping Irina and myself make it through such a difficult time. And to everyone at the Marin County and Tiburon Police Departments who worked tirelessly for justice, especially Sergeant Laura Judd, Ted Lindquist, and Paul Haakenson whose talent, skill, and passion humanized the legal system. To Suzi and Dr. Clark, for your wisdom, guidance, and friendship you showed Irina, thank you.

I'd like to recognize my family for their ongoing support and encouragement. Mom, Dad, Mike and Lori, Brian and Karen, and Gram—thank you for always believing in me.

Finally, I'd like to thank my wife, Irina, for her unyielding support, but most of all, for her love and friendship. With her at my side, somehow all things seem possible.

INTRODUCTION

The Compelling Story Behind
A Grandparent's Gift of Love

*U*nique events become etched in our minds and in our hearts—weddings, anniversaries, birthdays, graduations, days when a loved one died, or a life-altering event occurred. Often we share the joy or pain of that day with family, our community, and sometimes even our country. These times compel us to pause and ponder what we gained or what we lost, and reflect on why that particular day marks such a profound turning point in our lives.

July thirteenth is one of those dates for me.

I was sitting in my brick-walled San Francisco office about eleven A.M. when my fiancée, Irina, phoned, letting me know she wasn't feeling well and would be working from home. At the time she was relocating to a three-bedroom apartment with a friend and had scheduled a lunchtime appointment with a man who called about their ad in the classifieds for the third bedroom. She was eager to rent out the space, and I wished her luck before hanging up the phone and getting back to work. There are few moments when a subtle suggestion could alter the course of our lives—the seconds ticking by after that phone call marked one of those times for me, and for her.

Around two P.M. Irina's friend Susan called, telling me to come over to her apartment immediately. "I'm busy right now," I said.

"Eddie, you need to get up here immediately," she commanded. "Irina was attacked by the man who came to see the apartment!"

Like bombs, her words detonated around me. I stood there, slack jawed, paralyzed, gloom creeping over me like a virus. My strength pouring out of me like water through a sieve.

"What?" I shouted, my pulse suddenly racing. *"What happened?"* The combination of shock and concern caused me to hammer my questions into the phone.

"The man she was showing the apartment to attacked her. Now get up here!"

Slamming down the phone, I groped for my keys under a mountain of papers and yellow sticky notes, casting much of them to the floor. I hurtled down the stairs six at a time and dashed out the front door of the building, sprinting up the hill. The appalling look of fright that must have been on my face attracted bizarre glances from tourists strolling through the streets adorned in their San Francisco sweatshirts.

My mind bristled with thoughts of what had happened. *He attacked her! What does that mean?* I leaped into my car and at breakneck speed swerved recklessly through narrow city streets choked with traffic, thoughts of what I would find when I got there pelting me like ice balls in a hailstorm. The red lights were tediously slow and I lay on my horn, flailing my left arm out the window to urge pedestrians to get out of my way. Finally, unleashed from the confines of the swarming city, I sped over the Golden Gate Bridge and for a split second grasped the irony of the situation. Tourists strode lazily along the bridge snapping photos of Alcatraz, the cobalt water of the bay, and the orange towers of the bridge rising boldly into the diamond sky. And I knew that just a few minutes from that scene of tranquillity, my fiancée had endured a horrific experience. I pressed forward, keeping a heavy foot on the gas pedal, the scenery spinning by me in fast-forward.

Irina's new apartment was next door to her friend Susan's, and as I approached my heart galloped in my chest and my palms grew slick with sweat on the steering wheel. Moments after exiting the highway I veered impulsively into the parking lot, screeching to a halt before a barricade of three police cars, a news van, ambulance, and fire truck. That cluster of vehicles relayed the message—the situation was worse than anything I had imagined.

I sprang out of my car and scrambled toward Susan's apartment. Two fully armed police officers standing shoulder-to-shoulder blocked my path.

"Are you Eddie?" asked the stony-faced officer on the right.

"Yes. Yes, I am. What happened?" I urged, my chest heaving deeply.

"Irina was attacked. She's doing okay. You can go see her now." Their shoulders separated as if opening the gate to let me pass. I burst through, bounding up the steps three at a time. I was greeted by two more police officers in the entryway.

"Is your name Eddie?"

"Yes," I said, my mouth arid, pasty as I spoke.

"I'm Sergeant Judd. Irina needs you to be strong now. She's been through a lot," she said in a professional yet thoughtful manner. She prodded the front door open, letting me step inside.

The scent of despair engulfed the room, lying across my shoulders like a slab of concrete. Immediately I saw Irina, the woman I love, squatting on the edge of the couch hugging herself around her waist. The coffee table cluttered with tissues, Irina's tears. Two plainclothes detectives towered above her; another police officer and Susan, her friend, were at her side. I had raced frantically to get there, but at that moment I edged forward cautiously, unsure of what to say and fearing what she would tell me. The left side of her face was crimson, stained with tears. All eyes turned toward me as I inched closer, and I was impaled by a staggering vision. Her right eye was swollen shut, her face severely battered, the vestiges of what happened after coming face-to-face with evil. I couldn't breathe. Feeling like I'd been struck in the stomach with a steel-toed boot, I sipped fast shallow whispers of air, my heart thundering furiously against my chest. Leaping forward, I wrapped my arms desperately around her and we buried our faces, crying together.

Within seconds we lost ourselves, drifting on the periphery, isolated from the rest of the world. She braced her soft finger under my chin, my tears pouring over her trembling hand as she raised my eyes so they gazed directly into hers. I peered searchingly into her eyes, the right one swollen shut and blistering, her skin raw from his violent hands. Her eyes begged to be rescued, for time to be reversed, for this to be just a bad dream.

I swabbed the tears from her left eye; they felt warm, vulnerable. I watched the teardrops trickle down my cheeks, but I could not feel them. My face, my body was numb, as if I were shielding myself from the pain.

"I've never seen you cry before," she said, her voice low and defeated, her lively spirit extinguished.

Speechless, all I could do was hold her, shuddering in disbelief. "What happened?" I asked, mopping the tears from my cheeks with my right shoulder. Her tears erupted again; she clenched her hands in mine, lacing our fingers together, and fought uttering each word, as if she couldn't fathom the truth of what she was saying.

"He tied me up and raped me. He made my worst fears come true."

Her words, anchored by the weight of an abysmal sadness, floated in the air like a cold, still breath. I wanted only to shun them like a trivial comment, as if what she'd said were untrue. But I couldn't do that so I grabbed her words, took them into my heart, and together we cried a raging stream of tears. My skin rippled with chill bumps, like a snake slithering in a burlap sack. The room swirled around me as if I were on a dizzying corkscrew roller-coaster ride that had no end. It was hazy, surreal, and all I could do was hold her and hold on. Guarding her visions and whisking her to a place where evil had been banished and where she felt safe and loved was all I desired. I prayed that she would find it right there, nestled in my arms.

Everyone dispersed, leaving us alone to comfort each other. We talked, cried, hugged, and cried again.

The gummy remnants of duct tape around her wrists, mouth, and neck remained—a vicious reminder of what she had just endured. Few situations in life eclipse all our concerns, forcing us to draw deep from our faith and harness our emotions into surviving that one moment. Together Irina and I were enveloped in a chasm where our minds and hearts were adrift until the subtle interruption of the police sergeant alerted us to the painful reality we had yet to face. It was time for Irina to go to the hospital.

Flanked by two police officers, she was escorted hastily out the front door, a white towel draped over her head concealing her identity from the TV camera. The assault occurred in Tiburon, California, a quaint little town of sweeping hills dotted with lush foliage, picture-frame views of the San Francisco skyline, and hemmed on all sides by the turquoise water of the billowing Pacific. News of this sinister attack spread quickly, jolting everyone living in that normally tranquil community.

The police needed a few words with me, so I stayed and watched transfixed as the ambulance lurched forward, finally vanishing beyond the brow of the hill. "The assailant stole her car and purse. Could you give us a description of the car?" The officer's question tugged on my thoughts like a leash around a dog's neck, yanking me back to reality.

"Yes. I know the car well," I offered, eager to help in any way I could.

During the next few minutes the officers peppered me with standard police procedure questions about the make of the car, the contents of Irina's purse, and other details before letting me rush to the hospital. Upon arriving at the emergency room, I was told that Irina was being treated and to wait. Reeling with nervousness and questions of *What if,* I paced the waiting room, a skittish bundle of nerves. What if I'd told her to wait until later when I could go with her to show the apartment? What if someone had heard her? What if . . . ? What if . . . ? I was talking aloud to myself and could feel people staring at me, wondering what had happened. Their eyes darted away when I glanced in their direction. The clock above the TV read four-oh-six P.M. and I thought of how much had changed in the past couple of hours.

Frenzied, and needing to talk, I called my parents. No cell phone, no change, I dialed collect—a sign that something was wrong. "Dad, oh, Dad."

"Eddie, what happened?" he asked, hearing the devastation in my voice.

"Irina was raped and beaten," I said, panting. "How could this happen? She's kind, gentle, little," I wailed, the tears pouring down my cheeks. Sergeant Judd emerged from behind the ER doors, and I quickly gave my father the name of the hospital, telling him I had to go.

"Irina's parents have been notified," she said, rubbing my left arm. My skin swam with goose bumps as I thought of what they must be feeling living three thousand miles away—*helpless* was the only word that came to mind. I hugged Sergeant Judd, wrapping my arms around her steel-belted body. Her bullet-proof vest felt shocking and rigid against my arms, reminding me of the dangers lurking in society.

Waiting, pacing, impulsively exiting and entering the hospital doors in a vain attempt to escape the vivid images of my imagination and the relentless questions plaguing my mind was how I spent the next three hours. Wrapping my thoughts around what had happened and how together we would make it through tomorrow, next week, and next month was hard, like swallowing a pocketful of spare change. I gagged just thinking about it. And then finally, sometime after seven o'clock that evening, I was allowed in to see her.

She is petite—just five-foot-one—and as I inched toward the room I saw her curled up on the examining table, lying partially under a thick cherry-red blanket. She looked pitiful, her dark brown puppy-dog eyes drooping, her snarled hair lying rumpled over her left cheek, and her toes crimped up in a razor-thin pair of blue plastic clinic slippers. Wearing a scant blue hospital gown, her hands were clenched together and tucked under her chin, and her eye was bandaged. All I wanted was to scoop her up and cuddle her in my arms.

I tiptoed into the room, and before uttering a word she asked in a soft, weary voice, "How are you doing?" Her question knotted my stomach muscles like a rope, forcing a pathetic whimper out of me. I couldn't believe she had asked how *I* was doing when she was the one suffering.

I wheeled a stool over to the bed and dropped down beside her, weaving my fingers into hers. Each moment that ticked by was abrasive, like fingernails scraping along a blackboard. I wondered how many excruciating moments we would endure before things returned to normal, angry with myself for entertaining those thoughts.

I asked about the tests, and she pinched her eyes shut, struggling not to think about their obtrusive nature and the personal questions she had to answer. The nurse popped in to say that Irina was doing great, but she offered those encouraging words more for Irina's benefit than for mine. It didn't matter. As I gazed at her bandaged eye and rubbery pink skin, all I could do was wonder how one person could administer that much pain upon another human being.

The room was eerily silent as feelings of sadness and anger battled for my attention. The stillness of our environment, pierced only by a few tears from one or both of us, was shattered when Sergeant Judd peeked from around the corner, carefully asking if Irina could offer a description of her attacker. She gently nodded. And during the next thirty minutes, as questions about the color of his eyes, the length of his nose, and the structure of his jaw were posed, the predator's face gradually began to form on the computer screen. In the completed sketch he appeared sinister, because I knew the harm he was capable of inflicting. Irina said he had arrived in a clean white car, wearing khakis, a polo shirt, baseball cap, and new sneakers. He joked, appeared friendly—nothing to hint that behind his facade lurked a man with cruel intentions.

After a seven-hour hospital stay Irina returned to the scene of the crime, and with police cameras rolling she gave a painstaking account of what transpired. Feeling slightly embarrassed and wanting to spare me from the appalling details, she asked me to go home and wait for her arrival.

A few minutes past eleven a glistening white police cruiser crept into the driveway, crunching the gravel as the wheels rolled toward the front door. Irina arrived home traumatized, exhausted. Thinking all she wanted was a feathery pillow, her favorite blanket, and some sleep, I escorted her into the bedroom. "I'm starving," she said in a shallow voice, swerving back toward the kitchen.

Rifling through the refrigerator, I found a Tupperware container of fluffy mashed potatoes, the perfect comfort food. Two minutes later the shrill beep of the microwave blared through the kitchen, shattering the stillness surrounding us. "Would you like some butter?" I asked. She nodded, and I slid a knife across the top of the container, letting a curl of butter linger over the mashed potatoes before it plunged into the steaming pile below. It liquefied quickly, and I couldn't help but wonder if that's how Irina felt when she fell under her attacker's violent hands.

"Mashed potatoes are like a warm blanket," she said softly, nibbling tiny bites off the edge of her fork, the bruises to her jaw preventing her from opening her mouth fully. She took her time, eventually wiping the plate clean.

After a steaming shower and the sheltered warmth of her favorite pair of flannel pajamas clinging to her skin, Irina lay down searching for some semblance of peace, desperate to flee from the harsh reality of what occurred that day. But the vision that tormented her appeared on the dark screens of her eyelids each time she tried to sleep. As I lay there holding her, she shared with me the vision she could not escape. . . .

"I was showing him the bedroom," she said in a crackling

voice, "when he reached under the cuff of his pants and pulled out a knife. I screamed at the top of my lungs, but no one could hear me."

There was a sadness in her voice that paralyzed me. Lying there cuddled up under my arms, her legs and feet tucked snugly inside mine, overwrought with the horror she'd experienced that day, she wept. Drawing in hiccupy gulps of air, she cried out, "I can't see anything but him, and I can't feel anything but scared!"

His mocking words echoed in her mind. She was hearing again and again the same chilling voice she heard that afternoon. An evil man telling her what he was about to do to her. Delicately saying she was safe now in my hands had a hollow effect, the shield of fear engulfing her causing my words to echo as if I were yelling down a dark vacant corridor. My mind fumbled for the right thing to say, but it wasn't until I relented, allowing my heart to take control, that the soothing influence I so desperately wanted bubbled to the surface.

To this day I don't know how or why, but I began telling Irina stories about my grandparents, and soon found that the love grandparents are known for began working its magic on her heart and her imagination.

"When we're scared, the best thing we can do is imagine a place where we feel loved—a place of warmth, tenderness, and strength. Boating with my grandfather is one of those memories for me," I whispered. "The two of us floating aimlessly on the lake in an old rowboat pelted with dents. We'd sit out there for hours basking in the warm glow of the sun while our butts grew numb from squatting on those metal seats waiting for the fish to tug on our lines. He'd talk about life, the lessons he learned, his experiences, and what leads to happiness."

I wrapped my arms broadly around her, and she murmured, "I needed a hug like this one."

"My grandma taught me the art of hugging," I said with a sad smile. "She told me the secret ingredients are squeezing and tenderness—making sure your hugs have just the right amount of each.

"When we're scared, one of the best things we can do is laugh, because there's no room for fear in a smiling heart," I said. "Did I ever tell you about the time when I was a boy and screamed because I came face-to-face with my grandfather's false teeth? He accidentally left them in a glass of water on the kitchen table."

Irina chuckled, her body quaking slightly under my arms, and the sharp claws of fear began to relinquish their grip on her imagination. My simple tales kindled the memories of her own grandparents, and as she began talking about them, the tender, affectionate visions of her grandma and grandpa replaced the vicious images of her attacker. Thinking of her own grandparents, the sacrifices they had made and the obstacles they overcame, reminded her of simpler times, all the things she had yet to experience, and that anything is possible. Those thoughts began to fortify her spirit, giving her strength and hope when she needed them most. She reflected that her life might have ended that day. But she had survived, and lying there that night, as her panicked breathing subsided, she took the first steps toward acquiring an appreciation for life that comes only from facing your own mortality.

The essence and love of our grandparents enveloped us that night, enabling Irina to fall asleep peacefully despite the ghastly encounter she had faced that day. As she drifted off, I lay mystified at the soothing effect the memory and wisdom of our grandparents had on her during such a traumatic time. *What did other grandparents have to share that could enlighten and inspire people of all ages and under any of life's circumstances? What stories could people share who were dramatically influenced by a grandparent or significant elder?* I wondered.

Convinced that people from all walks of life would embrace a book of stories brimming with love, wisdom, sacrifices, and guidance from society's most experienced members, I began my search for the stories that fill the book you now hold in your hands.

The two-year anniversary of that day has passed. Irina has proven herself a poster child for possessing courage and gallantly conquering extreme adversity. On the first anniversary of her attack, instead of sitting around thinking of what had happened the year before, she decided to face fear on her own terms. She went skydiving. A symbol stating, *I am not beaten and refuse to live my life in a protective shell, fearful of the things I may face in this world.*

On the second anniversary, I accompanied her atop the South Tower of the Golden Gate Bridge, one thousand feet above the vast Pacific. Together we soaked up the spellbinding view, thankful that she was still alive, that we had each other, and that we were fortunate enough to live in such a magnificent environment. Standing there, a jerky breeze swirling around me, I gazed down at the tourists strolling carelessly along the bridge snapping pictures of Alcatraz and gazing at the bright orange towers rising boldly into the turquoise sky. I recalled the day two years earlier, overcome with gratitude that although Irina says a part of her died that day, she is still the same woman I grew to love. And as I watched her gasping in awe at the splendor of the bay and the panoramic view, I smiled, thrilled that her childlike spirit and zest for living still shone brightly.

Irina's attacker was captured five days after the crime was committed. The detailed sketch Irina gave of him appeared in newspapers throughout California and was the critical factor in bringing him to justice. He pleaded guilty eighteen months later and was sentenced to 251 years in prison. It was his third strike in a string of violent crimes and warranted the life sentence. On the day of sentencing, with her attacker outfitted in maroon prison fatigues, his arms and legs in shackles, Irina boldly stood before a packed courtroom and gave an emotionally charged speech, saying . . .

"I have turned many stones—trying to explain it, trying to make sense. But what happened to me is a senseless act. A part of me still feels scared—when riding alone in an elevator with a strange man my imagination sometimes gets the best of me. Every day I live with the memory of what happened, but I will not let it beat me. I will think of him every day for the rest of my life. My bad days don't seem as bad any longer, and on my best days I sometimes cry, remembering what he did to me and feeling thankful that I survived. I understand just how precious life is and that each moment is a gift I must use to the fullest."

Time; and the love she receives from her family, friends, and myself; and the stories of courage, sacrifice, and hope within this book have helped her to heal. There will never be closure, but she understands that if you are willing to make it happen, something good can arise from the ashes of life's traumatic events.

Today Irina and I are happily married. On the day of our wedding, as we stood before family and friends, I gazed into her eyes and thought of all we had been through together. *She was right*, I said to myself; standing there about to exchange vows, I thought of the day she was attacked, but my spirits were not dampened. Instead, I felt more grateful then ever, knowing that we had each other and since we had made it through that traumatic ordeal there was nothing we couldn't handle as long as we had each other.

Perhaps the best we can do is try to benefit from all our life experiences and learn from the insights of those who came before us to help enrich our community, our nation, and possibly even our world. And to always live by the philosophy, *It's not what happens to you, it's what you do with it that makes all the difference.*

Edward Fays

A GRANDPARENT'S GIFT OF LOVE

CHAPTER ONE

EMBRACING EVERY STAGE OF LIFE

Recognizing the beauty in each season of life and moving toward it with childlike curiosity and hopeful anticipation

Why do so many of us fear the aging process? As life moves forward, some doors close forever while new doors open, ready to provide us with fresh adventures that will hopefully enrich our lives even further. Welcoming each year with verve, by anticipating who we'll meet and all that we'll learn, is the finest way to live. Our life is a book that we write as we go along, and like any book, we must strive to make it interesting and, of course, make it complete.

Excuse Me, Mister, but Why
Are You So Wrinkled?

A little elementary school was set on a small parcel of land, complete with jungle gym and basketball hoop. From the school playground you could see the front porch of a nearby senior center. The kids were always too busy playing to pay any attention to the center, but many of the seniors delighted in watching the kids frolic in the schoolyard.

One day Ms. Valentine, the first-grade teacher, noticed the seniors watching the children and thought it would be a good idea to bring them together. So early one morning the following week, the children were escorted hand-in-hand out the door of their classroom, through the playground, beyond the school fence, and over to the senior center.

The students were allowed to mingle if they liked, and some were introduced to residents of the center. Remmy Evans, an enterprising little boy, was strolling around as if he were sizing everyone up when he spotted an older gentleman outfitted in a checkered flannel shirt and sky-blue baseball cap sitting off in the corner. Their eyes met, and the man waved Remmy over. "Hello, I'm Mr. Royce," said the man, extending his hand as if they were about to engage in a business meeting.

Remmy observed Mr. Royce's hand curiously and said, "Excuse me, mister, but why are you so wrinkled?"

Mr. Royce laughed heartily and said, "Now, that is a very good question. Would you really like to know?"

"Sure," replied Remmy.

"What's your name?" asked Mr. Royce.

Remmy hopped up on a chair and said, "My name is Remmy Theodore Evans. But most people just call me Remmy."

"Well, Remmy, let me tell you the story about wrinkles. Most people think wrinkles are a sign of age, but they're really a sign of use. When you're wrinkled, like me, it means you have lived a full life. It means you have more memories than most people do. I'll show you what I mean. How many times has Santa Claus visited your house?"

Remmy scratched his head, and his eyes rolled back before he finally responded. "Well, I'm six, but I can only remember the last couple of years, and Santa Claus came those times."

"So you know for sure that Santa Claus visited your house at least twice?" asked Mr. Royce.

"Yeah, that's right," replied Remmy.

"Listen to this," announced Mr. Royce. "Santa Claus has visited me eighty-nine times!"

Remmy's eyes opened wide, and with his mouth gaping he declared, "Wow! You must have a lot of great toys!"

"I did," said Mr. Royce, laughing. "Many of them are old now, like me."

"But when toys get old they don't get wrinkled," remarked Remmy.

Mr. Royce chuckled and said, "That's right. Instead they get chipped paint and broken pieces. It's kind of the same thing. The same way toys get used, people's bodies get used. Toys get old because we use them. My body is old and wrinkled because

I used it. Do you have an old toy that doesn't work well any-more?"

"Yeah, a couple of them," replied Remmy.

"Well, that's the way my body is now. Do you remember having fun playing with those toys?"

"Yeah! My best friend, Ronnie, would come over, and we would play with them a lot," Remmy said excitedly.

"So you have happy memories playing with your old toys, even though they don't work too well anymore?"

"I sure do, but I like my new ones, too."

"What if you never played with your old toys?" asked Mr. Royce. "They might still be like new, but you wouldn't have fun memories of playing with them, right?"

"I guess you're right."

"Which would you rather have, the good times playing with your friend or your old toys looking like new?"

Without hesitation Remmy exclaimed, "The fun with my friend! We laughed a lot."

"That's the same way I feel about my body," explained Mr. Royce. "I had fun in my life and did a lot of exciting things. If I wanted to protect my body and try to keep it looking like new, I would have missed out on some great times. The same thing goes for you and your toys. If you leave all your toys in the box and never play with them, they'll never get old and break, but you'll never have any fun with them either. Have you ever skinned your knee?"

"Yeah, look!" Remmy rolled his pants leg up over his right knee, proudly displaying a wound from the playground.

"That's okay," said Mr. Royce. "You're using your body and having fun. I had a lot of bumps and bruises in my life. I usu-ally got them while I was doing something I liked. It was worth getting a bump on the knee. The same way using a toy until it breaks is okay, because you enjoyed playing with it." With a concerned look on his face, Mr. Royce asked, "Am I making sense?"

"I get it," obliged Remmy. "I was having fun when I skinned my knee."

Mr. Royce smiled and continued. "When a baby is born, she's soft and smooth because she's new. But she also hasn't had any fun yet. She doesn't have any memories of playing with her friends either. But as she grows, she'll have fun, make memories with her friends, and, sure enough, skin her knee. When she gets old, like me, she'll have wrinkles, too.

"So now do you know why I have all these wrinkles?"

"Yeah!" said Remmy. "You're all used up!"

Laughing boisterously, Mr. Royce confessed, "Yes, that's a big part of it. I've also got wrinkles because I've lived a long time and had a *lot* of fun. I like to think of each wrinkle as a great memory."

"You must be really happy," declared Remmy.

With a nostalgic look on his face, Mr. Royce responded, "I certainly am, son. I certainly am."

As Ms. Valentine called for the students to say their good-byes, Mr. Royce reached out his wrinkled hand to say farewell, but Remmy didn't shake it. Instead he gave Mr. Royce an affectionate hug and ran off to join his classmates. A flurry of distant memories flashed through Mr. Royce's mind, and his eyes prickled with tears. He was delighted with the new memory he and Remmy had just created. He hoped it would be one Remmy would think of someday, many years from then, when he had wrinkles, too.

Inspired by Anita Hart

When There Are No Words to Say . . .

*S*he stood there shivering, raking her fingers over her head, strands of hair falling onto the sink; some snared under her nails. Her nerves were frayed, a violin string stressed to the breaking point. The wind and rain fueled the intensity of the moment, beating against the glass like an intruder trying to force his way inside.

I stood off in the corner, silently, out of sight. My eyes beaded with tears as I gazed at her, trying to comprehend what she was thinking. But how could I understand, even though I desperately wanted to? How could I possibly know what it felt like to be moments away from beginning a second round of chemotherapy treatments?

Standing there, I recalled the day more than a year earlier when she had first gotten the diagnosis. It was summer, one of those mornings when you step outside and are smacked by the sumptuous bouquet of flowers in bloom. We had planned on playing tennis that morning, but the phone rang, changing our lives forever. I walked inside, my cheery smile and sprightly colored yellow-and-white tennis outfit in stark contrast to the moment. She was sitting at the table, her face whitewashed, her hands fidgety. "I have cancer," she said crisply, so I would hear it the first time, so she wouldn't have to repeat those stinging words. The fresh-scented summer morning suddenly turned to gloom. "They want me to come in next week to discuss treatment options," she continued. "I just went in for my annual checkup the other day, and now they want to talk with me about treating cancer. My God!"

We made it through that morning, sharing our fears, which somehow made us both feel a little less frightened. We rode a tidal wave of emotions, crying together one minute and then convincing ourselves that she could beat the disease. The two of us shared our grief alone before sharing the news with family and friends.

She endured the chemotherapy treatments with bravery, losing more than fifteen pounds and most of her hair in the process. I had never bought her a hat before, but I purchased three in the next year. Once, as I placed a hat on the counter and handed my credit card to the saleslady, I broke down crying.

Then some good news came. Finally. The treatments worked. *They got the enemy,* I thought to myself. Thank you, God. It took some adjusting, but life got back to normal, that chapter of our lives behind us. Her hair grew back, she gained some weight, and we resumed our weekly tennis match. The hats she'd worn were happily stored in a box and stuffed in the closet of the spare bedroom. But now, in the time it takes to answer a phone call, a frightening new chapter has begun.

Standing there in the corner I asked myself, *What can I say to her?* I have asked that excruciating question a thousand times, and I asked it again. But at that moment, as she delicately caressed her cheeks and glared deep within herself, I realized that no word has been coined that can encompass a person's feelings. So hugs were invented instead. One loving embrace speaks volumes, so that's what I did.

I walked over silently, closed my eyes, and hugged her. I hugged my twenty-five-year-old granddaughter with all the love I had in my heart and soul, and then I accompanied her to the hospital.

Inspired by ROSALIE PACKARD

· · · · · · · · · · · · · · · ·

Getting Paid in Hugs

*J*ake was in the second grade when his parents told him that his grandpa would be retiring after working at the same company for forty years. With a look of amazement on his face, Jake said, "I'm only seven, so that means Grandpa has been there . . ." He thought for a second and finally exclaimed, "A really long time!"

His parents chuckled and said, "Yes, Grandpa has worked there a long time, and that's why we are throwing him a surprise party."

Jake loved his grandpa very much and wanted to do something special for the occasion. He offered to help with the party plans but was told that all the arrangements had been made. Undaunted, Jake knew there must be some way he could show his grandpa how much he was appreciated and congratulate him on his retirement.

Jake remembered the business card his grandpa had given him a couple of years earlier. It was wedged within the mirror's wooden frame in his bedroom, between a two-dollar bill and a picture of him and his dad on the Ferris wheel at the church carnival. He scrambled up the stairs and into his room. Taking the tattered card in his hand, he realized that his grandpa would no longer have that position. *Positions are good*, he thought, so he decided to create a new one for his grandpa. Jake told his parents about the idea, and they said it was wonderful.

When the big day came, Jake was ready. A collection of different-size boxes, all beautifully wrapped, were placed on a gift table—that is, all except for Jake's. He didn't want to include his gift with the others, so he carried it around with him the entire evening.

He watched his grandpa open the other gifts, "oohing" and "aahing" at each one. He wanted his gift to be the last one Grandpa opened, so as the evening drew to a close, he took his grandpa's hand and ushered him over to a chair in the corner, away from the crowd.

"I've got something for you, Grandpa," Jake stated with pride, offering up the gift.

With that, his grandpa propped Jake up on his left knee and declared, "Well, this sure is a beautifully wrapped present. Did you do this all by yourself?"

"Kind of," Jake replied, shrugging his shoulders. "Mom helped me a little."

Grandpa smiled. "Well, it looks wonderful. May I open it now?"

Jake enthusiastically nodded his head.

As Grandpa unwrapped the package, his cheeks grew moist with tears. Jake had given him the greatest gift he could have ever asked for: official business cards with his new title: FULL-TIME GRANDPA. There were no phone or fax numbers because now his time was his own. There was no business address because his new position didn't require one. Jake gazed lovingly into his grandpa's eyes and said, "Congratulations on your retirement. Now your full-time job is just being my grandpa!"

Holding one of the cards between his right thumb and

index finger and wiping his tears with the back of his hand, Grandpa asked jokingly, "Well, how much do I get paid?"

With his bright blue eyes expressing total devotion, Jake responded, "As many hugs as you want each day."

Beaming with joy, Grandpa gave Jake an affectionate hug and buoyantly replied, "Well, I guess that means I'm a rich man."

Inspired by BEN STEWART

Quite an Accomplishment

He hurried through the parking lot seconds after the bell rang signaling the end of the school day. The knapsack dangling from his left hand skipped along the ground. It had been seven long hours since he'd seen his mommy, so he was ecstatic. Once kisses were exchanged, she said they had to stop by her patient's house to drop off some medication for the evening nurse.

When they arrived, the little boy was introduced to his mom's patient—a sullen, crusty old man intently watching the Food Network with a rainbow-checkered quilt draped over his legs. The little boy's mom said she needed to talk with the other nurse and that she'd be back in a moment. The old man and the little boy glanced at each other, neither of them knowing quite what to say. The little boy looked around the room. He gazed over at the TV, an old shelf sagging from the weight of too many books, and a rumpled bed. Looking back at the old man, he asked curiously, "Did you just get out of bed?"

The old man scrunched the tuft of his eyebrows, peered at the boy, and in a disgruntled voice said, "Yeah. Why?"

"Well, it's almost dinnertime," replied the boy. "Didn't you do anything today?"

"Yeah, I got out of bed," declared the old man.

"That's it?" asked the boy, obviously unimpressed.

The old man focused his eyes, stuck out his gray stubbled chin, and said, "Hey, at ninety-six, that's quite an accomplishment."

Inspired by MAUREEN GALLOW

A Night to Remember

I spotted her at the Silver Fox's dance. A real looker. Usually the ladies there didn't arouse much enthusiasm in me, but she was like a brilliant rose in full bloom. Her eyes were gray-blue and matched the color of my titanium cane perfectly. She caught me looking at her and gave me a demure smile. I got the hint—it was time to make my move.

I sauntered across the floor as well as anyone can with a cane, but she seemed to like my confident swagger. Her smile got bigger as I approached. I said, "Hello, my name is Elvis."

"Really?" she replied. "Well, let me see you gyrate those hips."

"I can't. I just had hip-replacement surgery," I said. She laughed at my joke. Things were looking good.

We chatted for a while. Getting to know someone is much easier when your life has some history—there's simply more to tell. When you're young and someone says, "So, tell me about yourself," what is there to say? "I live with my parents and can't wait to go away to college." But when you're older, there's a whole treasure trove of things to discuss—children, grandchildren, career, travel, outlooks on living, and what's happening in the world. It's very engaging.

So we sat and talked. Her name was Rebecca and I finally told her my real name, Francis. It was a glorious evening. We enjoyed clever conversation and danced the night away. We laughed when a gentleman on the dance floor tried a courageous maneuver, something out of *Saturday Night Fever,* and couldn't get back up. Luckily, dance guards were standing by to rescue him. They're the equivalent of lifeguards at the beach; they help people on the dance floor who get in over their heads, so to speak.

Rebecca and I were both widowed. We each had family, but were lonely for something else: romance, intimacy, and—okay, I'll come right out and say it. Sex!

We strolled outside that night gazing at the stars, enjoying the crisp evening air and holding each other's hands. It was magical. I can't explain it other than saying that it just felt right. Perhaps I'm stepping out on a limb but I think I can speak for both of us when I say we fell in love that night, under the stars.

Standing there that evening, gazing into each other's eyes, I felt compelled to softly kiss her. I was about to take the plunge when an ambulance barreled into the parking lot, stopping abruptly at the entrance. Turns out it was nothing serious. Somebody spiked the punch bowl and someone else drank a little too much punch. I had to wait until the mayhem subsided before I could finally kiss her, but it was worth it. "The night was still and the world was ours," as they say in those old movies, but that's just how it felt. It had been years since I'd held a woman's face gently in my hand and graced her lips with mine and it was wonderful. And when I kissed her, I knew it was meant to be. She left me breathless.

Rebecca and I have been inseparable since that magnificent evening. We share a place together and not long ago I asked for her hand in marriage. She tearfully accepted and I am proud to say that my twenty-four-year-old grandson, Francis, will stand beside me as my best man. He has always been my best man, but on that wonderful day we'll make it official.

Life holds so many hidden treasures and true love is the greatest gift we can experience. There was a time when I wondered if I'd spend the rest of my life recalling the memories of my lost love. Those are days I will always cherish, but I am delighted to say I'm in love again, and it feels fabulous.

Inspired by FRANCIS HARMOND

The Perfect Moment

W hat will I know ten years from now that I don't know yet?" I peered at my grandpa Red Bart, eagerly anticipating his answer.

He took his time, savoring the first bite from an enormous slice of New York pizza and wiping his mouth with a crumpled napkin before he winked at me, smiled, and said, "That's a good question coming from a six-year-old with a mouth full of pizza. But that's for me to know and for you to find out."

"Come on, Gramps," I said, utterly disappointed. "Can't you tell me anything else?"

"All right, what would you like to know?"

"I'm not sure, that's what I'm asking you. What do sixteen-year-olds know that I don't yet?"

"Have you ever seen a sunrise early in the morning, just when it's peeking over the mountaintop?"

"On the bus ride to school I see it sometimes, shining in my window."

"That's what it's like to be sixteen," he said, dropping his folded slice of pizza onto a grease-stained paper plate. Gramps spread his arms out wide and said, "It's the age when people are beginning to understand the world. All the years leading up to sixteen are preparing you for that moment when you finally get a glimpse at life's possibilities. Your sun is rising from the day you are born, but you're protected under the shadow of your mom and dad until you're old enough to step out and begin exploring the world yourself."

"It sounds like sixteen-year-olds have a lot to do. What's it like to be twenty-five?"

"Sixteen is when the sun just begins peeking over the mountaintop, and twenty-five is when it's high in the eastern part of the sky, but still rising. It's warm and hasn't reached its highest temperature yet. Its full potential. Twenty-five is when people are out on their own and, like the sun, trying to rise and shine in a very competitive and complex world. Many twenty-five-year-olds are working hard at a new career. Others are still in school. The good part is at twenty-five you're an adult, so your mom and dad can't tell you what to do anymore. The bad part is they don't wash your clothes or make your dinner anymore either."

"You mean I have to cook my own food and clean my own underwear? I don't know if I like twenty-five. What's forty like?"

"By forty years old you probably will be married and have a boy just like you running around the house."

"Well, that's good. That way I'll have someone to cook and clean for me. Forty may be really old but it sounds good so far."

"Hold on, I'm not finished yet," Red Bart said, his voice charged with laughter. "Forty years old can be compared to the sun when it's highest in the sky, at its most influential. That's when people look up to it for warmth and guidance, like you do now with your mom and dad. Just like the sun at its peak, people in their forties have a great deal of responsibility—a house and cars to pay for and children like you who remain protected in their shadows. They also have demanding careers requiring plenty of time and attention. People in their forties, like the sun towering in the sky, can survey everything, and because of that they must learn to balance more responsibilities than most people. That means husband and wife have to chip in and help each other, throw one another's underwear in the wash every once in a while. Do you understand?"

"Yeah, but I think it's easier if I just make a lot of money and hire someone to clean my clothes. Don't you think? What's it like to be sixty?"

"Well, I'm not quite there yet, but I'll tell you what my life is like today. Have you ever seen the sun on a lazy summer's day when it's starting to sink just a little bit in the horizon?"

"Yeah, Gramps, it's bright orange a lot of the time."

"That's right. The sun has cooled off. It's no longer a blazing yellow ball of fire burning in the sky. Now it's slowing down, surveying all the things that have benefited from its hard work during the course of the day. People in their sixties feel the same way. Their ambition doesn't burn as hot as it once did. They prefer to look back and behold all the love they've shone on others and the lives they helped spring forth. People enjoy watching the sun dip lower in the sky because it has a certain wisdom, like it's done the work it set out to do and now it can rest. It's a cozy time of day and a cozy time of life. That's how I feel, like a warm orange sun that has worked hard and can enjoy the fruits of my labor. Like sitting here with you, eating pizza."

"Is there a time when everything is perfect, Gramps? An age where people can have everything they ever wanted? That's what I want to know, what age does that happen?"

"There is no perfect age where everything will go your way,

little guy. When the sun slides across the sky there are moments when it hits your eye just right, like a big pizza pie, That's Amore!"

"What? What are you talking about, Grandpa?"

"What I mean is that there are no perfect sunrises or sunsets, but there *are* moments when the sun's rays will hit you just right, making everything sparkle. That, my boy, happens at every age, making you happy that you're right there, able to enjoy that period in time.

"That's the closest thing I've ever found to a perfect moment. And if you're lucky like me, you'll have lots of them sprinkled throughout the course of your life."

Inspired by BART COLUCCI

A New Father's Confusion

$\mathcal{M}$y parents got my wife, Vickie, and me a Diaper Genie for our baby shower. They watched delighted as my wife peeled off the pastel wrapping and leaped from her seat when she saw what they had given us.

I glanced over at my father, hands open on my lap. "It's a Diaper Genie," he said, as if I should know. "Man's greatest invention. I just wish they were around when you were a kid. You stank to the high heavens!"

He smiled, got up, and popped the seal on a fresh can of Diet Coke. I still wasn't quite sure what it was but thought that any more questions might make me look stupid, so I just smiled and acted surprised when my wife opened up the next gift. A potty trainer. The Diaper Genie sat off in the corner of the baby's room for a while until my wife came home one day and smelled something awful fluxing throughout the house.

"What is that foul odor?" she said, her nose and lips scrunched up into one little spot in the center of her face.

"The baby's diaper, honey," I said. "Have a little compassion. Sheesh! He can't help it."

"What did you do, hang it up next to a fan?"

Chuckling, I said, "No, I put it in the trash in the bathroom. I meant to throw it outside but I forgot. I'll do it now."

"No," she said, looking at me only the way a loving wife could look at her husband. Like I'm cute and an idiot all at the same time. "The dirty diapers go in the Diaper Genie," she continued, pointing to the curious contraption in the corner. "It's a receptacle for diapers. It locks in the odor."

My first thought was Tupperware, and how that locks in freshness. Not a good association. Plopping down in my chair, I realized the baby opened me up to a bold new world. I felt comfortable tinkering with the car or painting a bedroom . . . but diapers and formula? I needed to consult with an expert.

"Hello, Dad?" He knew about Diaper Genies, so I figured he must have a good handle on the things every new father should know, like how to stay out of trouble with my wife and how to keep the house smelling "Mountain Fresh." I read that on a box of carpet deodorizer and for some reason it stuck with me.

"Dad," I said, "I'm in a bit of a jam here, could use your help. It used to be when I went out I grabbed my jacket and left. Now, with the baby, there are diapers, formula, little towels, toys, and he's always got to be bundled up no matter what the temperature. I feel like I'm doing laundry twenty-four seven and am confusing his pajama bottoms with my socks. They're about the same size. Also, I just got up to speed on the Diaper Genie. And now that I know what it is, let me say, many thanks. That will certainly come in handy."

"George," he said, his belly laugh coming over the phone loud and clear, "motherhood comes naturally to women. For men, fatherhood creeps along and gets there in its own good time. That's usually because the men would rather the women do the dirty work. Plus, men get confused. There'll be times when your wife and the baby will be crying at the same time and you'll just want to stick your head in the freezer. Now, remember, they'll be crying for different reasons. The baby will be hungry, and Vickie, she'll wonder about your common sense and why you threw the diaper in the trash rather than in the Diaper Genie."

"She told you about that?"

"Yeah. She called us a little while ago. We had a good laugh at your expense. Now, seriously, the most important thing a new father needs is patience and understanding. Much of being a good parent comes naturally, but details—like making sure you bring everything the baby needs when you take a trip—you will learn them over time. At first you'll pack every conceivable thing just to be on the safe side. That's why people with babies don't leave home; it's too much trouble. Remember, you've already got the most important ingredient for being a good parent."

"The Diaper Genie?" I said jokingly.

"No. Love," he said. "When you were a baby your mother bundled you up even inside the house, nervous about you catching a cold. The doctor—they still made house calls in those days—came over and said, 'Give this kid some air! What are you trying to do, bake him? He feels like a wet loaf of bread.' Even your mom, who is a great mother, needed to learn, and you will, too. That's part of the fun of parenting. And when your son gets older you'll have to figure out what the rules are in your house. But for right now, just play and make sure you put those diapers in the Diaper Genie. It locks in the odor, you know. Kind of like Tupperware locks in freshness."

"Yeah, Dad, I know. Thanks for the advice." I hung up the phone and stood there shaking my head, grinning. It dawned on me why kids have grandparents. New parents, like me, are only beginning our education. We're in "Parenting First Grade." Wondering if the formula is the right temperature, if the diaper is on securely, when we're being too neurotic, and if reading Shakespeare to our two-week-old child is actually going to enhance his IQ. Grandparents, however, have Ph.D.s in parenting, plus invaluable firsthand experience.

These days I'm beginning to figure out my son's patterns. When he sleeps, when he gets hungry, and when he, well . . . you know. Anticipating everything helps me feel more secure and in my wife's eyes, I really know what I'm doing. But every once in a while my son will throw me a curveball. Sometimes I can handle them; other times I call my mom and dad, his grandparents, and get some seasoned advice. Then I gaze at my son lying in the crib, grabbing his short pudgy toes with his plump tiny fingers, an innocent smile on his face, and think, *What an awesome responsibility. Thanks for the guidance, Mom and Dad. Thanks for being my child's grandparents.*

Inspired by GEORGE MCKINLEY

CHAPTER TWO

POWER OF LOVE

Inviting people to enter our hearts completely
and showing them just how vital
they are in our lives

When discussing the topic of love, I saw some people
reveling in happiness and others swept away by
feelings of sadness. I realized that love is the source of
our most splendid joys and our deepest sorrows . . .
and that none of us can live without it. Within these
stories the extraordinary power of love is revealed
from many perspectives, compelling us to be more
sensitive and open to expressing our true feelings to
the people we keep closest to our hearts.

So Long for Now

*I*t was one of those weeklong trips that seemed to end before it really got started. My bags were packed and sitting on the front porch. I didn't feel like lugging them through the rain and into the car. It was the closing moments of a visit to my folks' house, and I could see the sadness in my mother's eyes and my dad starting to get sentimental. I lived three thousand miles away, and good-byes are never easy. In the next few minutes, I would learn that my grandma dislikes saying good-bye so much that she invented a creative way to avoid the feelings of sorrow that accompany those moments.

My grandma stays with my parents for a few months at a time. Ever since she retired, she's had the funny habit of staying up half the night and sleeping late the following morning. She likes to watch Jay Leno and American Movie Classics into the wee hours. At three in the morning, when she finally gets tuckered out, she tediously climbs the stairs and crawls into bed. I don't think she has seen a sunrise in fifteen years.

Just before it was time for me to go, I went to say my good-byes. It was around twelve-thirty in the afternoon when I discreetly stepped into my grandma's bedroom. There she was, sitting in a wintry pink nightgown with her head bowed slightly and rosary beads draped in her hands. Her hair was still wispy from being slept on, and the wrinkled skin of her arms confirmed her age. I apologized for the intrusion, and she welcomed me anyway. "I'm praying," she said softly. "I pray every morning when I get up."

I chuckled, recalling the time.

I sat on the edge of the bed, and, with the rosary beads in her right hand, she gently touched my face. "You're a good boy," she said with a droopy smile.

"I'm in my thirties, Grandma," I replied, trying to convey that I was a man, not a boy.

She shunned my comment with the wave of her hand and said, "Ah, to me you'll always be a good boy."

"I think about Grandpa often," I expressed delicately.

She looked at me sadly and responded, "I know you do, honey. I pray to him every morning and let him know you think of him. I pray for you and your brothers and tell Grandpa how well you are all doing. Grandpa and I were looking forward to spending more time with the family, but I guess it wasn't meant to be. Sometimes I wonder why God took him so soon."

"Grandma," I whispered, "I would love to talk more, but I have to go."

She shook her head gingerly and said, "I know, I know. Our lives are so different. You have so many places to be and get so many phone calls each day. I have no appointments and hardly ever get any phone calls anymore."

I hugged her and said, "Good-bye."

"Good-byes are too permanent," she countered. "I like to say, 'So long for now.' That means that we'll see each other again soon."

So we hugged again and said, "So long for now."

I walked to the door and turned to see her one more time.

There she was, a gentle woman wearing an old pink nightgown and smiling. The love in her eyes told the story. I could sense a hint of sadness, a readiness to depart from the world and take her place in heaven, next to my grandpa.

"I love you," I said, and trotted down the stairs. When I got to the bottom step I looked up and pictured her sitting in that chair. Head bowed, eyes closed, hair wispy, skin wrinkled, heart filled with love. *No appointments today,* I thought to myself. *I hope this isn't the last time I see you, Grandma. From now on, I'll have to make each "so long" count, because one of these times it really will be "good-bye."*

My dad was kind enough to throw my bags in the trunk. I could see him waiting for me in the car and wiping the rain from his face with a napkin. My mom wanted to postpone the good-bye a little longer, so she accompanied me through the rain and into the car. Like so many people, we'd be sharing tearful good-byes in the passenger unloading zone at the airport.

As I slid into the car, I envisioned my grandma sitting up there in her room. *Grandma prays for me every day,* I thought. *How many people take the time to pray for me each day?* The answer to that question made the relationship I have with my grandma even more valuable. Two generations and fifty years separate us, but love and the special bond between grandparent and grandchild unite us. I gazed up into her window as the car rolled down the driveway. Behind a heavy downpour of titanic raindrops and fog clinging to the windowpane, there she was, peeking out. Hair wispy, rosary beads in her hand, smile on her face, eyes filled with love. I read her lips as she waved. "So long for now," she said. "So long for now."

I waved and thought, *So long for now, Grandma. I love you. Today there will be no good-byes.*

Inspired by MARY COLUCCI

Reasons Why

A young girl flinging stale bread to ducks in a lake stumbled across an older gentleman scrawling in a tattered notebook. "What are you doing, mister?" she asked, inquisitively.

"I'm writing down all the reasons why I love my wife," declared the gentleman.

The little girl arched her neck, peered into the man's notebook, and exclaimed, "Wow! This is a long list. Your wife must be a really nice lady!"

The man smiled, caressed the page with his hand, and, in a voice drenched with love, softly replied, "She was a miracle, and just the other day God decided to make her an angel."

Inspired by LORRAINE TOWLAN

Swinging on the Back Porch

There you are, my darling, gently swaying on our back porch swing. You look enchanting. Seeing you out there casts a smile across my face. It is my second favorite place to see you. You know what my favorite place is, don't you? When we embrace, and I gaze affectionately into your eyes. That's the moment I see how much you love me. Even after all these years my stomach fills with little butterflies when I behold the love in your eyes. I know you can see the love in mine. It's there. It's obvious to everyone how much I love you.

I could stand here forever just staring at you. You are the most exquisite vision I have ever laid eyes upon. I love how the breeze blows back your hair. It enables me to catch a glimpse of your soft cheek—a place I love to caress with my hand and kiss whenever the opportunity presents itself, usually anytime I'm near you.

Do you know that you've grown more beautiful with age? As I stand here watching you, I wonder how I got so lucky. What did I do to deserve a woman like you? You are beautiful, smart, tender, and a wonderful mother and wife. You're also a wonderful friend. That's one of the most important aspects of a successful marriage: We are lovers, husband and wife, but we're also each other's best friend.

I notice you're watching a bluebird bounce merrily on the thin branches hovering over our backyard. It's a pretty sight. This house and that tree hold many wonderful memories for us. Remember the bald tire we dangled from one of the sturdy branches many years ago? How our grandchildren loved to swing and spin until they were so dizzy they could no longer stand? I don't know how they could eat hot dogs for lunch and then hop on that tire and spin around and around. But I loved to watch the joy on their faces as they played together.

Right there, from where you're sitting now, we watched our family grow in years and in number. How many days did we spend cradling our new grandchildren to sleep on that very swing? The old wood we used to put that swing together has been transformed into a priceless family treasure.

As I stand here staring at you, I think about those quiet summer nights when it was just the two of us and we'd come outside and gaze at the stars in the sky. On more than one occasion we saw a shooting star. Enthusiastically, one of us would point to the star and follow it with our finger until it slipped into darkness. Once it disappeared, we'd sit with our eyes closed and our hands cupped in our laps and make a wish. I think we wished for the same thing, but we always kept our wishes a secret.

You've made my life wonderful, my darling. Sharing my life with you has been a blessing. Together we raised beautiful children. We have many reasons to feel proud. Our grandchildren are nearby, which gives us more opportunities to spoil them. It also means we have more reasons to smile.

As I reflect on our life together, I remember both ups and downs. The downs taught us some valuable lessons and helped us appreciate the good times all the more. I stand here quietly, leaning against the doorway and watching your feet softly swing to and fro. I feel like the richest man in the world. I have a happy and healthy family and that makes my life complete.

You turn and see me leaning in the doorway. I smile and reach out to touch you and suddenly you fade away. Spontaneously, I awaken from my dream and reality appears. You are gone now and I am alone. The pain of missing you engulfs my heart, but I know your spirit is with me. Through my dreams, I know we will remain together forever. Through my dreams, I have experienced the magnificence of everlasting love.

Inspired by ROBERT CULLEN

A Day in the Life

The room was dim. Half the fluorescent lights in the ceiling were off in an effort to conserve energy. Padded gray chairs were shoved against the matching gray walls, and the scent of despair loomed over everyone. No one was smiling. No one wanted to be there.

I was sitting in the emergency room of the local hospital with my fiancée, waiting for our turn. She had injured her back the day before, and our hopes that a good night's rest would help the situation went unrealized. She wriggled in her seat, trying to find a position that didn't cause blades of pain to fire down the nerves of her back. Finally, after two hours of waiting, she was called in. I escorted her to the door, where the nurse greeted us and asked me to sit tight in the waiting room. "This may take a little while," she said. I had no doubts.

Flopping back into my chair, I gazed curiously around the room at the other people who also preferred to be anyplace else.

An elderly couple was sitting across from me, his hand resting on top of hers—a symbol that she was there for treatment, he was there for support. A moment earlier my hand was resting on top of Irina's, and I wondered if in fifty years we would be like them, holding hands, possessing a long history together and still a support system for one another. I hoped so.

A few seats down was a boy who must have cut his forehead playing baseball; the mitt was still on his left hand. His mom sat next to him, looking frazzled and pressing a thick piece of gauze over his wound.

Off in the corner, where the two rows of padded gray chairs met, sat what looked like a young pair of grandparents and their little granddaughter. The girl looked like a teddy bear scrunched up sleeping in her grandpa's lap. The woman's hands were white knuckled, clutching her husband's right arm. Her eyes were pinched shut as if she was begging God for strength. The man stared at the floor, drowning in unpleasant thoughts; then his eyes rolled up and locked with mine before I could pull away. I gave him a nod; a sign expressing, *I hope everything turns out okay.* A subtle nod of his head relayed the response: *Thank you.*

Desperate for some fresh air, I wandered outside. The sky had turned the same color as the waiting room, pencil-lead gray. I let the wind gusts cast a cool mist across my face and rubbed in the moisture before heading back inside. Someone had claimed my seat so I stood near the registration desk, hoping that Irina would soon be released.

"Do you want to tell the family or should I?" Two nurses were talking in a small office across the hall.

"I'll do it," said the nurse on the right. Friendly looking, short, plump, experienced in matters like this, I guessed. "Where's his wife?" she asked.

"Flew home to see her mother, who was sick. Can you believe it? Talk about tough times," said the other nurse.

"So the wife doesn't know yet?"

"No. No one's been able to get in touch with her. The phone just keeps ringing."

"All right, let me go. Thank God that little girl has her grandparents here."

I watched as she passed me, chewing her lower lip, her hands clenched as though she were lugging the heavy weight of bad news. She moved slowly to the corner of the room, where the chairs met, where the little girl was sleeping, where the grandparents watched as she approached. The nurse said something and ushered the woman around the corner, leaving the little girl sleeping in her grandpa's arms.

A moment later curdling shrieks of agony echoed throughout that drab little room. Everyone perked up, jolted out of their drowsy haze. The same way people feel a little envious when it's someone else's turn to see the doctor, this time they felt grateful it wasn't them saddled with unwelcome news. The tension in the room was already thick and obtrusive, like too many people squeezed into an elevator on a hot summer's day. When that woman screamed, the walls closed in, forcing the boy and his mom outside. The grandfather scooped up the little girl and disappeared around the corner.

An hour later I walked through the doorway where the patients reclined in narrow beds, separated by thin beige curtains suspended on silver metal rings. I couldn't help but risk taking a glance as I paced by. The little boy getting stitches. His mom holding his right hand, the baseball glove still on his left. The elderly couple. Her resting with eyes closed on a bed and him sitting next to her, his hand resting on top of hers. And there was the little girl with her grandma and grandpa. Her daddy was lying in bed.

I had already learned that he was a carpenter working on a roof that afternoon when the sky turned gray. The rain cast a slick coat on the wooden slats and the man slipped, plummeting twenty feet into a pile of building materials. He was twenty-nine years old and paralyzed from the waist down.

It took me only a second to pass by that scene. The loving family huddled around that young man. His daughter, too young to understand the significance of what had happened, and the wife who didn't know how drastically her life had changed. The memory of that moment is burned into my mind.

A few curtains down I found my fiancée, woozy from a shot of morphine and eager to go home. The curtain was drawn when we walked by that family, so I recalled the scene from a few moments earlier. *That nurse was right,* I thought to myself. *Thank God that little girl's grandparents are here. She needs them more than she realizes, and the man lying in bed will need his family as he fights the battles that lie ahead.* That was my final thought as I stepped out into the darkness, basking in the refreshing coolness of the evening rain.

Inspired by a family I'll always remember

Cozy in a Snowstorm

*I*t was wintertime in upstate New York and a fresh snowfall had been forecast for that evening, many years ago. I was hoping to reach my destination before the snow blanketed the roadway, but unfortunately, Mother Nature had other plans. As I drove north, the snow fluttered softly on my windshield at first, but it wasn't long before the road was ensconced in snow and visibility was almost zero. I had only an hour to go, but in weather like that tragedy could strike in an instant. I decided to play it safe and checked into a quaint hotel I knew just south of the Catskill Mountains.

After arriving, I took a hot shower and meandered into the coffee shop adjacent to the hotel. There I relaxed with a hot cup of brew and a flaky slice of warm apple pie with a dollop of whipped cream melting lazily over the crust while watching the giant snowflakes pile up outside. Families and other motorists checked in and stomped over to the coffee shop for a hot treat and shelter from the cold. I was alone in my booth, but felt a sense of coziness as I watched people sigh with enjoyment as they took their first sip of steaming coffee or soup. Snowstorms have that effect on people. We were all stranded, but nobody seemed to mind. As long as you're snug inside, it's the perfect excuse for doing absolutely nothing and enjoying every minute of it.

The restaurant filled up quickly, so when a woman stepped in, dusting the snow from her brow, I gestured that she was welcome to share my booth. Her name was Victoria. We chatted over coffee and our conversation progressed from the weather to traveling and personal interests. We laughed, the time passing like the brisk wind outside. It became one of those mesmerizing evenings I wished could go on forever. Unfortunately, the owner of the coffee shop did not share my sentiment. When he wanted to close, I decided I couldn't let this chance encounter end over a few cups of coffee. I knew the roads would be cleared by morning, everyone back on their journeys and the cozy feeling of being stranded in a snowstorm just a fond memory.

Knowing that my true intentions were quite obvious, I said, "I'm visiting some friends at Wolfe Lake this weekend. I was wondering if you'd like to join me for another cup of coffee there, or perhaps dinner?"

There are moments in life when fate is on your side and things seem to work just right. For me, that was one of those times. She was also visiting friends at Wolfe Lake, but, as it turned out, neither of our friends saw much of us that weekend. I knew of a cozy little restaurant nestled in the woods, and I was able to rekindle the ambience and conversation we'd shared at the coffee shop two evenings earlier.

That was thirty-seven years, two kids, and five grandchildren ago. I often joked with her that if my parents hadn't taught me good manners, I might never have offered to share my booth and we never would have met. But I did share my booth with her, and she in turn shared her life with me. Occasionally we'd stop back at that coffee shop on our way to visit friends up at

Wolfe Lake. Even on sun-soaked days we'd cuddle up in the back booth and feel cozy all over again. We were both big fans of feeling cozy. I don't think there's a more delectable feeling in the world.

Today, when I think of Victoria, I always remember the last time I drove up to Wolfe Lake. Another snowstorm hit, and I found myself back at that quaint hotel just south of the Catskill Mountains. I took a hot shower and trudged through the snow over to the coffee shop for a steaming cup of brew and their scrumptious homemade apple pie with whipped cream. They had completely remodeled since we'd last shared the back booth. The staff, however, remained the same. As Gloria poured my first cup, she asked about my wife, and I guess the look on my face said it better than any words I could find.

"I'm sure she's still with you in spirit," she said. "It seemed the two of you shared a love that was carved in stone."

I smiled woefully as I nodded my head and raised the mug of coffee to my lips. And then, as the soothing flavor of the coffee smacked my taste buds, the tender love of my wife tugged at my heartstrings. When I looked down in sadness, I couldn't believe my eyes—there, etched in the tabletop, surrounded by a heart, was the word COZY. In that back booth she was with me after all.

Inspired by RON MCCARTHY

For Ever and Ever, I Do

Cole Anderson was enjoying a tranquil morning with his grandfather Michael. Floating aimlessly in a metal rowboat riddled with dents, they waited for the fish to bite and chatted about life.

Cole's grandparents had been married for fifty-four happy years, and on this particular day he needed the advice that came from that level of success. "My marriage is in trouble, Grandpa," he said, reluctantly. "Part of me wonders how I can fix it, and another part of me wonders if I even want to fix it."

They each tugged on their lines, hoping to entice some fish, and then Michael reeled in. He saw a few fish rupture the lake's glasslike surface and cast his hook and worm in that direction. As the bobber hit the water, he watched the ringlets amplify while the little red-and-white plastic ball recoiled on the surface. Cole could see his grandpa was contemplating just what to say.

And then, with the sanguine expression of someone who has all the answers, Michael, still staring at the bobber drifting on the water, softly said, "A happy marriage is a long falling in love. Marriage is very gradual—just a fraction at a time. The real ministers that join two hearts are the long, slow years; the joys and sorrows you face together; the children you create and raise; and the struggles within your family."

He continued, "A loving marriage is the service and support two people give to each other year after year. Long after the bridal bouquet has withered and the wedding bands are getting worn down. When the honeymoon wanes like the sun behind a mountain, that's when the real commitment to marriage begins. If, at that time, two people discover they don't love each other as they once did, they must redouble their attention toward one another. They should be jealous of everything that separates them—even in the slightest way.

"A marriage is too precious to be thrown away because of regrets or differences. If the romance from your marriage has taken wings and flown away, you must recapture it at once. Renew the attention you gave to each other in the earlier days and draw your hearts closer together. Acknowledge your faults and promise that you will be there for each other completely. And you must back up that promise with action and commitment."

Then Michael took his eyes off the bobber, peered intently at his grandson, and said, "You, as the husband, must honor your wife and show her respect as a beautiful lady. As she grows older and her physical beauty diminishes, let her know that her mental charms have grown more alluring. And she, as the wife, should be gentle to you. She should treat you like a man even as the years pass and, like me, you grow a little more fragile.

"As husband and wife, *never* say anything you will regret. Always remember that marriage is a blessing, and although it involves many weighty responsibilities, it is a gem in the crown of life. Care for it and it will last forever."

Cole cautiously reached over, fretful of rocking the boat,

and hugged his grandfather, thanking him for sharing his wisdom and guidance.

When the morning hours faded into history and another fishing trip reached its conclusion, Cole drove his grandfather home. As he pulled up to the house, he saw his grandma Ruth watering the tulips outside. She looked radiant as her shiny white hair glinted in the sunlight.

After kissing her hello and talking for a few moments, it was time to go. As he dropped into the driver's seat, he sighed and thought about what his grandpa shared with him out on the lake. But no words were as potent as the vision he saw through his passenger's-side window. There, standing among a rainbow of blooming tulips, stood Michael and Ruth waving goodbye—a charming couple whose love had grown deeper with the passing years. Cole thought to himself, *Now, that is a blessing—to grow old with the love of your life.* And so he headed for home, committed to falling in love all over again.

Inspired by COLE H. LEELAND

A Link in the Chain

The people we know the best are the ones we can hurt the most. And the people who have been brave enough to bestow their love upon us we can truly destroy. That is why love is so fragile, so precious.

What can we say to a stranger who hurts our feelings? What can they say to us? We have no time invested with them; we've never made ourselves vulnerable exposing our weaknesses, so it's difficult for them to hurt us deeply. The people we love, however, know the wounds we bear on the inside.

Trust is the chain that unites two people and is fashioned one link at a time. Through proving ourselves worthy of another's love, the chain grows stronger, more robust. When two souls share love, the same scars often mark them. This reinforces the chain, because both people walk with similar wounds on the inside, so they protect each other and possess a unique understanding of one another's feelings.

There are weaknesses within ourselves that we express to our loved ones; and there are other flaws we wish to hide but are eventually exposed through our behavior. The same way people notice our imperfections, we notice theirs. It's easy, even tempting, to use the knowledge of their vulnerability against them in times of turmoil and stress—but that undermines trust and works to break the chain.

We must be sensitive to the feelings of those who have offered us their love. It is not only the words we say but also the tone in which we speak that can hurt those closest to us. The feelings of the people we love are more precious than a diamond, yet more fragile than an egg. It's not because they can't withstand struggle or disappointment; it's that they don't expect us to be the ones to spark those feelings.

Think of the people you love and what they have entrusted to you for safekeeping—their most intimate thoughts, their secrets, their hopes, and their dreams. Picture your children. They pay strict attention to everything you say and do; make sure their link to you is healthy and timeless.

There is a risk in loving; you take a chance on another, and the other on you. There is a risk in raising a family because suddenly a life is wholly dependent upon you. Does it make sense that the people we love the most we can also hurt the most? Yes, because love cannot exist until we abandon ourselves to another's hands and risk getting hurt. Love is the most exquisite feeling in the world and that reward, like anything precious, comes at a price.

Be keenly aware of the effect your words and actions have on the ones you love. Their hearts lie in your hands.

Inspired by JEAN MOORE

CHAPTER THREE

COURAGE AND SACRIFICE

Admiring the strength of the human spirit that endures tragedy and celebrates triumph

Unexpected circumstances may usher us to the brink and force us out of our comfort zone. They demand that we possess the courage to step forward and make the sacrifices required by the moment. Although we may tremble with uncertainty, we are sure to emerge from the situation with a greater understanding of life, a heightened belief in ourselves, and the assurance that we are in control of our own destiny. Meet ordinary people who, under striking conditions, performed with valor. Their actions and insights will help all of us summon the courage within ourselves.

Captain Courageous

*O*ccasionally we're lucky enough to learn about someone so remarkable that it's almost impossible to comprehend. For most of his professional life, John ran an international finance company. I never met him, but was fortunate enough to hear vivid stories about his courage and determination despite what most of us would consider insurmountable challenges.

No matter how much power an individual may wield in business, politics, or any other arena, no one is immune from affliction. John is a victim of Lou Gehrig's disease, and at sixty-seven years of age he is confined to a bed, paralyzed from the neck down. He cannot breathe on his own, feed or bathe himself, or even swallow food. He can blink his eyes and purse his lips, but that's the limit of his bodily movements. His physical world is restricted to the point at which most of us would welcome death. John, however, does not live in the physical world; he lives in a mental one. His strength of mind far outweighs his physical handicaps, and in the realm of his imagination he is not confined to a bed and getting fed through a tube. In his mind he is free, strong, capable, and determined. When John stood at the helm of a vast corporation his time was consumed with work; minute by minute his schedule was broken down, assistants making sure he stayed on track with his commitments. But now, with all that behind him and nowhere to go, he has time to pursue a lifelong dream—to write a book, his autobiography. He had just one enormous obstacle to overcome: He could not move a muscle or speak a word. But he has found a way and begun writing.

John first used a special computer mechanism that allowed him to type without the use of his hands. A computerized headset with a flexible wire and special lens at the tip positioned in front of either eye allowed him to register letters on the computer screen each time he blinked. It was a tedious, toilsome process, but he persevered.

When the incessant blinking caused his eyes to burn with irritation, he was forced to find another option. The headset was reconstructed with a narrow tube and a pacifier at the tip, which the nurses had to carefully position in John's mouth. Now he lightly presses his lips on the pacifier, and a letter registers on the screen. Because saliva builds up quickly, he needs continuous oral suctioning to work.

Like counting the stars in the sky, writing his book appears to be an unending endeavor, but day after day John's inner strength allows him to stay focused on his goal, take an active part in his care, and maintain an interest in the world around him.

What compels someone to attempt such a daunting task and continue to live when all hope seems lost and there is no chance for recovery? John's family holds the answer to that question and says it's simply "love." Love for his family, for life, and for each moment he is alive, despite his paralysis.

John is not just a keen businessman, eloquent writer, and courageous soul but a proud grandfather of eighteen as well. Those who know him say that his greatest pleasure is visiting with his grandchildren. He talks with them through his voice-synthesized computer. The love he has for them and the joy he receives just seeing their adorable faces are his inspiration to persevere. Although he can't reach out to them, he tenderly embraces them with his eyes, and they wrap their arms over his rigid body.

John is not concerned about when he will die; he's only inspired by how much living he can squeeze into each minute he is alive. His gallant attitude has enabled him to carry on as the courageous captain of his life and become an inspiration to those who meet him or learn of his remarkable story.

Inspired by JOHN ANDERSON

Rosie's Roller Skates

*I*t was many years ago now when a little girl named Rosie was growing up in a low-income neighborhood in New York City. During the summer months when the scorching sun beat down upon the city, local firemen would come around and turn the spigots on the fire hydrants, letting an endless surge of refreshing water flood the streets. The kids splattered gleefully as the water spewed out from the hydrants and cascaded over their legs and feet. It was a primitive swimming pool, but for the poor kids growing up in the Bronx, it was a special treat.

Rosie lived with her grandparents just a few blocks from Tremont Avenue, a main thoroughfare in the neighborhood. She'd been orphaned when a tragic car accident claimed the lives of both her parents. Rosie was a genteel little girl who got straight As in school, always wore her thick black hair in a ponytail, and was adorned in her favorite red dress for church each Sunday morning.

One day, as they strolled home from church, Rosie saw a girl glide by wearing a brand-new pair of white roller skates. She stared in wonder as the girl rolled effortlessly up the street with her hair blowing gently in the breeze. "Grandma! Grandpa! Can I get a pair of roller skates?" Rosie asked. Her grandparents glanced at each other sadly, knowing they couldn't afford such an expensive item. "My birthday is coming soon, and if I could have anything in the world that is what I would want," she declared.

Her birthday was a month away, and that evening as her grandparents lay in bed staring at the ceiling, they tried to figure out a way to get Rosie a pair of roller skates. "I could see about getting some overtime," professed her grandpa.

"But Rosie loves spending time with you each evening," Grandma said.

Shaking his head, Grandpa replied, "I know. I love spending time with her, too, but it would only be for a few weeks. I think the joy on her face if we could give her a new pair of roller skates for her birthday would be worth it."

Over the next four weeks, Rosie's grandpa worked a few extra hours each night at the loading dock, arriving home just before Rosie's bedtime. He was exhausted from putting in fourteen-hour days, but the twinkle in Rosie's eyes always rekindled his energy a little bit.

Rosie's birthday arrived on a sparkling Saturday in early September. That afternoon a few friends came over to enjoy birthday cake and join in a small celebration. Most of the people in the neighborhood were poor, so the gifts were simple— a hair ribbon, a drawing, and ten cents she could spend when the ice cream truck jingled the bell on its daily tour through the neighborhood.

Finally, Rosie's grandparents gave her their gift. The sheer size of the box thrilled her, and she wildly ripped off the birthday wrapping and placed the bright pink bow in her hair. Her face illuminated and she leaped for joy when she popped off the box top, peeled back the tissue paper, and saw a pair of brand-new white roller skates tucked neatly inside. Her grandma and grandpa cried tears of delight as she gave them both a loving embrace.

That afternoon when the party ended, Rosie's grandma and grandpa watched as she skated up and down the block with her hair blowing in the wind and a smile of sheer bliss on her face. Her grandpa turned to his wife and said, "Those were tough nights working at the dock after laboring all day in the blistering summer sun, but seeing the happiness in Rosie's eyes makes it all worthwhile."

The next morning after church, Rosie hurried to her room, changed out of her red dress, and grabbed her skates. A moment later she was outside coasting down the block, a smile fixed permanently on her face. As she turned and headed up the block, she spotted her grandpa talking with his friend from across the street. "Grandpa! Grandpa!" she yelled out, "watch me skate over to you!" And she hopped off the curb, skating briskly toward him.

"Stop, Rosie! Stop!" Grandpa shrieked, but she didn't hear him. She darted into the street, never seeing the bus barreling toward her. Grandpa ran screaming for her to stop. As the bus driver slammed on the brakes and the tires screeched and smoke from burning rubber drifted through the air, Grandpa reached Rosie and threw her out of the way. She tumbled back to the curb and watched in horror as her grandpa was struck by the bus and killed instantly.

Today, embedded in the sidewalk at the scene of that tragic accident is a plaque dedicated to the memory of Rosie's grandpa. Rosie never skated again. She took the skates off that morning stained with blood and dirt and placed them back in the original box. Every once in a while she holds the box in her hands and remembers, with longing, the day she lost her grandpa, and the day he saved her life.

Inspired by BART COLUCCI

Integrity

The temptations were high in his neighborhood. Cutting corners in order to get by was the accepted method for growing up on his block. Unfortunately, his situation was common among the kids in that area. Drug abuse and alcoholism were his mother's hobbies, and his father vanished when he was a baby. For the past six years, Trey had been raised by his grandma Reggie.

Reggie had lived in the neighborhood most of her life and knew the odds that a young man growing up there faced. A juvenile boys' home and state penitentiary were haunting possibilities and became a reality for many of the neighborhood's young men. The fight to stay alive often took precedence over strong principles and family values. But for Reggie, the moral fortitude of her grandson was the top priority. She expected Trey to have integrity and demanded nothing less.

Each evening they prepared dinner together, thanking God for the food on their table, that they had each other's company, and for the battered secondhand stereo Trey bought for his grandmother with the money he saved bagging groceries and stocking shelves after school.

The racket from the streets was an intruder, shattering the

intimate conversations they shared, the sanctity of their little home. Trey had thought a stereo and some of his grandma's favorite music would help muffle the biting sounds of the street and keep her entertained while he was at school, even if the records were scratched and skipped sometimes.

Trey listened to his grandma speak about character, honesty, and trustworthiness as essential elements for a successful life. He heeded her advice, becoming a "big brother" for some of the younger kids in the neighborhood. She said those traits would catapult him out of that area, enabling him to get a good education and lead a prosperous life. But on the streets he saw things differently. The drug dealers with their fancy cars. People who lied and stole. They all seemed to be doing well. Trey saw "success" awarded to the people his grandma called "the base of humanity," and couldn't help but question if his grandma was right or just naive.

"Why do they have it all and I have nothing?" he'd ask in frustration. "I'm being honest and I don't have a dime. People can trust me but I have no friends, except for the young kids on the block. You say you're proud because I have character, but it's not getting me anywhere." Seeing others in his neighborhood prosper while he worked for petty wages at the grocery store only fueled his temptation to join them.

"I know you're enticed sometimes," Reggie said. "You see those boys on the street and think they have it all. But what do they really have? *Not trust. Not love.* They live in fear, one eye looking over their shoulder making sure someone isn't sneaking up behind them."

"But I have to watch my back, too, Grandma," he countered.

"That's the world we live in," she explained. "But you can be sure those boys have made enemies, and enemies seek revenge.

Many will not see their thirtieth birthday. That's a high price to pay for a fancy car and expensive jewelry."

She peered into her grandson's eyes, and with his face braced firmly in her hands, she said, "*You* have integrity, and that is the foundation of all that is great with humankind. Those boys out there, they surrendered their integrity in exchange for some high-priced toys. *You* possess truthfulness and goodness; those qualities, along with a mighty will, are irreplaceable. They will carry you to any noble destination your heart desires. Strong character consists of two things—will and self-restraint. A strong will can move mountains. Self-restraint is what you need *now* to resist the temptations beyond that door.

"There is nothing the world esteems more than a man who stands by his convictions and is regarded as an honest individual. The person preceded by that reputation is welcomed with open arms wherever he goes. Men and women of every generation have chosen to die rather than forsake their integrity. Be stronger than you think you can be and your future will have wings, whisking you away from here, above and beyond your wildest expectations."

For a time Trey heeded his grandma's words, continuing work at the grocery store and spending time with the kids in his neighborhood. But he eventually quit his job and neglected his grandma, leaving her at the dinner table alone, spinning records on her old stereo, waiting for him to return home. Trey surrendered to the lure of the streets, shattering the relationship he shared with his grandma and telling the kids in the neighborhood that he could no longer be their "big brother," unaware that the boys and girls who depended on him suddenly felt abandoned, unloved. He justified his actions saying, "My grandma has nothing. These kids growing up here have nothing. I have nothing. By making some money, real money, I can give my grandma some nice things and do the same for the neighborhood kids with their shabby clothes and beat-up shoes."

It didn't last long, however. The self-loathing backed up like a bitter swell in Trey's throat, like cough medicine. Through the thin clapboard walls he listened to his grandma sobbing late into the night while he tousled the sheets and sat at the edge of his bed, his head bowed in shame. And when one of the kids he mentored started skipping school, he realized that his grandma was right. It wasn't what he could buy, but who he was that mattered most to his grandma and to those kids in the neighborhood. He wanted out of the path he had chosen—but once he'd entered that world there was no easy way out. His actions had sealed his fate. The warning Reggie had given him about people prowling for revenge was an ever-present fear nipping at his imagination like a thousand tiny little teeth. Until early one Saturday morning, before dawn, as he stepped out the front door of his apartment house headed for work at the grocery store his fear was realized. A car lurched from the alleyway across the street, tires screeching as it headed toward him. A man hung out the rear window on the driver's side and took aim. Trey was gunned down, his body collapsing at the steps of his building.

Reggie was awake and ran to the window when the booming sound of shots fired smothered the peaceful music emanating from her old stereo speakers. From her angle all she could see was a pair of sneakers, the ones Trey kicked off and left near the front door each evening when he came home.

She spent the following months sitting in the doorway of Trey's room, contemplating the tragic loss. She never entered his bedroom again. Instead she just sat in the doorway staring at the picture sitting on his dresser, a photo taken of them at his elementary school graduation, forever a reminder of the hope destroyed and the life lost. She couldn't bring herself to walk out the front door of that building either, refusing to step over the very spot where her only grandson lost his life. Sadly, she lived out the rest of her days brokenhearted, drowning out the noise from the street on her old stereo, and secluded from the world in her tiny apartment.

Inspired by GAYLE VANCE

More than a Second Chance

*I*f you had the chance to save a life, would you? That's the question my dad asked himself before making a very important decision.

He liked to joke and say that one day, he would donate his body to science. He'd flex his arm, suck in his tummy, and remark, "How could they pass up a body like this?" But my dad wasn't joking. He sincerely hoped that someday his organs—or any part of his body that could help people in need—would be used to that end.

I cringed at the thought of my dad being used for "spare parts," but I understood his motives. My mom had died of liver cancer and chances are she could have been saved if a donor had been found in time. My dad wanted to save someone from the anguish he endured, so he became an organ donor.

My daughter, Faith, was thirteen when my dad passed away. When I sat down to tell her the news, her lips and cheeks quivered frantically and the tears quickly plunged down her cheeks. We had discussed organ donation already, so she stammered, "I . . . I guess that means we have . . . we have to share Grandpa with other people now."

"That's right," I whispered, holding her hands in my lap. "Hopefully your grandpa will make a sick person well and bring some happiness to a family in need."

The few months following my dad's death were wearisome. There were trigger spots everywhere reminding me of the wonderful times we'd shared together. My dad and I had spent many evenings in the backyard lazily gazing at the stars. Once he passed on, Faith took his place, and together she and I frequently sat out there sipping iced tea and babbling about life or whatever topic happened to arise.

One evening, as menacing clouds loomed in the sky, masking our view of the stars, we talked about Grandpa and his decision to become an organ donor. "Do you think Grandpa's organs went to help some people?" she asked inquisitively.

"I think so," I said. "But I don't know for sure. There are long lists of people waiting for all different organs, so Grandpa probably did help someone."

"Mom," said Faith, "when I die, I want to donate my organs and help someone, too. I think what Grandpa did was a very generous and brave thing."

"You're too young to worry about that," I said, uncomfortable with where our conversation was going. "When you're much older you can make that decision."

"No, Mom. I've already decided. I want to be an organ donor, like Grandpa."

"Okay, Faith," I said, anxious to change topics. "But you're young and won't have to worry about that for a long time."

The following week basketball season began, and Faith was a starting guard. Her grandpa had been her number one fan, never missing a game. Now I felt the pressure to cheer extra loud. When the buzzer sounded at the end of the fourth quarter Faith's team, the Stars, had beaten the Hornets, eighteen to fourteen. Faith contributed four points and fought gallantly for the rebounds under the net. I felt like my passionate cheering had paid off.

Only a dusting of snow had been forecast for the evening, but when we stepped out of the gymnasium doors an inch had already carpeted the ground. I'd never liked driving in the snow, and tonight I had to take Faith's friend Charlotte home, too. We hopped into the car feverishly rubbing our hands together, trying to keep warm until the heat came on. The parking lot was jammed from the combination of snow and everyone exiting the gymnasium together. There was a chaotic array of red taillights and exhaust fumes wafting in the frigid night air as drivers tried to merge into a one-way exit at the south end of the parking lot. It took a few minutes, but by the time we were on the main road the car was toasty warm and I felt better. The busy traffic melted most of the snow on the main road, and we lived only a few miles away.

I was approaching Herring Avenue, where I needed to turn right, when Faith and Charlotte spotted the McDonald's up ahead and asked if we could stop for some french fries. I smirked at both of them and said, "Okay. Since I've got the green light and you both played a great game, we'll drive through."

As I crossed through the intersection a car came speeding through from the right side. Faith screamed, *"Mom, watch out!"* I panicked, slamming the brakes with both feet. The car collided into our right side, ramming us into the telephone pole on the left side of the intersection. Stunned, my first reaction was to move, but my legs were pinned under the steering wheel. Faith's upper body was thrust onto me. Blood was streaming from her forehead and she appeared unconscious. The passenger's-side door was demolished and the dashboard had collapsed, trapping her legs underneath.

"Help! Somebody please help us!" I screamed.

Charlotte was shrieking in the back and jumped from the car in a panicky fit. Within seconds other cars stopped to help, but Faith and I were trapped.

"The ambulance is on its way," someone yelled. A moment later I heard the piercing sound of sirens; knowing they were coming for us made the situation all the more terrifying. It was surreal. I was getting claustrophobic, and though my legs were stuck, I started squirming in a mad panic to get loose and help my daughter. "This can't be happening," I bantered, trying to convince myself that it was just a dream. "Faith, honey, please answer me," I begged. "Faith!" She said nothing.

Suddenly a team of firefighters, police, and EMTs barricaded us. It was a chaotic scene and I felt utterly helpless. "Please take care of my daughter," I pleaded.

"We'll get you both out," assured a fireman. "You'll both be okay."

"My legs are trapped, and my daughter's are, too!"

"What's your name?" he asked. His calm, self-assured manner was the polar opposite of how I was feeling and I couldn't help but notice it.

"Joan. My name is Joan. My daughter's name is Faith," I muttered.

"My name is Roger, and I need you to remain still. The more you squirm, the harder it will be. Stay calm and we'll get you out. All right?"

"Okay. Okay," I mumbled, gulping down each breath. "How is Faith?" I asked, fearing his answer.

"There's a team of people helping her right now," said Roger. I reached out and grabbed her hand. It was eerily still, and I urged them, "Please, take care of my little girl!" They unbolted my seat and wriggled it backward, allowing me to extend my legs and slip them out from under the steering wheel. My forehead was cut and my body was trembling uncontrollably as I ran frantically to the passenger's side to be near my daughter.

Charlotte was crying and being treated for some minor abrasions in the back of an ambulance. The firemen brought out a saw and shaved through the front passenger's door. Sparks were soaring, lighting up the night sky, and I couldn't fathom what was happening. It was maddening. I turned and saw a police officer directing traffic and the onlookers' faces gasping in horror when they saw my daughter trapped inside. All I wanted was to awaken from that nightmare and then I heard someone shout, "We need the Jaws of Life over here!"

The procedure was agonizingly slow but ultimately they slid Faith out of the car and onto a board, stabilizing her neck and back before rushing us to the hospital. She was unconscious and bleeding severely. I clenched her right hand in both of mine as the ambulance raced toward the hospital. "We've got a young girl, thirteen, in critical condition, head trauma, possible broken back, multiple lacerations," I heard the driver alerting the hospital. My stomach wrenched knowing he was talking about my Faith.

A surgical team greeted us upon arrival, whisking Faith into the emergency room. I was asked to wait outside. In a precarious state of mind, I ran to the bathroom. Staring at myself in the mirror—my clothes torn, my forehead cut, blood on my hands, and my body shivering—for the first time it felt more like reality than a harrowing dream. I splashed cold water on my face and came out of the bathroom asking for some news. Nothing yet. They were still in the operating room, but I was assured they were doing everything they could. "Your daughter is in the best of hands," said the nurse, trying to comfort me.

I was frantically pacing the hallway when the police said they would like to ask me a few questions. "I can't think straight right now," I blurted. Then, in a burst of manic energy, I grilled them about what happened. "What caused the accident? Who was driving that car?"

The officer calmly replied, "A drunk driver ran a red light and broadsided you at the intersection."

My mind flashed to the appalling stories of people being killed by drunk drivers—two girls going to rent a movie being killed on their way home because a drunk driver ran a red light; a drunk driver striking a young boy walking home from school . . . the list goes on.

The sight of the doctor emerging from the operating room ruptured my thoughts. He looked weary—stained with blood and holding the surgical mask in his hand. The look on his face told me the news I couldn't bear to hear. "She was bleeding badly and suffered severe head trauma. I am sorry."

"No! No! Please. I want to see her!" I wailed. "I have to see my baby!"

The doctor said nothing and simply took my hand, escorting me into the operating room. There on the table, her clothes bloodied and torn, lay my Faith, my thirteen-year-old daughter, my baby girl. Suddenly I remembered the night just a week earlier when we were sipping iced tea on the deck in the backyard. We spoke about Grandpa and how much we both missed him. She said that she admired him for being an organ donor and that someday—when she died—she wanted to donate her organs to help people. I told her she was too young to think about that. Sobbing profusely, I thought of how fast life can change and how fragile life really is. *Do I honor her wish? Do I want my baby being taken apart?*

I held her hand and cried a river of tears. Then I thought about my dad. Faith asked if he had helped a sick person by being an organ donor, and I said that he probably had. *Should I give her the same opportunity to help someone else?* I had told her about the long list of people waiting for transplants. *Could she help a young girl or boy in need of a transplant?* I pressed my lips to her forehead and said, "I love you, Faith, my courageous little girl."

Awash in tears, I told the doctor, "Faith wanted to be an organ donor."

Overwhelmed, he responded, "Her liver wasn't damaged, and there is a young boy in the hospital waiting for a transplant."

I told the doctor, "Just last week, Faith said she wanted to be an organ donor . . . someday. If she can help you save this young boy's life then please, give her that chance."

The doctor quickly alerted a team, and I went to speak with God. I sluggishly entered the hospital's tiny chapel, just six pews on either side and a small cross suspended on the far wall in front of me. The place was empty. My feet dragged forward as I thought about my plans for that evening and how things had now changed forever. After we got home and Faith went to bed I was going to take a bath and finish reading a mystery novel I'd begun a few weeks earlier.

Now here I was in a chapel, and my daughter was gone. My sadness was beyond measure, so I knelt down and prayed. We weep from our eyes but at that moment I felt like every pore of my body was sobbing.

I sat in silence as if I was expecting an answer, and then I felt a chill run down the nape of my neck. It was the delicate touch of a hand on my skin. I turned, hoping to somehow see Faith standing there telling me that everything was okay, but instead I saw the pallid face of a stranger crying. Fighting back her tears, she discreetly asked, "Joan? Is your name Joan?"

"Yes, it is," I whispered.

"My name is Veronica. I was wondering if we could talk for a minute? I was just told my son, Todd, will be getting a liver transplant. My son has been hanging on, he's a fighter, but his time was running out. The doctors are optimistic about his recovery now that he is getting a transplant. I don't mean to intrude, I just wanted you to know that you and your daughter have saved not just my son tonight, but my family."

When I asked God, *Why did this happen?* I didn't expect an answer. But He gave me one. I said, "My daughter's name is Faith. Her grandpa, my father, was an organ donor. She admired his generosity and the idea that he could help someone live even after he died. Last Friday evening she told me she wanted to follow his example. I told her it was a nice gesture, but she would have years to make that decision. Tonight I made it for her."

Standing there in a dimly lit chapel, surrounded by silence, Veronica and I hugged each other. "May God bless your child and her grandpa," she whispered in my ear. "They are both extraordinary people."

Inspired by JOAN ALDEN

The Hero

 he life of a truck driver is a lonely one. Miles of blacktop, all-night coffee shops where only the waitress knows your name, and all the time in the world to reminisce—or dream—about almost anything.

Ike Fisher was a trucker. His usual route included the states south of the Mason Dixon line and east of the Mississippi, but once every few months he would head out west. Ike didn't have any family and never minded a couple of weeks on the open road.

Late one drizzly night, as his giant rig roared through the dense fog looming over the deserted highway, Ike spotted the alarming sight of flashing red lights shrouded in the mist and weeds about twenty feet beyond the edge of the highway. Ike snatched the CB from its mount and called for help.

"Breaker, breaker, this is the Road Hound searching for the Midnight Patrol. I came across a vehicle that took a turn for the worse out here at highway marker seventeen. I'm steering my rig to the shoulder, see if there's anything I can do. I expect you boys will be here in a minute."

"Breaker, breaker, thanks for the wide eyes, Road Hound.

We'll be there pronto," squawked the reply from a police cruiser a few minutes away.

Ike steered his massive semi until all eighteen wheels stamped tumultuously along the gravelly edge of the road. He seized the flashlight and first-aid kit stuffed under his rumpled bed and hopped down from the cab. After quickly scanning the area with his flashlight, he hurried down the hill to the distressed vehicle.

"Is anyone hurt?" he called out. "Are you hurt?"

All he heard were the abrasive sounds of crickets in the weeds. As Ike got closer to the car, he saw that it had flipped upside down. Inching even closer, he heard a pathetic whimper coming from inside. Beaming the light in the passenger's-side window, he spotted a brown-and-white puppy cowering in fear. Ike cast the light in front and discovered a woman and young girl, both unconscious. He jerked vigorously on the passenger door, but the door frame was wedged solidly in the ground.

Desperate to get the women out of the car, Ike smashed the window with his flashlight and peeled off his shirt, using it to clear away the shards of glass on the window frame. Then he carefully slid the girl out of the car, swung her over his shoulder, and dashed up the hill, laying her gently on the ground beside the rear of his truck.

Scanning the highway in both directions, he saw no signs of police yet. He scrambled back down the hill to the driver's side and yanked the door open. Ike pulled the woman out and carried her to safety. He heard the police sirens echoing in the distance and as he examined the two women for any severe wounds, he remembered that the puppy was still trapped inside the vehicle. Sprinting back down the hill, Ike pushed the driver's front seat forward and crawled midway through the driver's-side door, trying to rescue the little pup. The dog recoiled in fear on the passenger side.

"Come on little guy, come on," Ike said, his arms extended outward. The puppy was unswayed and huddled in the corner. Getting desperate, Ike crawled completely into the car and wrapped his arms around the terrified animal. Inching back toward the door, he suddenly smelled gas and panicked. While scrambling to get out, the front seat fell back, trapping Ike in the car. The rear window had splintered in the crash, so Ike kicked the rest of it out with his foot. Feetfirst and on his knees, Ike braced the dog in his left arm and pushed his body out with his right hand. When a fragment of glass jutting out from the window frame punctured Ike's right thigh, he screamed in agony and the puppy wriggled loose, scampering back into the vehicle. Instantly, the car burst into flames. With both hands, Ike forced himself out the rear window and rolled down the hill, snuffing out the flames as he tumbled. With his skin charred and smoldering, Ike lay in the wet dirt and weeds about thirty feet from the burning car. Rescuers arrived on the scene and within minutes firemen were dousing the flames.

For Ike, however, life would never be the same. The paramedics whisked Ike to a burn unit forty miles away, where he underwent emergency surgery. He had sustained third-degree burns on 40 percent of his upper body, including his face and hands. Luke, the puppy, perished in the fire.

Ike spent the next four months in recovery at the hospital. In addition to his burns, he had severed some of the veins and muscles in his right thigh, preventing him from driving a big rig again. His leg no longer possessed the strength and stamina needed to stop an eighteen-wheeler.

He did save the lives of two people, however. The two women he rescued, Gayle and Christina Florio, were both taken to the county hospital. They each had suffered a concussion and minor scrapes but were okay within a few days. Ike, Gayle, and Christina became friends and stayed in regular contact through letters and phone calls. But after the accident and his long rehabilitation, Ike felt alone, having to face the world with deformities he could not hide. He had no family, only a few acquaintances. They were sympathetic to his plight but didn't know what to say and in time found ways to avoid him. Even when staring at himself in the mirror, Ike felt as if he were peering at a stranger. For fifty-six years he saw the same face mature and change over time. But the vision he saw now was beyond anything he could endure. His skin looked like burned plastic—frizzled, pulpy, and painful to the touch. He wore long-sleeve shirts to cover up his arms, but his hands, neck, and right cheek were also partially burned.

Ike's doctor recommended a psychologist to help him deal with his disfigurement, but Ike resisted. "How could a psychologist understand what I'm feeling?" he cried.

"Then at least let me put you in touch with a support group," urged the doctor.

"Maybe later," Ike said. "Not now. I need to sort out my own thoughts before I start sharing my feelings with strangers."

The encouraging words Ike received from Gayle and Christina lifted his spirits, but his depression remained crippling. The trucking company he worked for gave him a severance package but Ike was not entitled to worker's compensation because, as it said in the report, "Ike Fisher's accident was not caused while performing the duties required of the job."

He needed work, scouring the classifieds for something he could do without much human contact, such as night security. He landed a janitor's job at an elementary school about an hour north of his home. He worked the four-to-midnight shift

Monday through Friday cleaning the bathrooms, waxing the floors, and straightening up the classrooms. On nights when it snowed, he had to return to the school at five A.M. and plow out the parking lot.

Ike hated those snowy nights. Not only because he had to plow the lot at five A.M., but because he couldn't avoid bumping into the students and teachers as they arrived for school. He was a gentle man, but his disfigurement made people treat him like a monster. The teachers were respectful but simply tried to avoid him. The students were at first frightened of him but soon recognized his timid manner and took advantage. From around the corner, Ike heard clusters of kids calling him a freak as they giggled and scooted down the hallway.

He never got mad. When he looked in the mirror he felt like a freak. Sometimes he would sit alone in the school basement sobbing, unable to conceive of what his life had become. *Is this all that's left?* he wondered desperately. *A deformed body, living alone and cleaning toilets for the rest of my life?*

As Ike emerged from the basement one day, his eyes red and inflamed from crying, a boy from the third grade wandered by. "What's the matter, mister?" he asked.

Ike looked down at him, wiping his eyes with his fingertips, and said, "Aren't you supposed to be in class?" The boy flashed the bathroom pass in his right hand. "Oh," said Ike, "well, maybe you should be getting back now."

"I will in a minute," replied the boy. "What's the matter? I can see that you were crying. Maybe I can help you."

"You can't help me, kid, you wouldn't understand."

"Is it because of your skin?" asked the boy.

Startled by the boy's candid question, Ike said, "Yeah, that's part of it."

Then, without hesitation, the little boy raised his shirt, revealing a fragile torso with skin that was charred and fleshy. "You see, mister, I do understand," he said sympathetically. "But it's not what people see that makes us who we are; it's who we are on the inside that counts. My grandma taught me that."

Ike stared at this child—so thin and delicate. He winced, knowing how painful it was getting burned and imagining that for a little boy, the pain must have been more excruciating than he could ever imagine.

The boy dropped his shirt and stared up at Ike. Still teary-eyed, Ike asked, "How did you get that burn, little guy?"

"The oven in my parents' house blew up because of a gas leak. I was sitting at the table doing my homework when it happened," he replied, his voice cracking as he described the incident.

"Was anyone else hurt?"

"No. My mom was the only one home and she was in the washroom putting clothes in the dryer. How did you get burned, mister?"

"I rescued two people from a car and it exploded when I tried to save their puppy," Ike uttered.

"So you saved two people's lives?" the boy asked in amazement.

"Yeah," replied Ike, thinking of the cross he now had to bear.

"So, mister, those burns you have are just your scars for being a hero. All heroes have scars, you know. Don't be sad about your burns; be proud that you saved two people's lives," declared the boy. "I better get back to class now. It was nice talking with you, mister."

"Uh, what . . ." Ike was going to ask the little boy his name, but he ran down the hallway so fast Ike never got the chance.

When Ike got home after work that day, he glared at his reflection in the mirror, gently fingering the scarred areas of his neck and face. The words that little boy had heard from his grandma echoed in his mind—*It's not what people see that makes us who we are; it's who we are on the inside that counts.* For the first time Ike didn't see a disfigured man with a bleak future gawking back at him. For the first time Ike felt proud of himself and saw new possibilities for his future.

I saved the lives of two people that night, Ike thought. *I can no longer treat what happened to me on the side of that highway as my death sentence. As long as I have life, I have possibilities,* he professed. *Now I guess it's time I begin to seize them.*

Ike lived for another twelve years. He continued his job at the elementary school for two more years. During that time he got to know the students and teachers, and he gave speeches on the topic of possibility and the different types of scars we wear as we journey through life—mental, emotional, and physical scars. Ike spoke at other schools and community organizations. He told the story about the little boy in third grade who helped turn his life around and urged his audiences to listen to children, because often they say miraculous things.

When Ike died there were two pictures of him on either side of his casket, representing the two dramatic stages of his life and who he was during each of those times. For a person who at one time wanted only to isolate himself from the world, Ike Fisher had an overwhelming number of people eager to say their good-byes and pay homage to a unique and special man. Of course, among the crowd were the two women who, through shared letters and conversations over the years, had grown to love this man. Gayle and Christina Florio came to say farewell not only to Ike Fisher, but to a hero.

The little boy whose words influenced Ike and helped him turn his life around moved to a different school a few days after their fortuitous meeting in the hallway. They never saw each other again. Ike died believing that the little boy in the third grade was somehow there to rescue him from a life of misery and for that, Ike was eternally grateful.

Inspired by GLORIA RAMSEY

CHAPTER FOUR

Believing in Ourselves

Celebrating the gifts we possess,
recognizing what we are capable of accomplishing,
and finding the boldness to take action

Sometimes it's easier for us to see the potential in
others than it is to see the possibilities within
ourselves. Often this occurs because we are unaware of
other people's insecurities and see only their
confidence, while at times we wrestle with feelings of
doubt within ourselves. Through introspective stories
bubbling with the rich wisdom that comes from
experience, we discover how to peel off the layers of
insecurity, finally revealing what lies just below the
surface—elevated self-confidence, our unique talents,
and a gallant willingness to risk and succeed.

Pluck

*K*evin Carpenter stumbled home from school one day downhearted and in despair. The final selections for the basketball team had been made and the roster posted in the school gymnasium—his name omitted, same as always. He'd given it his all during the tryouts; he even practiced on the weekends and evenings after school. But like the last boy to get picked for kickball when team leaders choose sides, Kevin felt utterly rejected.

Kevin's grandma lived with him and his parents. As he floundered through the front door that afternoon, she noticed something was wrong. "What's the matter?" she asked, genuinely concerned.

"Nothing, Grandma," Kevin mumbled, thinking that she wouldn't understand.

But she insisted. "Why don't you tell me? Maybe I can help."

"I got cut from the basketball team, okay?" His voice seethed with frustration.

"You mean even after all the practicing you did?" she pointed out, not realizing the stinging effect of the words she chose.

Kevin snapped, "You're not helping me!"

"I guess you'll just have to practice more," she responded, unfazed by his remark.

"No, Grandma! I quit! I'm never trying out again. I gave it everything I had and I still didn't make the team."

"It sounds like you need more pluck!" she declared.

"Pluck?" He looked at her as if she were crazy. "You mean *luck*, don't you, Grandma?"

"No. I mean pluck," she insisted. "You know—courage, determination, spirit, chutzpah! Those things that keep people going when the tide turns against them. Let me share with you a little fable I read years ago," she continued.

"A mouse that lived near the home of a great magician was so fearful of cats that the magician took pity on the tiny mouse and turned it into a cat. Immediately, it began to fear dogs, so the magician turned it into a dog. Then it began to fear tigers, so the magician turned it into a tiger. Then it began to fear hunters, so the magician, in disgust, said, 'Then be a mouse again! Since you have only the heart of a mouse it is impossible to help you by giving you the body of a braver animal.' And the poor creature once again became a mouse."

Kevin's grandma glared at him sternly, pointing a bony finger in his direction. "Any worthy achievement demands that you have the determination to see it through by always putting forth your best energies," she said, thrusting a fist in the air. "Electrify yourself with passion and the drive to get what you want. In the end you'll think better of yourself and the world will think better of you." Then she smiled and softly said, "Always remember the fable I just shared with you. And when the time comes that you're scared or feel like giving up, ask yourself, *Am I a man or a mouse?*"

Inspired by TERRY J. SCOTT

Taking a Chance

My friend Chris and I were attending a charity fund-raiser—one of those pretentious functions where small talk consists of people bragging about their philanthropic endeavors rather than the size of their stock portfolios. We were tracing the odd sequence of events that had led to us being there—neither of us had enough money to be "philanthropic"—when suddenly, an exquisite woman strolled confidently through the doorway, her red hair aflame against her sparkling black dress. Jaws dropped and heads turned as people gasped at her exquisite beauty. Chris was struck right between the eyes. She was tall—six feet in heels, elegant, and sophisticated. In other words, she was out of his league. Normally he wouldn't have the nerve to approach such an irresistible woman, but after some cajoling, I convinced him that he couldn't pass up the opportunity. Plus, watching him make a play for such an attractive lady would be an entertaining way to help pass the time. When he saw her standing at the bar waiting for a drink, he primed himself and made his move. I wished him luck and watched, smiling, as he paced over, wiping the sweat from his palms on the back of his pants just before making contact.

What followed astounded me. I stared dumbstruck as they laughed, enjoying great conversation. He ordered a drink and stood there leaning against the bar, self-assured as James Bond. I wondered if he was sipping a vodka martini, shaken not stirred. About twenty minutes later he strutted toward me, gleaming with pride.

"So what happened?" I asked, barely able to contain myself.

"I think I'm in love," he said, shaking his head in disbelief. "She was beautiful, intelligent, and funny. And you know what the best part was? I sounded intelligent and was funny. She even laughed at my jokes. What more could a guy want? She brought out the part of me I like about myself. And a part of me I never knew existed."

"Well, what happened?"

"I felt so confident I asked her if she had any plans later tonight. That's when she said to me, 'How old are you?' "

"Did you tell her the truth?"

"Are you kidding? When a woman asks how old you are she already has doubts, so the best course of action is to lie. Make yourself older or younger, depending on the situation. So that's what I did. I added four years and told her I was thirty-two."

"Did she believe you?"

"I guess so. Then she asked me to guess how old she was. Dangerous territory, but I thought clearly. I deducted five years and told her I thought she was thirty-eight."

"So when are you going to see her again?"

"Next Saturday. Her place."

"Get out of here. That's great!"

"It's not what you think. She's throwing a twenty-fifth birthday party for her granddaughter, and since a lot of people my age will be there she thought I would have a good time. She told me to bring a friend, so you're invited, too."

"Her granddaughter! She's one of the most beautiful women I've ever seen. I can't believe she's a grandmother. Are you still going to the party?"

"Sure. If she looks that good, could you imagine what her granddaughter must look like?"

"Good point. Hopefully she won't mention that you were hitting on her tonight."

"Hopefully. But I've got to tell you, my confidence level shot through the roof. The last time I spoke with a woman that good-looking I was sixteen years old and talking to the poster hanging on the wall in my bedroom."

Inspired by CHRIS MCDONALD

Why Am I Special?

*G*randma, am I special?" my granddaughter asked sheepishly. "If there's somebody just like me, does that make me less special?"

"Why, of course you're special, Andrea," I replied, trying to assure my young granddaughter that she was, indeed, unique. "There is no one else like you anywhere in the world."

"Then why do people always say that my best friend Samantha and I look alike?" she asked curiously. "We even like all of the same things."

Snickering, I said, "What makes you special is not what you look like or what games you play, but who you are on the inside."

"What do you mean?"

I thought for a moment before posing a question to her. "Each person in your class is a what?"

"A student?" she said quickly, satisfied with her answer.

"Yes, they are all students," I replied, "but each person is an individual. That means there has been no one exactly like her in the past and there will be no one exactly like her in the future. The same thing goes for you. Let me show you what I mean."

I thought for a moment, then asked, "Who do you know that thinks exactly like you do all the time?"

"Nobody," she answered.

"You and Samantha may appear similar, but have you ever looked really close and noticed a lot of little differences?"

"Sure, Grandma. Her nose is bigger than mine."

Chuckling, I said, "Okay, well, she'll probably get that fixed someday, but that's another subject. How many people go to your school?"

"A lot, Grandma," she answered. "Over three hundred people, I think, but most of them are older than me."

"How many people are in your grade?"

"Twenty-four, Grandma. Oops, no, wait, twenty-five. I forgot to count myself."

"Okay. How many people sit in your row?"

She counted slowly, picturing the familiar faces before exclaiming, "Six, and that includes me, too. I have the first seat in the second row."

"How many people are assigned to your seat?"

"Oh, Grandma, just me," she said with an infectious little giggle. "There wouldn't be room for anyone else in my seat."

"Now do you see what I mean? Out of over three hundred students who go to your school, there is only one person assigned to the first seat in the second row in your class. That's you. That makes you special. When you're at a dance recital and stare out beyond the bright lights and into the audience for your mommy and daddy, how do you recognize them?"

"They've got the biggest and brightest smiles and they're usually already waving at me."

"That's because for you they're one of a kind and stand out in a crowd, making them extra special. And someday, when your mommy and daddy come to your graduation, their eyes will be darting through the crowd trying to find you. There will be twenty-four other students all wearing the exact same graduation gown, but they'll be looking for you. And when they recognize you, their hearts will burst with pride, as will mine. That's what makes you special. It's also why each life is so precious. We all have something so unique, one of a kind—it's something no one else can ever give."

"What is it, Grandma? What do we all have that's so special?"

"Ourselves, my dear. We have ourselves to give to the world."

Inspired by JOAN REYNOLDS

Practice Makes Perfect

One day I was watching my grandson, Stevie, shoot basketball. For hours he practiced shooting from the left and right sides, just under the hoop. Every shot sprang off the backboard and *swoosh*, slipped gracefully through the net. Finally I said, "Stevie, do you plan on shooting from anywhere else on the court?"

Cupping the ball in his lap, he declared, "Not yet, Grandpa. Since I'm in a wheelchair, I won't be able to run around the court. So I decided to master my shots close to the net. This way, when my team gets the ball they can just pass it to me and we've got two points."

"I guess they'll be calling you the Point Man," I said, offering him some encouragement.

"No, Grandpa," he replied. "They'll call me the Leading Scorer!"

Inspired by CALVIN RYDER

Message in a Bottle

here I was, perched at the edge of the wooden dock my grandfather had built when I was a little girl. The sun, dipping low behind the mountain, cast a warm orange glow across the lake right to the brink of the dock, right to me— as if the exquisite sunset was meant for me alone. Perhaps it was a message that there would always be a glimmer of light illuminating my path. Plunging my feet into the water, I noticed that they looked distorted, large and hazy, as if I were peering at them through a plastic bubble. I could hear the faint roar of speedboats droning in the distance.

The edge of the dock was the ideal place to think. I needed a fresh look at the challenges I was facing and hopefully some answers on how best to proceed. I was thirty-six years old, a mother of two, in the midst of a divorce, and facing the unknown.

I had dedicated the last twelve years to my family and loved it. But while I was changing diapers, cleaning clothes, and preparing lunches for school, it seemed the world had passed me by. I couldn't help but ask, *What will happen now?*

I needed a job, but sitting in front of the computer to write my résumé I felt lost, the blinking cursor on the white page taunting me. I had seen people performing low-wage jobs they obviously didn't like and I had to wonder, *Is that going to be me?*

I went on interviews, sitting in front of huge oak desks where people ten years younger than I quickly decided my fate. One morning, after an early-twenty-something rolled his eyes at what he considered my insufficient résumé, I said, "Do you appreciate all the things your mother did for you when you were growing up?" Before he could utter a word I added, "Because that's what I've been doing for the past twelve years!" I snatched my résumé off his desk and marched out, feeling proud that I'd spoken my mind but still scared, my eyes prickling with tears as I jabbed the elevator button.

After a few weeks of interviews I decided to run away for a couple of days to the home where I'd spent my summers as a child. The kids were with their dad and I hoped a weekend spent absorbing the fresh country air would shed new light on things. Turns out it was just what I needed.

Sitting there on the thirtieth plank, I spotted a bottle floating nearby, its long neck tossing in the water. *It must have fallen off one of the motorboats,* I thought. With my toes wedged between two planks and my upper body dangling off the brink of the dock I plucked the bottle from the water, snaring the cork with the tips of my fingers. It was dark and felt empty and I was planning on throwing it away when I wondered why an empty bottle would have a cork in it. *If it fell overboard by mistake, wouldn't it just fill with water and sink to the murky bottom?* Yanking on the cork, I turned the bottle over, my heart leaping with surprise when a note toppled onto the dock. "This is something out of the movies," I said aloud. "I can't believe this!" Hastily, I grabbed the paper, unrolled it on the dock, and grew absorbed in the message scribbled on the page.

A mother is the morning and evening star of life and nature has set her on a pedestal. The light of her eyes is always the first to rise and often the last to close at the end of the day. Her love glows in her sympathies and reigns in all her thoughts and deeds. A mother is brave in her actions, wise in her advice, and tender with her feelings.

Seated Indian-style with tears drizzling down my cheeks and the paper clenched in both hands against my chest, I felt grateful. For twelve years I had held the most important position in the world—mother. Venturing into the business world and threading my way through offices honeycombed with cubicles had intimidated me, but no longer. I am a mother. I'll find a career that enriches my life, perhaps even go back to school, further my education.

As I got up to leave, there was Judy, my grandmother, behind me on the dock. She asked if I was okay and where I got the bottle. I felt the words springing from my mouth but I refrained, saying, "It's just an empty bottle I pulled from the lake. Probably fell off a speedboat." I hugged her and together we meandered arm-in-arm up the path, back to the house.

Not until this very moment did I unleash the words that I desperately wanted to share with her that night, about that magical note in the bottle. I never told my grandma that I had curiously watched her earlier that evening, sneaking down through the thickets along the rim of the lake. It wasn't until reading the note and tracing my fingers over the familiar handwriting that appeared in so many of my birthday cards that I realized what had transpired. It wasn't until reading those words that I learned it was my grandma who'd uniquely understood what I needed to hear, what I needed to discover by myself. And so she decided to send me a message in a bottle.

Inspired by JENNY GIVENS

You Can Do It

A little boy stood by his grandpa's hospital bed. Even on his tippy-toes he could barely peek above the silver safety rails, but his words reached far and wide.

"Grandpa," he said, "when I couldn't get a hit on the baseball team you told me not to quit. You said if I was determined, I could do it.

"When I had all those lines to memorize for my class play and I couldn't remember them, you told me to try harder. You said if I was determined, I could do it.

"When I missed the shot in basketball and lost the game for my team, you told me to practice so it wouldn't happen again. You said if I was determined, I could do it.

"Grandpa, I know you don't feel good and you're probably tired, but don't quit, Grandpa. If you're determined, you can do it."

The little boy's grandfather, with tears rolling down his cheeks, gently reached for his grandson's hand and whispered, "I'll do it for you."

A short time later he was released from the hospital. The doctors said he made a miraculous recovery. When asked what made the difference, his eyes sparkled and he softly replied, "My grandson told me I could do it, and I wasn't going to let him down."

Inspired by MEL DESMOND

CHAPTER FIVE

HOPE AND SPIRIT

*Finding the faith to guide us
through life's darkest moments*

There will be times in our life when things look
hopeless and we feel alone. During those moments it's
essential that we connect with people who have rallied
the faith within themselves and learned to triumph
over the barriers they faced. The human spirit is
resilient, but when our hope is waning it's hard to
remain robust. Startling illustrations of what is
possible through the power of hope, faith, and love
will compel us all to make sure we have those "life
essentials" in our corner.

Strength of a Whisper

*U*p at four-thirty A.M. The shrill beep of the alarm was an unwelcome but necessary intruder in the darkness of my bedroom and the depth of my sleep. I acted quickly, shutting off that piercing sound before stumbling to the bathroom muttering, "I can't believe it's already time to get up."

Twenty minutes later, still groggy but inching closer toward complete awareness, I poked the buttons on the StairMaster at the gym. MANUAL SETTING—TWO HUNDRED TWENTY POUNDS—LEVEL SEVEN—START. Within five minutes I was fully stimulated, beads of sweat amassing on my forehead.

As those steps rotated and my eyes darted from the TV to the time I had left on that grueling machine, I thought about the conversation I'd had with my grandmother, "Gram," about seven hours earlier.

"Edward, I finally started exercising," she said in a feeble voice, her words grainy, as if they were being dragged over sandpaper. She strained just to eke out a whisper. "I can't swallow too good . . . the muscles in my throat are weak, so the doctor said I've got to build them up."

I already knew about Gram's throat problem. My mom told me that Gram needs her food diced up and has to concentrate when she eats, making sure those little morsels don't get lodged in her throat. She said Gram exercises while lying on her bed—neck and throat stretches, swallowing, and talking to herself.

My mother said, "I told her to try singing so the vocal cords and throat muscles get stimulated. When she was getting in the shower I peeked in and told her to sing in there. She belted out a tune right away, singing, 'Geeeet Oooout oooof Heeereee . . . !' Closing the bathroom door, I laughed and told her she had the right attitude."

Ever since Gram let me know about her weak throat muscles and trouble swallowing, I couldn't get her out of my mind. The frailness of her voice as she lay on the bed, staring at the ceiling and talking out loud. *What does she say?* I wondered. Prayers to my grandfather, Benny? Talking with God? Counting numbers? I admired her courage yet wanted to rescue her from the vision of helplessness gripping my thoughts.

As my thighs burned and my heart drummed against my rib cage while on the StairMaster that morning, the question *What can I learn from Gram's experience?* flashed before me. I glanced around the gym at the hard bodies. Glistening biceps flexing in the mirror, step aerobics classes with people kicking up their heels in unison—all of us striving to improve ourselves, the same way Gram was working to better herself. I felt so superior to her at that moment, gazing at my reflection in the mirror briskly climbing those steps while she was barely able to swallow, eating only mushy food. It seemed I had every advantage—youth, health, time, and opportunity. It was easy to understand how young people often don't give serious thought to what their grandparents may be facing. That night I picked up the phone and called her. "Gram," I asked, "how is your throat today? Still having a hard time eating?"

"I have to swallow slowly so I don't choke," she said in a brittle voice. "I don't mind though; taking my time . . . means I can savor the taste of my food, and you know how I've always loved to eat. Thank God I haven't lost my taste buds, that would really . . . stink!" Her words crept along, and although I could anticipate what she wanted to say I remained quiet, waiting for her to speak. "How are things going with your book?" She meant this one, the book you're holding in your hands right now.

"Good," I said, "very well."

"I'm praying for you every day that things go well with your book and everything else you'll do in the future."

I envisioned her sitting there, her decaying body, her left breast missing from an operation she'd had six years earlier, counting each breath, belabored, tedious. A few pieces of food left on her plate, too troublesome to get down. And the blue-and-white nightgown drooping over her sagging body. I remembered myself in the gym that morning—strong, vibrant, driving myself hard on the StairMaster. *If only I could give her a little of that,* I told myself.

"I know I'm a few thousand miles away, but is there anything I can do for you, Gram?"

"Just think of me honey," she said. "When I know you're thinking of me it makes things easier. I'm sorry I talk so slow. The vocal cord on my left side doesn't work anymore so it's hard to speak. I went to the beauty parlor today, though, got my hands and feet done. That was a nice treat.

"Edward," she said, "don't feel sad for me. This is my time to be eighty years old but that's just my body. My mind is much younger—twenty-four, I like to think. That's when I married your grandpa, one of the happiest times in my life. I remember being young and seeing people the age that I am now. It seemed like another world, one I would never reach—

but here I am. Many of the things I once had are gone now. Getting to this place in life meant I had to give up what I once possessed, my youth. But in return I have lived a full life, and if any of us could have one wish when we are born I'd say that would be it—to live a satisfying, happy life. I've got to go now, it's time for me to do my exercises. Okay? I love you."

"I love you, Gram. I'll see you soon." Hanging up, I slouched back in my chair and stared at the man in the window. I've noticed a few signs of aging on him lately. A couple of gray hairs on his temples that he hastily plucks out and his skin, not as tight as it used to be. He blinks when I blink, mirrors my every move. It's like looking at a stranger sometimes, when I stare at myself. The subtle signs of aging often catch me by surprise. The first gray hair, a tiny wrinkle—*This can't be me*, I think, but it is me, experiencing life's stages. I'm only thirty-four and have begun identifying the trade-off Gram had spoken about. I was in better shape at twenty-four, but looking back on the laundry list of mistakes I've made in the past ten years makes me realize that a few gray hairs and a couple of extra pounds are a worthwhile exchange for the wisdom I have gained. By my eightieth birthday I should be awfully smart—but what makes me gasp is thinking of all the mistakes I'll make over the next fifty years. I'd better give Gram another call tomorrow. Maybe she can't do forty-five minutes at level seven on the StairMaster, and maybe she talks slow these days, but she can tell me about life and some of what I may encounter over the next half century. And in that way she is vastly superior to me.

Inspired by MARY COLUCCI

Puddle Jumping

*D*riving west on Bay Street in San Francisco toward the Golden Gate Bridge offers one of the most sumptuous views in the United States. To the right lies the icy cobalt water of the bay, with the cell block of Alcatraz perched atop a rocky foundation. Angel Island, a lush uninhabited retreat that is a preferred locale for hikers and picnickers, looms large in the distance. Ahead are the Marin Headlands—the rolling mountains that ascend above the west side of the Golden Gate Bridge and are the last bastion of solid ground before the vast Pacific.

It's a sight I've seen hundreds of times, and it never ceases to captivate me. But today, while rolling down Bay Street, my eyes were diverted from one form of natural beauty to another. It had rained that morning, and although the sun now cast a tepid glow over San Francisco, there were still plenty of puddles lingering on the street. While waiting for the light to turn green, I spied a woman wearing a thick blue sweater, black pants, and walking shoes. She was propelling an ivory-colored baby carriage. Marching alongside her and holding on to the carriage with his right hand was a little blond short-haired boy bundled up in a red jacket and black boots.

They were approaching a dip in the sidewalk where a puddle had formed, and the woman put her hand on the boy's shoulder as she steered the carriage to the right. Abruptly, the boy ducked out from under her hand and, with his head hung low, stomped through that puddle flat footed in a gallant attempt to splatter as much water as he could with each step. It was pure innocence, and I couldn't keep from smiling.

When the light flashed green I stepped on the gas and watched that little boy shrink away in my rearview mirror. I couldn't help but think that children often have the best attitudes. As adults, why don't we jump in a puddle when we're in a bad mood? If we did it with a carefree attitude, like a child, it would change everything.

The blond boy who stomped affably through that puddle reminded me of C. J., another little blond-haired boy who has faced things head-on and whose courageous attitude paints a smile on people's faces. At six years old, C. J. was battling leukemia. I learned of this courageous boy from Nancy, C. J.'s devoted nurse and someone he came to see as a surrogate grandma.

The wonder of children is that they are unaware of the impossible. For many of us, getting leukemia would be a death sentence. For C. J. and other kids his age who lived on the floor of the children's cancer ward, it was a fight they didn't know they could lose. Nancy describes the environment:

> The floors are cold and the distinct hospital smell, a dreary odor in anybody's opinion, permeated the air—but the staff made every attempt to create an animated environment where children can feel normal, even though they are faced with a very abnormal and frightening disease. The walls are decorated with crayon sketches, and pictures of

former child residents are posted in a glass display case in the main hallway. A towering stack of children's movies is available in the playroom; dispersed on the rainbow-checkered carpet are toys, dolls, air-filled chairs, handheld video games, and building blocks.

C. J., like most of the children there, was forced to wheel an IV pole with the bag of solution dangling from above. He knew what time I arrived each day, and if he wasn't getting his treatments he'd wait for me in the hallway and run when he saw me enter the double doors at the far end of the corridor. It took all my might to hold back the tears as he clumsily hurried toward me, wheeling his IV pole behind him.

C. J.'s favorite movie was *The Lion King;* we watched it every day. We'd plop down in an overstuffed chair cuddled up together with his head tucked snugly under my chin. "This is my favorite part," he would say just before quoting a line from the movie, word for word, with his best character impersonations.

When he laughed, I wanted to cry. When he gazed up at me with his cheerful blue eyes and little pug nose, I smiled and kissed his forehead. And when the harrowing sounds of a child screaming infiltrated our peaceful space, I turned up the volume of the movie.

"Nurse Nancy," he often said to me, "I'm going to get better. I promise you, I'm going to get better." I wondered where he got the strength.

I often found myself standing at the entrance to the playroom watching a dozen bald-headed kids with sunken cheeks and blotted skin play and cackle together as if they didn't have a care or a worry in the world. Standing there I wondered, *Where do these children find their faith?* And then I realized it was because they are children, fortunate enough not to know their limitations. For some of them, that ignorance will save their lives.

Nancy wasn't just a surrogate grandma for C. J.; she was a part of his family. His parents looked to her for strength and support. She would accompany them to the chapel, where they prayed together for C. J.'s complete recovery.

Tender love and prayers seem to have worked their magic. As of this writing, C. J.'s cancer has gone into remission. His hair has grown back, black and curly, and for now his prognosis is a good one. When the doctor announced the good news C. J. looked up and confidently declared, "Nurse Nancy, I told you I would get better. I made you a promise and I don't break my promises."

A few days later C. J. left the hospital. Nancy drove the wheelchair, parking it on the sun-drenched sidewalk outside the hospital's main entrance. She wished the family well and promised to remain close, but she knew that for now her job was becoming a surrogate grandma for another child who needed support and whose family had so many frightening questions that needed to be answered.

The IV pole that C. J. had wheeled everywhere stood stoically in a corner with an empty bag hanging from the hook and the tube dangling a few feet above the ground. Sadly, within days a needle would be inserted into the end of that tube and another young boy or girl would be wheeling it around.

Children haven't learned of their weaknesses yet, so they remain pillars of strength. As adults, we are often so aware of our weaknesses that our strength is inhibited. As adults, we know too much about ourselves, so maybe the best we can do is merrily flail through a puddle on the sidewalk and relish the feeling of immaturity for a moment. It's okay to behave like a child sometimes. Kids are the most courageous and loving people in the world.

Inspired by NANCY FOSTER

A Search for Happiness

*T*he disease almost killed me. If it hadn't been for the support of my loving family, it would have surely been my demise. Some days I felt good and eager to fight; other days I just wanted to throw up my hands and surrender.

My mother had had it, and so did a few other people in my extended family. I remember being young and seeing the effect it had on them. But I never dreamed the same thing would happen to me. I didn't understand how it could. I took good care of myself mentally and physically, so how could it creep up on me? But it did. I didn't realize I had a problem until I was forced to look at the obvious. Like many people, I didn't want to admit this was happening, afraid of what I would lose if I tried to treat it and scared of what I would sacrifice if I simply ignored it.

Finally I could no longer deny it. I needed help—professional help. I was referred to experts in the field and met with others who'd lived through the same ordeal. At first we were strangers united by a common bond, but over time they became my friends. They helped me find within myself the courage to fight. They made me realize that hope for the future was the most important thing, and that if I didn't take the necessary steps to remedy my problem, all would be lost.

With the backing of my family and new friends, I took the necessary steps. I'm fifty-six years old and have been a recovered alcoholic for three years. Today I am blessed with a baby grandchild. I used to look for happiness in a bottle. I finally found it. These days the most precious moments for me are holding a bottle of formula for my granddaughter, Carly, at dinnertime.

Inspired by JOSEPH SANTOS

This One Day

This was her day. She radiated in her glimmering white gown, and everyone was vying for just a twinkling of her attention. She'd married the man of her dreams, and her closest friends and family members were there to join in the celebration. Like an angel, she danced the night away, and when she spoke people hung on her every word.

But there was one person her sparkling blue eyes returned to again and again—the one who spent the entire evening with a bashful smile beaming across his face. He sat at the number one table watching her, the memories spinning through his mind. He remembered the days when she was a baby, and he had cuddled her in his arms. He reflected on the times when she was a little girl and skinned her knee, and how he'd kissed it and made it all better. He reminisced about her teenage years when their relationship was strained because she wanted to spend time with her friends. And he thought about how, when those years had passed their relationship had flourished again. He was her grandpa.

And now she was dancing in front of him, a full-grown woman embarking on a magnificent new experience. As she spun barefoot on the dance floor, her eyes passed him sitting at the table. With each twirl, she waved and smiled.

A moment later, glistening and slightly out of breath, she took the seat next to him and laced her fingers into his.

They looked deeply into each other's eyes. Only the two of them fully understood the significance of that moment. "Do you think they see us?" she asked with childlike anticipation.

"Somehow I think they're here with us," her grandpa said with a smile. "Don't you feel the awesome presence of love in this room?"

"Yes, I do, Grandpa."

He whispered in her ear, "Well, then, that's how you know they're here. This is your day and they wouldn't miss it for anything in the world."

She kissed her grandpa delicately on the cheek and whispered "I love you" in his ear. Then, with a bridesmaid on either side, she promenaded back to the festivities on the dance floor. Grandpa smiled sadly and reminisced about that part of their history.

She had been spending the weekend at his house while her mom and dad escaped to the seclusion and comfort of a bed-and-breakfast nestled deep in the Blue Ridge Mountains. On the drive home after a sun-drenched weekend, the rain began to fall lightly, casting a thin sheen of water on the roadway. The two-lane mountain road they were traveling on grew slick; a truck barreling the other way lost traction and careened across the double yellow line, hitting them head-on. Her father was killed instantly, and her mom died in the life flight helicopter en route to the hospital.

Grandpa's house turned into her permanent new home. She was six years old. Grandpa was there to support her, and she became a pillar for him to lean on, too. Together they helped each other cope with the catastrophic loss of their family. She had lost her mom and dad, and he'd lost a son and a daughter-in-law.

Over the years the anniversary of that tragic day took on a special significance. Each year they traveled to the scene of the accident and planted fresh flowers. Afterward they'd visit the cemetery to pray and talk with the family they had lost. During the first few years it was a sad, very painful tradition, but as their emptiness diminished and their love for each other grew stronger, it took on a different meaning. Instead of crying and reminiscing about the times they'd missed, they came to feel it was the one day of the year all four of them could be together.

So when this young girl grew up and met the man of her dreams, there was only one day of the year she could get married—the day she knew her parents would be there. That afternoon, as her grandpa walked her down the aisle and more than two hundred pairs of radiant eyes studied their every move, only the two of them could understand the true significance of that day and that moment in time. For there, among all those friends and loved ones, were the presence and love of her parents. The tragic anniversary date of their death became the one day of the year when all four of them could be together, and so it became her wedding day.

Inspired by VERONICA WHITE

Strength of Spirit

*W*hat if you could never get out of the seat you're lounging in right now? How would you feel if the bones and muscles in your feet and legs never supported your body weight again? What would it be like to lie in bed glaring at the lifeless stems extending from your hip sockets and terminating at the tips of your toes?

Those are the questions I pondered the first time I saw Shane Gailey midway between two stainless-steel parallel bars, cautiously letting the weight shift from his arms to his atrophied legs and feet dangling an inch above the floor. He flexed his arms, inching his body lower until the cold rubber mat kissed his toes, signaling the boundary line. The strength in his arms was assured, but he felt that his legs would buckle with just an ounce of pressure applied to them.

I watched his face grimace as his body weight exhausted his arm muscles. After a few seconds, the therapist rescued him from that rickety position and eased him back into the wheelchair. After catching his breath, Shane rolled through the parallel bars and swung a hard left at the far end. That's when he saw me standing in the doorway.

"Alex," he said, "I didn't know you were here. But now that

you are, I'm gonna make you an offer you can't refuse. How about taking me to lunch in the cafeteria? The food is terrible, the prices are too high, and the place has a funky smell. Whaddya say?"

I laughed and said, "Now that *is* an offer I can't refuse." Shane's favorite movie was *The Godfather*, and he quoted it often.

I offered to wheel him to the elevator but he insisted on maintaining his independence. "My legs are like string beans so I've got to keep my arms muscular," he said jokingly. I forced a laugh, hoping it would keep me from crying. Shane had been my dearest friend since we'd fought over a Tonka truck in the first grade and our teacher forced us to share it.

While boarding the elevator, Shane's therapist came running over, her arms flailing and a manila folder braced in her right hand. "Shane, you need to sign off on this," she said, drawing out the *a* in his name.

As she explained the form, I thought about the day of Shane's accident. He was helping his uncle move an armoire. They got it into the hallway and were sliding it on a blanket across the slate floor when Shane's uncle went to answer the telephone. Shane decided to surprise his uncle by pulling the armoire onto the elevator himself. When he heard the familiar *ding* signaling that the elevator had arrived on his floor, he stepped back—and tumbled three stories down to the basement. An electrical malfunction had caused the doors to open when the elevator car was on a different floor. Ironically, there I was holding the elevator door open as Shane signed off on some paperwork.

A few minutes later Shane and I arrived in the cafeteria for some bad food and good conversation. His sprightly disposition amazed me. I had other friends who were irritable when it rained or when the pizza delivery guy was ten minutes late.

Shane couldn't walk and he still maintained a positive attitude. That day, over dry roast beef sandwiches and lukewarm iced tea, he told me where he'd acquired such a heroic outlook on life.

"Right after the accident I was devastated. I'd spend days writing out lists of all the things I'd forfeited to fate," he said. "I felt trapped in cement boots . . . as if the world was zipping past me and I was reaching out trying to latch on with my fingertips, but was left behind. I'd lie in bed at night hyperventilating as my heart raced from the panic-stricken realization that everything I cared about was gone.

"During those first weeks when Michelle kissed me good night and the door closed behind her I feared she was walking out of my life forever. 'Why would she want to stay with a cripple!' I'd say, smacking my legs and not feeling a thing. The possibilities of what could have been and what I now had to face were eating me alive. I was never so scared and angry in my life, but a very wise man took the time to point out all the things that I was failing to see.

"He said, 'It's easy to be courageous and optimistic when there's nothing to fear, but the true heroes are courageous and optimistic in the face of fear.' So he introduced me to people facing the same situation I was, but they were doing it with courage. I wondered if they were delirious or just in denial, but it was neither. I spoke with a woman named Denise whose legs were crushed in a car accident. She's here five times a week for rehab, has two young kids, and when I asked how she does it she simply said, 'I found a way.' Her kids stay with their grandparents sometimes, but Denise and her husband make the sacrifices and stick together. It's the most courageous thing I've ever seen. Like many of the people here, she has resolved to get better and use what she is learning from this experience to her advantage. I've learned a lot from Denise and the other people here, and they've become my friends. It has taught me that common sufferings are a stronger link than common joys. When things are good, we don't feel the need for support. When times are tough, that's when we create the ties that bind.

"One evening, after my mom left the hospital broken-hearted, this man whispered the following words in my ear: 'There is only one way of dealing with fate—whether you are faced with blessings or afflictions—and that is to behave with dignity. You must not lose heart, or it will worsen for you and for the ones you love. All people are born with the traits of a hero, but only by fighting the toughest battles does one's hero-ism take shape.'"

Shane peered at me with his right fist clenched on the table and said, "His words struck a chord deep within me and I vowed at that moment to never be defeated. It's easy to accept pity from others," he confessed. "What's hard is remaining brave when facing exceptional challenges. My legs are feeble—you can probably wrap one hand around my thigh—but they're sensitive to temperature, and that grants me a sliver of hope, urging me to endure whatever is necessary to achieve complete recovery."

"So who is this wise man who enabled you to adopt this Herculean attitude?" I asked.

Shane snapped a bite of his pickle and smiled wistfully before revealing the truth: "He's my grandfather Earl. He fought in World War Two. He owned a convenience store that burned down and was forced to rebuild from scratch. He lived through the Great Depression, lost a son in Vietnam, and just last year his wife, my grandma, passed away. Through everything he has maintained his dignity and learned as much as he could for himself, and now for me. He's the strongest man I know.

"One day I will walk again," pledged Shane. "The quote *What doesn't kill me makes me stronger* never meant more to me than it does now. Not a day goes by that I wouldn't prefer to be charging down the field with a football in my hand or strolling in the park with Michelle, but I can't do that today. I will, however, do those things again someday. And when I do, they will taste sweeter than ever.

"What my grandpa and the people I've met helped me to see are the possibilities. Initially, those were tough to notice—it's not easy seeing beyond the limitations of this wheelchair—but I have, and now I am more resolute than ever. When one stage of life ends, another begins, and with it comes different challenges and rewards. I'll never quit, so I'll never be defeated, and in the end I'll emerge a better person, and that's a noble pursuit."

Shane's tenacity is beginning to pay off. His legs can withstand pressure, and he recently took his first few steps without the support of a therapist or parallel bars. It was a milestone on his journey toward complete recovery. His parents, grandfather, and girlfriend, Michelle, were there to see it. Everyone cried and cheered. Shane has remained strong for them, and they have for him. It seems that the combination of strength and love will enable Shane to prevail and, one day, walk again. I guess a strong spirit really does conquer all.

Inspired by ALEX VOGEL

・　・　・　・　・　・　・　・　・　・　・

Remember Me?

*W*ill Sanford was Ashley Cartwright's grandpa, and together they were two peas in a pod. They swung on the swings together, munched on vanilla ice cream in waffle cones together, and read stories to each other while lounging in a fishnet hammock tied between two oak trees in their backyard. They were, indeed, the best of friends. This is quite remarkable when you consider that a year earlier, they hadn't even known each other.

Ashley was eight years old when her grandpa was afflicted with a rare disease affecting the area of his brain controlling long-term memory. The familiar faces and wonderful times that Will Sanford had shared with his beloved granddaughter and the rest of his family vanished.

The symptoms tediously began revealing themselves when Will started forgetting the names of people he had known all his life. When paying bills, his own address evaded him. And when driving home, he often forgot which street he lived on. The deterioration of his memory continued at a brisk pace until he awoke one day shrieking, because his very surroundings were suddenly unfamiliar. The last bit of light casting a glow on his past was sealed off forever. Will and his wife,

Carol, had been staying with their daughter Melissa, and she fled to their bedroom when he cried out. "Dad, Dad," she stammered, "what's the matter?"

The answer to her question was swift and severe as he gazed into her eyes and asked, "Who are you?"

The doctor had warned the family that this day would come. But for Carol, Melissa, and the rest of Will's family, it was a shocking and heart-wrenching realization that the man they loved suddenly didn't recognize them.

Instantly Will was catapulted back in time, forced to undergo the same feelings of discovery children face. He went from being an educated man who had raised two children to feeling like a youngster, naive in the ways of the world.

Carol and Melissa showered Will with love. They took him to areas in the neighborhood he had been a thousand times, and played his favorite music, hoping to ignite the memories they felt were buried somewhere deep in the caverns of his subconscious. But to Will, life was a sudden mystery. At fifty-five, he was just being introduced to the world when he should have already possessed a lifetime of experiences.

Melissa delicately explained to her daughter, Ashley, what had happened to her grandpa. "So he's learning new things just like I am," Ashley exclaimed.

"That's right," replied Melissa. "Grandpa learned a lot, but all the memories that were stored in his brain got lost. Even the way he recognizes you as his granddaughter disappeared somewhere. That doesn't mean he doesn't love you; it just means he lost the ability to recognize the people he loves."

"So we just have to start over again, right, Mom?" Ashley said with confidence.

"What do you mean, honey?"

"I don't remember when, but there was a time when I

learned to love Grandma and Grandpa. Now we have to make sure Grandpa can learn to love us." Spontaneously, Melissa's eyes were soggy with tears and she graciously wrapped her arms around her daughter.

"Each person should continue living life normally," the doctor said. "It's the best way to introduce Will to an unfamiliar world, while keeping everyone else engaged in familiar activities." Upon hearing the doctor's advice, Ashley quickly scribbled down a list of the things she and her grandpa had enjoyed doing together. She wanted to introduce him to each of them again, for the first time.

It was promptly apparent that Ashley would be the one to arouse her grandpa's curiosity and reduce his fears of the unknown. Her inquisitive nature inspired Will to take the plunge and reacquaint himself with foods, places, and people that he had loved for a lifetime.

One by one Ashley went down the list of things they enjoyed doing together. The feeling was bittersweet when they splurged on vanilla ice cream in waffle cones for the first time. Will loved the frosty smooth texture of the ice cream and the crunch of the crisp cone, but it was a reminder of all the memories that faded away—the other times he had shared a waffle cone with his granddaughter, the Christmases they'd spent together, and his younger years. Even the memories of his life with Carol, their wedding, and the years spent raising a family together were erased from his memory.

Perhaps the hardest part was that Will could no longer teach Ashley about important life lessons because, like her, he was learning them for the first time. He couldn't dip into the memories of what things were like when he was a child because in a unique way, he was experiencing childhood all over again. The opportunity for them to continue a normal grandparent–grandchild relationship had been stripped away and this affected Ashley's mother, Melissa, terribly. She remembered how things were before Will lost his memory and how Ashley had learned many poignant lessons about life from her grandpa.

Within a few months, however, Melissa began noticing the beauty blossoming in the new relationship between Will and Ashley; the delight they shared when discovering something new, from amusement park rides to visiting the Grand Canyon. For both of them, life was fresh, bursting with animation.

The broken hearts in Will's family may never completely mend, but they pore through old photo albums with him, looking for a glimmer of recollection and introducing him to his past life. "He deserves to know the people in these pictures," they say, "and his family and friends deserve to be reintroduced to him."

Understanding that Will has no memory of his past is especially hard for Melissa because they were so close. She now feels that the precious memories the two of them shared together are permanently lost.

Melissa understands that she can't change the past or bring it back to life, so she seeks solace in the budding relationship between Will and Ashley and seeing her parents slowly begin to fall in love all over again. She knows that at least these memories will remain in the heart and mind of her father, forever.

Inspired by MELISSA SAMUELS

CHAPTER SIX

KNOWING HOW TO
LEARN FROM LIFE

*Making the most of every experience by reflecting
on our mistakes and being aware of each step we
take on the road to fulfillment*

Too many of us are in a constant hurry. We scramble
from one activity to the next, often unaware of the
direction we're heading and seeking comfort in the
belief that if we're busy, we must be doing something
right. What we need to do is stop and acquaint
ourselves with where we are, how we got there, and
then ask, *Am I happy?* In these stories people have
pondered such questions, receiving answers that have
altered the course of their lives.

A Time of Discovery

*D*id you ever lie on the cool grass at night and gaze in wonder at the twinkling stars? Reaching up, trying to grasp them with your hands?

I have always been fascinated with astronomy. My grandpa, whom we called Grandpa Jack, was a retired navy man and spent many nights staring at the stars and studying their formations. He taught me how the moon's gravity affects the ocean tides and the theory of the planets forming from an immense cloud of gas and vapor. The vivid imagery Grandpa Jack used in telling his stories made me feel as if I were there, floating in space or aboard the *Santa Maria* when Columbus discovered America. These true tales inspired my fascination with outer space, ancient sea voyages, and the discovery of new worlds and planets.

On my fourteenth birthday Grandpa Jack presented me with a savings bond and Darwin's *Origin of Species.* I couldn't help but think, *Thanks for the book, Grandpa, but I would have preferred cash instead of a savings bond. I can't buy a pizza with a savings bond.* What I did do, however, four years later, was cash in that bond and use it for part of my tuition at MIT. I was going there to study physics and the farthest reaches of outer space.

Upon my acceptance into college, Grandpa Jack presented me with another gift—a relic that had stood proudly on his desk during his service in the navy. It was a bronze telescope he had purchased from an antiquities vendor in Europe forty years earlier. It was something I'd always admired, and although it didn't work well anymore, it still reminded me of the ambitious stargazers from centuries ago. They were true pioneers, exploring the unknown and hoping to expand humankind's knowledge of the universe. I possessed a burning desire to do the same.

I took the telescope to my bedroom, holding it in my hands and studying it as I had done so many times in the past. The bronze shimmered brightly in some places, but other areas were dull and faded. It was riddled with indentations and mounted on a two-inch oaken base with the word EXPLORE engraved on a bronze plaque bolted to the front. The scope squeaked slightly during adjustments, and the grip on the knobs was worn down like an old tire. I owned a modern telescope, of course, but this was a part of history and would be my most treasured possession in my room at MIT.

As I sat contemplating all the changes I would encounter within the next few months, Grandpa Jack knocked hastily on my door. He always knocked three times with the same amount of pressure and speed, so I knew it was him.

"Come on in," I shouted. He meandered in and smiled when he saw me hunkered in my chair, the telescope cradled in my hands.

"I've got something else for you," he said. "It's something I picked up the same time I bought that telescope. I always had a fascination with the stars, and the first line of what I am about to give you compelled me to buy it. As the years passed it became a beacon for how to live my life. Like me, you love to explore, and now you're about to embark on a new exploration in your own life. You'll discover many new things about yourself on this journey. What I'm about to give you isn't a road map; rather, it's a guiding light."

Grandpa Jack handed me a scroll of crusty old parchment paper. I held it up to my nose—it was musty, like the pages of an aged book that hadn't been opened in decades. On each end was a hand-carved chestnut-colored wooden handle. "I'll leave you alone to discover what's inside," he said softly, obviously satisfied that he'd just given me an important element of his past.

My back was to the door when I heard it close behind me, and I gently unrolled the scroll on my desk, the paper crinkling as I expanded it. The edges were frayed and the writing was in calligraphy. Following is what was written.

The Trials of Life

Stars shine brightest in the darkest nights. Diamonds are formed through constant pressure. Gold radiates the greatest shine after it's been scoured. Spices smell the sweetest after they have been pounded. Success comes only after a great deal of sustained effort.

Those people who live without facing life's trials will die never having lived. It is only by struggling, fighting for what we believe in, that we know we are truly alive. The satisfaction of the struggle and subsequent reward is the greatest joy in the world.

Opposition is not our enemy, it is our friend. This premise holds true in man as well as nature. The acorn is not an oak tree when it sprouts. It must endure long summers and fierce winters. The oak will only grow mighty battling fierce snowstorms, heavy rains, and side-striking winds. These elements of nature are rough, but they force the oak to grow stronger. In life, we can look for the easy road or blaze our own path. Those who take the road less traveled will encounter rough teachers, but they will emerge robust pupils.

A man is not a man when he is born; his life has only just begun. The same goes for a woman. The strength of manhood and womanhood comes through the years and trials they face during that time. In war, who does the general select for some challenging endeavor? He chooses the soldier who he knows will not flinch in the face of danger.

In all of us, there are desires waiting to be fulfilled. Remember that within you there is a battle raging: the fight between staying focused on your dreams and the temptation to succumb to immediate gratification. You cannot expect to strive for a professional position and live a life of leisure. You cannot expect to be healthy and indulge in rich foods. To live for your immediate desires and expect to achieve your long-term dreams is to ask for the impossible.

You can see it anywhere in the world—people who have achieved fantastic success. What is rarely ever seen is the amount of effort and sacrifice that was involved in their early years. You cannot get the reward without risk and hard work. But if you ask anyone who has achieved above-average success, they will say the sacrifice was a small price to pay for the feeling of great accomplishment.

As you go forward this day, believe in yourself. March to your own drummer. If you break with tradition and separate yourself from the crowd, you will stand alone for a time. But if you persist and hold steadfast to your beliefs, the crowd will join you and you will emerge the leader.

Today is your day. Go forth and do not look to step in the footprints of those who have gone before you—they may have gone the wrong way. Make your own footprints and blaze a trail for people to follow you.

After reading that scroll, I sat there thinking about life. I realized that as we go through life, every day is a process of discovery and exploration—the same as looking into outer space. The stargazer studies formations, hoping to find patterns that have some profound meaning. In life, we must do the same. What patterns and choices lead to happiness and satisfaction? Like the planets that humankind has not detected yet, there are points in each of our lives we have yet to discover.

I am nearing forty years old now. That bronze telescope and parchment scroll have been with me for half my life. Each morning, before I embark on the challenges and excitements of a new day, I read "The Trials of Life." It reminds me that each day should be relished and enjoyed, but that I should also remain on guard. Challenges and opportunities arise quickly, and I must be swift to slay the challenges and expeditious in seizing the opportunities.

Sometimes in life, it's the people we never meet who have the most dramatic impact on us—a grand hero who thrived centuries ago or a writer whose words reach the depths of our soul. Other times, it's someone we see each day who helps mold us into a stellar human being. Grandpa Jack's gift of storytelling transformed the way I perceive the world and the universe, and his legacy and teachings continue to influence my decisions.

Often I have broken from the crowd and stood alone. I found it difficult, but he was right—with the courage to stand alone and risk being wrong also comes the sweet vindication of having the foresight of knowing what's to come and what is waiting to be revealed.

Thanks to his advice I have stepped into the abyss, and—like looking into an unfamiliar region of outer space—I have been delighted with what I discovered about myself and my ability to perform in an uncertain world.

Inspired by WILLIAM J. KEATON

A Lesson Learned from
a Life Lived

*S*omeday we will all depart from this world.

The significance of that statement has changed for me over the years. When I was young, it didn't faze me. Death was a distant star, beyond my realm of thought. Like most young people, I didn't see any point in thinking about my own mortality. I was too busy living to spend time worrying about dying. What I failed to realize, however, was that thinking about my death could have helped me better plan my life.

Now that I am faced with the reality that my life is drawing to a close, I see things differently. I don't sit around thinking about it all day, but I don't ignore it either. I can't. I have learned not to.

These days I think about the choices I have made and the legacy I'll leave behind. *What will people think of me? Will they think of me? What should I have done differently?* These are the questions people ponder as they near the end of their lives.

It's disturbing to think that someday I will be forgotten. Where will the pictures of me end up ten, twenty, or fifty years from now? There is something scary about dying and being forgotten. Did I make a difference? Did my life have meaning?

For me, being forgotten is like drifting aimlessly in space. You are out there, somewhere, but no one knows you exist. So now, with the time that I have left, I am working to build myself a lifeline to the future.

I have always admired people whose names grace the pages of history books, their lives studied by students across the country and around the world. Visionaries such as Einstein and Edison have achieved immortality, but there are also millions of unsung heroes who have helped shape the future for the better. Maybe you know some of them. Perhaps you are one of them. Some are teachers who took an impressionable young soul under their wing and helped guide an ordinary life to an extraordinary adventure.

I could have been a teacher, but that role requires us to learn from our mistakes so we can then pass our knowledge on to younger generations. Unfortunately, I was too focused on my future to ever stop and learn from my past, so I repeated the same mistakes many times. I went through life with blinders on, seeing only what I wanted to see. I did what I thought I should do as the provider for my family, but never questioned if it was the *right* thing to do. I assumed too much and questioned too little. Late in life, I learned that assuming leads to mistakes and wasted time, while questioning leads to clarity and correct answers.

I valued money more than time, working extra hours to make a few more dollars and always thinking I could make up the time with family and friends . . . later, tomorrow, or next week. I never did. Now that my time is running out, I would trade all my money for just another day, one that I would spend with my family rather than at the office. But of course I can't, which is why I have shared my feelings, my remorse. I am hoping this will be my lifeline to the future. Whoever hears my words—my grandchildren, my great-great-grandchildren, anyone, I hope you learn from my mistakes.

Now that my final hours are approaching, my family is here with me. My son talks quietly with the doctor and has a concerned look on his face but has yet to shed a tear for me. My daughter holds my hand like a mannequin; she's here out of courtesy rather than love. And my grandchildren look at me as if I were a stranger, which to them, I am. I could have lived on in their minds if only I'd taken the time to love and teach them about the things I learned. The mistakes I made.

The end of my life has impelled me to reflect and recognize what I would have done differently. I cannot change the past but I can still learn from it, even in the short time I have left. The wisdom I glean from pondering my history I share with my family and hope it will make a difference in their lives. Because of the actions I take today I pray that someday in the distant future, when my headstone has endured the severity of many frigid winters, someone will find an old picture of me and say, "He was my teacher."

Inspired by KENNETH TRACY

The Long and the Short of It

*I*t was a whimsical spring day, and Grandma was sitting silently on the front porch of our vacation home. I was a rambunctious six-year-old and hurried over to her eagerly, asking, "Whaddya doin', Grandma?"

She chuckled and said, "I'm thinking about my life and writing down some of the most important lessons I've learned."

"Can I do that too, Grandma?" I asked zestfully. "Now that I'm in first grade I'm learning new stuff all the time."

Grandma smiled and peeled off a piece of paper from her yellow legal pad. She handed me a sharpened pencil and I plopped down next to her, eager to remember what I'd learned.

"I learned to share the toys at school with other people." I wrote that down. "I learned to color inside the lines." I jotted that down, too. "I learned to finger paint." I scribbled that one on my paper. I was on a roll—I had three lines filled up! I peeked over at Grandma's page, and she had all the lines filled up.

"Grandma," I asked, "why do I only have three lines of things I learned and you have a whole page?"

"That's because I'm older than you," she stated without hesitation. "I've learned more, because I've been around longer."

"But how can I make my list long like yours?" I asked. "I have a short list but want a long one because that will mean I'm smart."

Grandma giggled and said, "Well, there are two ways most people learn. The first is through reading books and doing projects at school. The second is through experiences, or what people call trial and error."

"What's that, Grandma?"

"That's when you learn by making mistakes," she said sharply.

"But aren't mistakes bad?"

"No. Mistakes help us to learn. Let me show you what I mean. The list of things you learned has three lines. The list of things I learned is longer. Now let's make a list of the mistakes we've made."

"Okay."

After a few minutes we compared our lists. Grandma said, "You see, your list of mistakes is short and mine is long. Making mistakes is a natural part of learning."

"So, Grandma, are you saying that learning and making mistakes go together?"

"That's right."

"Well, when I start second grade next year, I'm going to tell my teacher I want to make more mistakes than anyone else in the class!"

Inspired by TRACY GREEN

Stairway to Heaven

*H*is mother was standing at the workbench in the basement, slipping open those shallow drawers where different sizes of nails and screws are kept. She looked peculiar there among the tools. Her lily-white hands and shiny red fingernails were eye catching amid the ruggedness of the gray cutting saw, hammers, and wrenches. He was used to seeing her standing at the sink or the stove and asked, "Mom, what are you doing down here with Daddy's tools? Building something?"

"No, honey," she replied. "I'm looking for a nail to hang this picture."

Taking the framed photograph in his hand, the boy asked, "Who is it?"

"My grandma Gloria. I'm going to put it at the top of the steps so each morning as I head downstairs to start my day I'll see her face, hear her voice in my mind, and be reminded of all the wonderful things she taught me." The little boy followed his mom up the stairs and watched as she drove a thin nail into the wall with a couple of light taps.

"Stand back a few feet and tell me if this is straight," she said, holding the picture and looking back at him, her chin resting on her right shoulder.

"Up a little higher on that side, Mom," he said, pointing to the left.

"How about that?"

"That's good. Mom, how come that's the only picture hanging on our wall?"

"Because we've been lucky so far and still have the people we love right here with us. Your great-grandma," she said, pointing to the picture, "has joined God and the angels in heaven. And this will be our stairway to heaven."

"But Mom, the first thing at the top of these steps is the bathroom."

Chuckling, she said, "I know that, honey. What I mean is this wall will be a display for the people who have shaped our lives and have now moved on to the next stage of life."

With the passing years, as the young boy grew older, more faces were added to that stairway to heaven. It became a shrine for the people who were loved and a way to keep their memories alive. When he was nineteen years old he took the long walk into the basement with his mother to the same workbench and grabbed a nail from the drawer while she slipped a hammer from the leather holster on her husband's tool belt. That day they hung a picture of her father and his grandfather Nicky on the wall. He was six steps down from the top now.

At thirty-five, that teenage boy had become a man, had his own house and family, and continued the tradition by beginning his own stairway to heaven. For years the only photos that hung on the wall were of his grandparents. When his daughter, Elizabeth, was old enough she asked him, "Who are these people, Daddy?" pointing her delicate little finger high above her head.

"These are your great-grandparents. They were very special people in my life who I loved dearly. You never had the chance to meet them, but they taught me many things and much of what I learned from them I'm sharing with you, so in a way they're playing a very important role in your life."

Explaining this to his daughter helped him realize that hanging photos on the wall not only kept the relationship he had with his grandparents alive, but also allowed him to introduce the family from his past to his present family.

As the years rolled on and the man grew older, his stairway to heaven stretched from the top step to the bottom. Photos of his mom and dad were displayed. He hung them with Elizabeth, who made sure they were straight, just as he had many years before. Elizabeth eventually married and gave birth to a little girl. Suddenly her father was a grandpa, but the time he had to spend with his granddaughter would be short. A heart attack claimed him before his grandchild was old enough to know him and appreciate the place he occupied in her life. Until one day, not long after he passed, the little girl saw Elizabeth carrying a hammer, a nail, and a picture and asked, "What are you doing, Mommy?"

"I'm hanging a picture of your grandpa, honey," she said. "He loved you very much, and even though he didn't have much time to spend with you he did his best to teach you things. This picture will keep him close to us. I'll take it down sometimes and tell you stories about him, what he taught me and how much he loved you."

"What was his name, Mommy?"

"Nicholas. He was named after his grandpa, and I named you after him. That's how you got the name Nicole."

She drove the nail into the wall and hung the picture. Standing back a few feet with her hand gently stroking her daughter's hair, Elizabeth said, "Do you think it looks straight?"

"I think so, Mommy, but who are all these other people hanging on the wall?" she asked.

"Our family, honey. Reminders of where we've come from, of the people who have made a difference in our lives, and that my dad and your grandpa will always be with loved ones."

Inspired by ELIZABETH RYDER

The School of Hard Knocks

My grandmother Mary is not an educated woman. She made it through only the sixth grade before quitting school to help support her family. Although her paycheck was meager, she helped put food on the table and pay the rent. It was a vastly different world than when I was in sixth grade.

There were times when I felt confined to a classroom and preferred to be almost anyplace else, but looking back, sixth grade was the perfect place to be. I was getting an education, completely unaware of the burden my grandmother had faced at the same tender age. How would I have reacted if I had had to quit school and work sweeping floors at an old factory or washing dishes in the back of a restaurant? The thought of it made homework and the occasional trip to the principal's office look pretty attractive.

Now that I'm out of school I find myself thinking about my grandmother and how hard she labored. Because of her limited education she never got a well-paying job with a desk, comfortable chair, and wall-to-wall carpeting. Instead she dumped fifty-pound bags of flour in giant mixing bowls in the back of a bakery. She worked from the predawn hours until nighttime. My parents took my brothers and me to visit her there when we were kids. For us it seemed like the ideal place to work. Doughnuts, cookies, and sweet rolls were piled high on trays in the glass display cases, and she let us have our share. My grandmother always seemed so happy and at the time I thought it was because she liked her job. *Who wouldn't love to work in a bakery?* I thought. But looking back I know it was because she was thrilled to see her grandchildren, so any sign of fatigue washed away. At least for the moment.

During my teen years she worked as a cook at a day care center. Each day she prepared breakfast and lunch for three hundred kids. In between, she cleaned and did prep work. One morning I discreetly wandered in to surprise her with a giant bear hug—but I was the one who got jolted. Peeking from around the corner, I saw my grandmother on her hands and knees scrubbing the floor. The air in the place was hot and gluey; giant pots of soup simmered on the stove. I was thirteen, and old enough to know that I didn't want *my* grandma working so hard and in such a dismal place. *She's too good for that,* I told myself. When she peered over her left shoulder and saw me standing there, her eyes sparkled. Her hair was a mess and beads of sweat were trickling down her face, but her grim countenance transformed into a smile the moment she saw me. I could see the weary look in her eyes and it broke my heart, but she never complained. I guess a lot of grandchildren feel the same when they hear similar stories of loved ones in their family.

Despite her lack of education, Mary preached the importance of studying hard in school. Although she had virtually no formal education, she valued learning more than most people. Perhaps she saw the significance in it because it was something she never possessed, making it even more valuable.

She liked to say, "I attended the School of Hard Knocks.

There are no classrooms and there's no diploma to hang on the wall. The teacher doesn't take attendance but the boss checks the time cards. Instead of assigned seats there are assigned stations. And if you keep your eyes and ears open, you can learn a lot about human nature."

Mary doesn't know much about politics or that you shouldn't end a sentence with a preposition, but she knows about goodness—she can spot it in people a mile away. For where she is now in life, I think that's the most important thing. Each day she looks for the goodness in others and gives the best of what she has to each person she meets. For an uneducated woman, that's a brilliant approach to life. For an uneducated woman, it turns out my grandma is very wise.

Inspired by MARY COLUCCI

The Confession

My son, Matthew, was twenty-four and a proud new father, which thrilled my wife, Helena, and me. Matthew spent four years serving his country in the armed forces and met a lovely girl, Erica, overseas. Like many young soldiers living abroad, he matured quickly and was eager to start a family. Arriving back in the States, he began his career in the computer industry and took night and Saturday classes at the university.

Matthew and Erica purchased a small home, a fixer-upper that was pop-in distance from where my wife and I lived. Of course we visited every day, unable to keep our hands and eyes off our new granddaughter. One Saturday morning Matthew called needing my help.

"Dad, I was wondering if you could spare a few minutes," he said. "I just got out of class and realized I locked my keys in the car. Would you mind picking me up? I've got a spare set at home."

"Sure," I said, "that happens to the best of us. I'll be there in no time." I arrived fifteen minutes later and saw my son leaning up against his red Honda reading one of his mammoth computer textbooks.

My life was about to change forever.

Matthew had only been stateside a few months and between the baby being born, buying a new house, starting school and a new job, he didn't have much time to share the details of his years overseas. And he didn't know about what I'd been up to either. Matthew had no idea that my casual drinking had escalated into a daily ritual. He didn't know I hid bottles of vodka behind the trash cans in the garage. He never would have guessed that I drank alone, and I was sure he wouldn't find out that I had been bingeing that morning, gulping down a mouthful before looping into the parking lot where he was waiting for me. He didn't see that I had braced the bottle between my legs and sealed the cap before stashing it under the passenger seat of the car. I wanted desperately to tell him, hoping that I would find the courage to share my feelings, but the truth was about to emerge on its own.

I hated myself for drinking, so I drank more to numb the biting pain of disappointment within myself. It was a vicious cycle, feeling like I was wrapped in a straitjacket and the only move I could make was hand to mouth.

I'll never forget the day I caught my reflection in the midst of a binge. A weak man with gimlet eyes, hands trembling, mouth puffy and glossy with wetness, lips twisted under the rim of the bottle. I clenched my eyes, unable to look at myself, and tilted my head back until I drained the final drop.

"Please, you have to stop this! It's tearing us apart," my wife wailed on numerous occasions. "There are plenty of support groups and you know I'm behind you every step of the way."

"I've tried quitting a hundred times!" I shouted, but stopping drinking is tantamount to pushing a boulder up the side of a mountain. I just didn't have the strength. We'd gotten in a heated argument the night before I picked up my son. The feud ended abruptly when I locked myself in the basement, breaking the seal on a fresh bottle. The alcohol was my crutch. Without it I felt like a man zigzagging across a stream of slick, moss-covered stones. Little did I know that the sip I had before rounding the corner to pick up Matthew that morning would be the last time liquor would ever touch my lips.

The road leading from the university to Matthew's house was four lanes, two in either direction, no buffer between the road and the curb. Heading downhill doing about forty-five, the booze I consumed that morning went to work.

"Dad, are you all right?" Matthew asked, after I made a sudden swerve left, away from the curb.

"Yeah, yeah, fine," I said, shrugging it off, convincing myself I was okay and we only had a few miles to go anyway.

About a hundred yards ahead the road curved slightly to the left, but I didn't. My senses were shot and my eyelids felt heavy, like someone was tugging them closed with tiny strings. My focus was on staying awake, leaving little attention for the course of the road.

"Dad, look out!" Matthew screamed, a second before impact.

The right tire hit first, tossing us like corks as the car trampled over the curb, the impact from the other tires adding to the mayhem. I didn't even slam on the brakes; I felt like I was in a dream I couldn't control. The brush scraping the undercarriage of the car and the tree limbs skidding along the sides slowed us down before the trunk of a giant oak halted us dead in our tracks.

Dazed, I rubbed my eyes and shook my head, wondering what had happened. I saw Matthew's head lying on the dashboard, the windshield splintered. I sobered up immediately. "Matthew!" I screamed, "Matthew!" I nudged his shoulder trying to wake him up. No movement. Within seconds the police and ambulance arrived, rushing us both to the hospital.

He had sustained a concussion and gash to his forehead requiring twelve stitches. I emerged from the accident physically unharmed but dealing with suffering of a different kind.

The police notified my wife and daughter-in-law, who arrived while Matthew was being treated. Erica didn't know about my drinking, but my wife knew and demanded an answer.

"Yes," I said, answering to a spot on the floor. Ashamed, unable to look her in the eyes, my hands were stuffed deep into my pockets like a child who'd misbehaved. She slapped me full force right in front of the nursing station. The side of my face ignited with pain.

The investigating police officer marched down the hallway asking for a word. "A bottle of alcohol was retrieved from under the passenger seat of the car. You can give me a straight answer or I can give you a test," he said. "Were you drinking this morning?" I answered the policeman's question, sharing with him as many details as my warped memory of the incident afforded me. It marked the first time in my life I was fully honest about my problem, but it took a desperate situation to force me to the edge—to be truthful. That's the thing about drinking and denial—the places we fear to tread are where most people live their daily lives. Honestly, safely, not trying to cover up bad habits. For a drinker, however, honesty is the edge, because our biggest fear is being fully exposed, having to face the truth and the wrath of our family or—even worse—their love and sympathy. It's salt in the wound to have loved ones come to your rescue after spending years being dishonest to them. It amplified the guilt I was already feeling, cutting through me like a frigid wind. Alerting me to the suffering I had caused. But facing my weaknesses and overcoming them was the only way I could reclaim my life. I sat there in the hallway weeping, grateful that my son would be okay, disgusted with myself for putting him and his family at risk.

Matthew recovered. The stitches were removed a few weeks later, but he lives with a small scar on the right side of his forehead. I see it every time I look at him, a reminder of my mistakes, the fears I let control me for so long.

The judge thought my time would best be served teaching others from my mistakes. I was sentenced to community service—talking candidly about my experience, how I eventually kicked the habit, and what I learned. My son and his wife had a second child, a boy, and I always tell people about my grandchildren. Standing before a room full of students, a bunch of adults at an AA meeting, or writing a column for a community newsletter, I speak from the heart . . .

I wish I could tell you that at some point you'd outgrow making mistakes. When people learn that I'm a grandfather, they often assume I should "know it all" or at least "have known better." Unfortunately, I'll never know it all, none of us will. As for having known better, I did, but I couldn't help myself and that's what makes the memory of that day and that period of my life so painful. All of us will make decisions we know are wrong but we'll do it anyway. Usually it's for the gratification of the moment and the expectation that nothing bad will come of it. I tell my story not with pride that I have finally faced my addiction, but with embarrassment and regret for the suffering I caused and the weak judgment I displayed for so many years.

I speak humbly, painfully aware of my mistakes and the challenges facing the people sitting before me. For a long time

I felt like my life had lost meaning, even though I was blessed with a loving family and a career I enjoyed. Now I'm in the unique position of having gone through the darkest part of the storm, and although everyone's situation is different, I am helping to guide people who are out there completely lost and desperately wanting to find their way home. After sharing my story, people ask how my life is different now that I am recovering. They ask it from an anxious standpoint, unsure how they can survive in a world without alcohol. The answer is simple. I say, "Life is best enjoyed when our emotions are at their peak. Drinking dulls the senses, causing us to linger in a dismal clouded state, like living our lives inside a steam room."

My wife, Helena, and I work together, helping couples heal the wounds in their relationship and within their family. She shares her unique perspective, and every time I sit there listening to her, I feel ashamed at what I put her through and grateful that she stuck with me. Together we have helped save a few marriages.

I have learned that there are no secrets in life, just making decisions and dealing with the outcomes. The best any of us can do is make the right choices; when the selection is a tough one, step back and evaluate, don't act hastily, get some guidance. Everyone makes wrong decisions from time to time, and unfortunately some of those will hurt the people we love. But if we learn something and share that knowledge with others, we can enhance lives as well. Life is a winding road, and it's important to tell the people traveling behind us what to look out for so they can avoid the pitfalls we fell into. Teaching others helps heal the pain of past mistakes and, in my experience, has led to a very satisfying life.

Inspired by MICHAEL ROBERTSON

CHAPTER SEVEN

PURITY AND INNOCENCE

*Seeing the world through childlike eyes
simplifies life's complexities by
combining the wisdom of age with
the clarity of youth*

The child's heart and mind are like a blank canvas,
unscribbled with the observations of the world. As
adults, our opinions frequently force us to make hasty
decisions, which we later wish could be undone. We
often dismiss the remarks of children as naive and
immature. The things children say are indeed
sometimes immature, and therein lies their wisdom
and purity. Grandparents are wise enough to recognize

this and listen, enabling them to have patience and notice the good in all things. Through sprightly illustrations of children and grandparents, we can all learn to do the same.

Assigned Seats in Heaven

One day a little boy asked his mom and dad if they could drive him to the cemetery where his grandpa was buried. The family had recently moved, and now visiting Grandpa was just a short drive away.

When they arrived the boy asked his parents to wait in the car. "I want to talk with Grandpa alone," he said, solemnly. His parents smiled and watched as he scampered down the hill and canvassed the area before stumbling upon his grandpa's final resting place.

Kneeling down, his knees sinking into the spongy turf, he carefully read the inscription and date. *Grandpa has been gone for two years,* he pondered, sadly. He reached out and lightly fingered the inscription on the headstone: IN LOVING MEMORY. His eyes prickled with tears as he remembered the fun times they had shared together and how much he missed his grandpa.

"I'm at a new school now, Grandpa," he said aloud. "I was assigned a seat next to a boy in my class and now we're friends." Somberly, he added, "I wish you could meet him."

Then the boy noticed the new headstone next to his grandpa's. "I'll be right back, Grandpa," he whispered. He took a few steps over, knelt down, and introduced himself to the man. "From the date I can see that you're new here," he said. "I know how you feel. I just started at a new school." He paused, pointed to his grandpa's grave, and stated, "My grandpa has been here a while. He's right next to you. Maybe since you have assigned spaces next to each other here, you have them up in heaven, too. Well, I just wanted to say hi in case you and my grandpa become friends. It was nice talking to you."

The little boy returned to say good-bye to his grandpa. Kneeling down with his hands placed firmly together and his head bowed slightly, he whispered, "I love you, Grandpa, and I think about you every day. I've got to go now, because Mom and Dad are waiting for me. 'Bye, Grandpa." He smiled and hurried up the hill.

As he slid into the backseat of the car, his mom turned to him and asked, "Why were you standing in front of the headstone next to Grandpa's?"

Smiling, but with a hint of sadness, the little boy replied, "I saw that the man was new and thought he might need a friend, so I told him Grandpa was next to him. I thought they might like each other." He paused, reflecting for a moment, and softly said, "It's always nice to make at least one new friend in a strange place where you feel all alone."

Inspired by CATHERINE BUCKLEY

Froot Loops and Frosted Flakes

t was early Saturday morning when I heard the jig of little footsteps tapping on the ceiling. It sounded like a chorus of tiny feet, but unless my two grandchildren had had a few friends over for the night, there were only four feet up there. Then suddenly, the pitter-patter of pint-size foot flops came galloping down the stairs.

"Good morning, Grandpa!"

"Good morning, Grandpa!"

"Why, good morning, Timmy. Good morning, Tommy. How are you boys this morning?" I asked, despite their gleeful attitude.

"Good!" said Timmy.

"Yeah, we're good! Where's Grandma?" asked Tommy.

"She's outside talking with the neighbors. Do you boys want some breakfast?"

"That sounds great, Grandpa," declared Tommy.

"Yeah, that's great," added Timmy.

"Do you have any Froot Loops?" inquired Timmy

"Hmmm, Fruit Loops. Let's check the kitchen cabinet, see what your grandma bought at the store."

"How about Frosted Flakes?" asked Tommy.

"I think we have Frosted Flakes," I said. "Yep. Sure do. And look at this, we have Fruit Loops too. Oh, they spell fruit F-r-o-o-t.

"How about we plan our day while you boys eat your cereal?"

"Okay, Grandpa," declared Tommy.

"Can I pour the milk for you, Timmy?" I asked, anxious to avoid a mess on the kitchen floor.

"No thanks, Grandpa," he replied, as drops of milk splattered on the floor. "I do it all the time."

"Are you sure that spoon isn't too big to fit into your mouth, Tommy?"

"I can make it fit, Grandpa," he said with supreme confidence. "The bigger the spoon, the more cereal I can scoop at once. That way I eat all the cereal before it gets soggy in milk."

Hmmm, good thinking, I thought to myself.

"Tommy! You're spilling milk all over your shirt," I blurted in surprise.

"I know, Grandpa," he said calmly. "I have to turn the spoon so it fits in my mouth. My shirt always gets a little milk on it. That's why Mom cleans it so much."

"Oh, okay," I said, rubbing my forehead. "Do you boys want some orange juice or toast?" As the words leaped from my mouth I had visions of orange juice splashing onto the floor, a sticky mess.

"No thanks, Grandpa," responded Timmy. "This is good. Two bowls of cereal usually fills us up."

"You sure are pouring a lot of cereal into that bowl, Timmy. When you pour the milk, how do you know when to stop if you can't see the rim?" I asked, envisioning milk flooding all over the table and onto the floor.

"I usually can tell but sometimes milk spills on the table and then I know it's time to stop," he said, obviously satisfied with his method and unaware of the little river of Froot Loops trickling over the other end of his bowl.

"Watching you boys eat breakfast is very interesting."

"Thanks, Grandpa," Tommy replied. "Want some?" he asked, holding out his spoon, a trail of milk dripping onto the table.

"No. It looks delicious but I already ate."

"Can we give some to Sundance?" asked Tommy.

"How are you going to feed the dog cereal?" I asked, dreading the answer.

"Just drop a couple of spoonfuls on the floor," declared Tommy. "Sundance will lick it all right up. You'll never even know it was there."

"No, let's leave Sundance upstairs. I fed him this morning anyway."

"That was good," said Timmy, gulping down a spoonful of Froot Loops. "I'm done with those. Tommy, can I have some of your Frosted Flakes?"

"Only if I can have some of your Froot Loops."

I watched as the two boys reached over, plunging their spoons into each other's bowls, a trail of milk and cereal crisscrossing the table as it sloshed from their spoons before they gulped it down.

"Now I'm done," said Timmy, a few colorful Froot Loops clinging to his white shirt.

"Yeah, me too," said Tommy, dropping his giant spoon back into the bowl. A splash of milk landed on my unread newspaper.

"We'll change so we can go out with you and Grandma," said Tommy as he pushed against the table, causing the legs of his chair to skid backward over the freshly buffed wooden floor.

Ouch! "Okay, boys. I'll see you in a few minutes.

"It looks like I get stuck cleaning the dishes—and the floor—and the table," I said, after my charming grandsons scurried upstairs. "Oh, hi, honey. Finished talking with the neighbors already?"

"What happened?" my wife asked. "Why is there milk and cereal all over the floor?"

"Timmy and Tommy ate breakfast," I said, shrugging my shoulders.

"Did they eat the cereal or throw it at each other?"

"No, they ate it," I said, chuckling. "But maybe I should have given them Pop-Tarts instead. Less mess."

While spinning a few sheets from the roll of paper towels my wife said, "I guess a little spilled milk is a small price to pay for spending time with our grandkids. Where are the little monsters of mayhem now, anyway?"

"Upstairs getting dressed. Is that rushing water I hear?"

"Grandpa! Timmy overflowed the toilet."

"Well, dear," my wife said jokingly, "it looks like you finally taught your grandkids something. I'll stay here and clean up the kitchen. The other mess is all yours."

"Thanks, honey," I said. *But how could they have clogged up the toilet so quickly?* I thought to myself. And then I saw it. Along with a continuous gush of water surging onto the floor were Timmy, Tommy, and their dog Sundance. All three of them trying not to get their feet wet. They looked so pitiful standing there I couldn't help but laugh. And then Tommy said, "We were just trying to give Sundance a haircut and threw his fur in there," while pointing to the toilet bowl.

Timmy decided to state the obvious and, with the pair of

fur-covered scissors dangling from his right hand, said, "Grandpa, it was a bad idea."

So my wife cleaned the kitchen, my grandsons and I cleaned the bathroom, and Sundance went outside to roll in the grass. Within an hour the place was sparkling—that is, until lunch. But I'll save that story for another time.

Inspired by JACK STEPHENS

Grandfather for Hire

*M*y wife, Sarah, and I lived in our neighborhood for more than thirty-five years. We'd seen a lot of people come and go—new families moving in, and older ones whose children had grown, moving out. Many headed to Florida— "God's waiting room," as some call it. Sarah and I had raised our kids and spoiled our grandkids in the home I live in now. The lines on the wall marking my children's growth spurts are still there; I look at them and fondly smile. I've now started a new set of lines for my grandchildren. The stains on the carpet and the scuff marks on the wall, which once annoyed me, are pleasant reminders of the memories this house holds. I could never leave.

Sarah has been gone for a few years now, and the chores around the house recently became a little too much for me to handle. I could still wheel the garbage can to the curb for the Tuesday-morning predawn pickup, but the lawn mowing and weed pulling took their toll on me. Shoveling snow in the wintertime was literally too much for me to handle.

The new families in town meant that there were always some kids eager to make a few extra bucks. Over the last couple of years, I started hiring a boy from the neighborhood to mow the lawn and shovel the driveway. During winter we would share hot chocolate and gooey chocolate chip cookies together. In summer I always served a pitcher of sweet iced tea. The kids jabbered on about school and friends while gobbling up a handful of cookies or gulping down a tall glass of chilled tea. None of them ever kept the job too long. I guess they got bored and wanted to spend more time with their friends.

One fall day, when gusts of wind sent the crisp leaves scratching along the pavement, I asked a few neighbors if any of their sons wanted to make some extra money shoveling my driveway that coming winter. I didn't get any takers. I offered ten dollars for each time but realized I wasn't keeping up with the cost of living for young kids anymore. One boy's father told me that with the inflated price of candy and video games my offer was just too low. I conceded that I was out of touch.

I guess word got around, however, and Sally, a new member of the block, knocked on my door. She was recommending her ten-year-old son for the job. I told her I'd like to meet the boy and that I was sure we could work something out. The next morning I was introduced to a stringy kid named Billy. He was awkward and shy, but a lot of kids are at that age. He looked like ten going on eight. I wasn't sure if he was up to the job, but his mom said, "He's a little guy, but he's a tiger. I know he can handle it." I said okay and welcomed Billy aboard as my newest and only employee. Together, I showed Billy and his mom where I kept the tools of his new trade.

It wasn't long before the first snowfall blanketed the neighborhood. It began Friday evening, and early Saturday morning Billy arrived ready to tackle the driveway. I'd left the car out the night before so the job wasn't too intimidating. From my upstairs window, I watched him plunge the plastic red shovel into the deep pile of snow and heave a load over his right shoulder and into a growing mound of white powder. He looked small, lost in his coat, but he was strong for his size and intent on doing a first-rate job. After about forty-five minutes, I called to see if he would like to warm up with a hot chocolate. His hat was slipping down over his eyes so he raised his head up to look at me before nodding enthusiastically, the hat slipping farther down onto his face. Billy shed his puffy winter jacket, thick blue knit hat, gloves, and snow-covered red boots in the garage before plunking into a chair at the kitchen table. He wiped his runny nose with his sleeve before I could offer him a tissue. His ears were crimson and his hands shivered from the cold. Cupping the steaming mug in his palms, he sat there quietly, unsure of what to say. So I began talking, not knowing at the time that it would be the first of many conversations Billy and I would share.

Billy was timid at first but he soon opened up. He was different from the other boys his age, not saying much about school or friends. I didn't think he had any friends. As we sat chatting, thick snowflakes started falling again, so I told him not to worry about the driveway. I'd pay him for that day, and he could come back once the snow had stopped.

The winters are long and cold in Maine, and Mother Nature provided Billy with a full day's work most weekends—and often after school, as well. Over the next few months we went through a few family-size boxes of hot chocolate together, and I got to know this curious little boy who seemed to have a lot on his mind.

Sometimes he would come by even when my driveway didn't need to be shoveled. That made me feel good. My grandkids lived out west so Billy's company was always welcome. One day he appeared at my door with a brown shoe box and a piece of paper bound snugly under a thick rubber band. He said, "Mr.

Hanson, do you have a few minutes? I've got something to ask you."

He seemed to mean business, so I suggested we step into my office. I offered him the big leather chair and smiled as his feet dangled a few inches above the floor. I slipped open an old metal folding chair and set it across from him. Leaning forward with my hands clasped in front of me, I said, "What's on your mind, Billy?"

"Mr. Hanson," he uttered nervously, "I love my mom, and I know she is doing her best for me, but I need something else. You see, I never got to know my grandpa, and my dad, he left my mom and me a long time ago. Since I'll be a teenager soon I feel like it's important to have a father figure in my life. After hearing how much you miss your grandchildren, I had an idea." Billy paused for a moment, his feet flopping nervously, his fingers tugging at the rubber band around the shoe box before he took a deep breath and looked me straight in the eyes. "I would like to hire you as my grandfather. I saved all the money you paid me for shoveling your driveway, and now I'd like to hire you. What do you think, Mr. Hanson? Can I pay you to be my grandfather?"

My heart thumped in my chest, and like a cloudburst, tears rushed down my cheeks. It was the most wonderful question and biggest compliment I had ever received. With my eyes closed I gave Billy an oversize hug that felt like it lasted forever. When we released he took that as a yes, and with his face beaming, he handed me the shoe box. I slipped out the paper he had folded neatly and tucked under the rubber band. At the top of the page, in a ten-year-old's handwriting, was the word CONTRACT.

"This contract states that Billy Flannigan will become the 'Special Grandson' of Mr. Hanson and Mr. Hanson will be the

'Special Grandfather' of me, Billy Flannigan." Following was a list of his references. His mother, Sally, Ms. Vance, his teacher, and Ricky, his new friend at school, had all signed the paper. They vouched for Billy, stating that he was considerate, fun, appreciative, and would make a wonderful grandson. I grabbed a pen from my desk and signed my name, Henry Hanson, in the spot he had for me, under SPECIAL GRANDFATHER. I handed him the pen and he signed the spot where it said SPECIAL GRANDSON. We sealed our agreement with a hug and a kiss on the cheek.

"When would you like to start your new position?" Billy asked.

Grinning, I said, "My schedule is pretty clear, so I'd like to get started right away. How about we go out for burgers, fries, and some miniature golf? Does that sound good to you, grandson?"

"That sounds great, Grandpa," he said with a wide-eyed smile. And then he asked curiously, "What are you going to do with the money you just made?"

"I'm not sure yet, but I've got one idea that I think will bring great returns someday," I said as we headed out the door, bound for my favorite burger joint.

With the permission of Billy's mother, I spent the next few years investing what he gave me and added some of my own money as well. Today that small amount has blossomed into enough to pay for his college tuition.

Billy is in high school now and has a job paying him more than I ever could for shoveling my driveway. He's saving for college, unaware that the investment he made the day he hired me has paid huge dividends, for both of us. I'm looking forward to his graduation day, when I can finally give him his present. And now, when those blustery autumn winds send the brittle leaves scratching along the pavement, I know it's time to ask around, see if I can hire an ambitious young boy from the neighborhood to shovel my driveway. I've raised my offer to twelve dollars now; a small price to pay to get my driveway shoveled, enjoy fun conversation with a young spirit, and perhaps make even a slight impact on his life. There was a time when I looked toward winter and saw only the frustration it would cause me. Today when the snow falls I know it won't be long before I hear a plastic shovel scraping along my driveway. That's when I heat up the water for hot chocolate and the oven for cookies and see what an old-timer like me and a fresh-faced young boy might have in common.

Inspired by HENRY HANSON

Time for a Bubble Bath

So there I was, seated at the kitchen table enjoying a hot cup of freshly ground French roast coffee, when my three-year-old grandson, Benjamin, stood in the center of the kitchen and proceeded to take off all his clothes.

Laughing, I asked, "Benjamin, what are you doing?"

"Going to take a bath," he said, as if that wasn't obvious already.

"How come you didn't get undressed upstairs?" I asked, chuckling at him standing there buck naked next to a little pile of dirty clothes.

"Because Mommy washes the clothes down here," he said, pointing to the laundry room.

I admired the little guy's logic. I never did like carrying my bundle of dirty clothes down to the washing machine after I took a shower, but getting undressed in the kitchen wasn't an option for a fifty-two-year-old man. I envied him, naked in the middle of the kitchen. The dog came over, sniffed his feet, and went under the table.

"What are you going to do now?" I asked.

"I'm waiting for Mommy. She has to turn on the water."

"I can turn the water on for you."

"Thanks, Grandpa, but Mommy knows how to do it just right."

"Okay. Where is Mommy?"

"I don't know, but she'll be here soon."

As if that were her cue, my daughter, Katie, emerged from the family room. She laughed when she saw me, a fully dressed grown man having a somewhat intelligent conversation with a naked three-year-old.

"We're just talking politics," I said. "Benjamin is obviously a liberal."

She laughed and, while gazing down at her only son and tousling his hair, asked, "Benjamin, are you ready for your bath?"

"Yes, Mommy. I've been waiting for you. 'Bye, Grandpa."

"See you later, little guy." As they turned to walk away, I thought to myself, *Ah, the beauty of childhood. There he goes, hand-in-hand with his mother, about to enjoy a warm bubble bath.* I felt a little envious. Some of the best things about childhood we never outgrow. A few weeks later, however, after a two-mile Saturday-morning run, I came home to an empty house. My wife was shopping, and I remembered Benjamin getting undressed in the kitchen. Since I didn't feel like toting my sweaty workout clothes downstairs after my shower I peeled them off right there, in the center of the kitchen. I was standing naked and drinking a glass of water when the front door sprang open and my wife walked in carrying a bag of groceries.

"What in the world are you doing!" she shrieked.

I looked at her, shrugged my shoulders, gazed down at the pile of dirty clothes on the floor, grinned, and said, "Going to take a bath. Care to join me?" The edges of her mouth crept up into a smile.

Two hours later I picked up my clothes and threw them in the wash while my wife put the groceries away, both of us grateful that we hadn't outgrown our childlike instincts.

Inspired by BEN MARTIN

A Lot in Common

One day the kindergarten class of Cedar Creek elementary school was taking a trip to a nearby nursing home. They were scheduled to perform a show for the residents and afterward join them for lunch. The show went off without a hitch and they soon sat down for hot dogs and sodas—a treat for everyone.

One curious little boy perched himself up on a chair next to one of the residents and asked, "So what do you do for fun around here?"

The man responded, "There really aren't too many fun things to do here."

"No toys?" asked the boy.

"No toys," replied the man.

"Can you watch TV?"

"It's too much trouble," the man said, his voice steeped in frustration. "There's only one TV and people argue about what to watch."

"Yeah, I know what you mean. I've got the same problem with my two brothers. But I guess you can stay up as late as you want, that's pretty good."

"Nope. It's lights out by ten o'clock," said the man, shaking his head.

"That's a bummer."

"Tell me about it," the man replied, thankful that he'd found someone who understood his frustration.

"At least you can eat whatever you want for dinner. I have to eat what my mom makes."

"I have to eat what the cook makes in the kitchen," said the man, sticking out his tongue, a sign that he didn't like the food. "And sometimes I even get yelled at for spilling milk!"

"You too?" replied the boy in amazement.

"Sure. The staff here makes me clean my room, too!"

"My mom makes me clean mine. Wow! I've only had to deal with these rules for a few years and sometimes they make me mad. How old are you?"

"Eighty-four."

"No wonder a lot of old people are cranky. I'd be mad too if someone had been yelling at me for eighty-four years."

Inspired by ROSALIE LAWTON

The Dinner Table

Once there was a frail old woman whose husband passed away and left her all alone, so she went to live with her son, his wife, and their little daughter. Each day the old woman's sight dimmed and her hearing faded just a little bit more, and sometimes at dinner her hands trembled so much that the peas rolled off her spoon and the soup splashed from her cup. Her son and his wife grew annoyed at how she spilled her meals all over the table. One day, after she knocked over a glass of milk, they reached the breaking point and decided that enough was enough.

So she would no longer disturb them during dinner, they set up a tiny table for her in the corner next to the storage closet and made the old woman eat her meals there. She sat all alone, her hands trembling as she carried the food from her plate to her mouth. With teary eyes she would look across the room at the others, unable to hear what they were saying. Sometimes they spoke to her while they ate, but usually it was to scold her for dropping some food onto the floor.

One evening, just before dinner, the little girl was busy playing on the floor with her building blocks and her father asked what she was making. "I'm building a little table for you and

Mommy," she smiled, "so you can eat by yourselves in the corner someday when I get big."

Her parents sat staring at her for a moment before they both burst into tears. That night, they led the woman back to her place at the big table. And from that day forward she sat with the rest of the family and no one ever yelled at her if she spilled something every once in a while.

A tale shared by MARJORIE BANCROFT

CHAPTER EIGHT

HEALING A BROKEN HEART

*Mending the relationships we once held dear
and understanding how others deal
with the pain of a shattered spirit*

The quality of our life is rooted in the quality of our
relationships. We won't always agree with our family
and friends, but nourishing the relationships we have
is vital to our happiness and well-being. Also, we must
learn to listen when others are asking for our support.
Too often we are absorbed with our own concerns
and miss seeing that someone close to us is grieving
or needs to be rescued. By becoming more aware of
others' feelings, we can fortify our relationships and
enhance the quality of our own lives.

A Chance Encounter

The date was January third. Three years ago this day my son lost his life in a catastrophic car accident. The road was icy; his car careened off a steep embankment and plummeted thirty feet to the ground. He had moved away almost twenty years earlier, feeling that our relationship was beyond repair. I didn't try to stop him. I was notified of his death by mail, a month after the accident happened.

It felt strange. It was the anniversary of a tragic loss, and I had no one with whom to share my sorrow. I didn't even know anyone who knew my son, so I found myself alone, eating breakfast at a little restaurant not far from my home. When he was young, my son and I always enjoyed getting breakfast together. But now I sat in isolation at the counter, my head bowed down in my hands and my eyes staring blindly into my coffee cup. Thoughts of what I would change, if I only could, infused my mind.

As I sat there lost in my own world, a young man propped himself up on the stool next to me. He ordered waffles, two eggs scrambled, and coffee. I gazed at him curiously. That was the same thing my son used to order.

"Are you from out of town, honey?" asked Bernadette, the

waitress. She knew all the regulars and was always curious about the stories of strangers.

"Sure am," he replied. "I'm doing some traveling during the school vacation. I decided to treat myself to breakfast because today is my dad's anniversary, and we always had breakfast together."

Again I gazed at him curiously. "I hope you don't mind me asking," I said. "But did your dad pass away on this date?"

"Yes, he did," said the young man, taking a sip from the glass of water Bernadette had just poured for him.

"If I'm intruding let me know, but how did your father die?"

"Car accident. Three years ago," he uttered, shaking his head as if to say, *Sometimes life just isn't fair.*

"My son died in a car accident, too," I replied. "Three years ago today. We always enjoyed breakfast together."

"Well, to your son and my dad," said the young man as he raised his coffee mug.

Twenty minutes and some polite conversation later, Bernadette placed the check on the counter and I offered to pay for the young man's breakfast. "You remind me a lot of my son," I expressed.

"I appreciate the compliment but prefer to pay my own way," he replied. He paid the check, thanked Bernadette for the pleasant service, and shook my hand. "Sorry about your son," he mumbled, and headed for the door.

As I watched him walk away an icy chill rippled through my veins. He had my son's walk—a confident swagger. He wore cowboy boots and faded jeans, just like my son. And a denim jacket draped listlessly over his right shoulder. As he swung the door open and the rusty old bell fastened to the hinge resonated a dull clank, I called out, "Was your father's name John?"

He froze in the doorway before slowly rotating until he faced me. His face was bleached and he gazed at me with prying eyes and furrowed brow. He said, "Is your name John?"

And at that moment we both knew, his father, my son, were one and the same. This young man who had enjoyed breakfasts with his dad was my grandson. And out of nowhere, the chance to make a change appeared before me.

Inspired by JOHN MITCHELL

Quiet Desperation

We have all felt the pit of desperation in our stomachs. Some people experience the kind of despondency that gnaws away at them like termites through rotting wood. The kind that permeates their thoughts during the day and the inner sanctums of their dreams at night. These people go to extreme measures to safeguard themselves against the source of their hopelessness, making sure what they endured before will never, ever happen again.

Kimberly was twenty years old, a junior in college, and there wasn't a week when she didn't break down crying with uninhibited abandon. Often, in an emotional outburst, she would run sobbing out of the classroom in a mad rush to find seclusion in the bathroom. Locking herself in the corner stall, she would cry for hours, the sleeves of her shirt stained dark with tears, her wet fingers slipping on the cold green-tiled walls.

In the seven years since her thirteenth birthday she had gained fifty pounds. The snide remarks from people in school and her father's bitter attitude at home made her life unbearable. No one could comprehend the fear Kimberly was trying to insulate herself from; her father was furious that she was no longer the charming girl she'd been during her preteen years—

the one who loved to dress up and look pretty. Now most of her clothes were oversize. She always wore sneakers or flat shoes, never makeup, skirts, or high heels. Baggy sweatshirts and sweatpants or jeans were what she felt most comfortable in.

When she started gaining weight, her mother, Allison, expressed concern, attempting to find the root of the problem. Her father, Philip, stringently voiced his opinion, claiming, "She has no discipline and we shouldn't waste time asking her what's wrong because nothing is wrong. She just lacks willpower!" Philip's outbursts were frequent and vicious, causing her mother to recoil in fear and never question anything again.

Kimberly's depression felt like a noose around her neck, making suicide a tempting option. The few friendships she did have deteriorated, and while most people her age got together for parties, Kimberly spent her weekends alone in her room or taking lonely walks in the park near her parents' house. She would stare at her reflection in the pond—pudgy face, pale white skin, body shaped like a pear. She never walked away without throwing a rock in first, wishing the ripples of the water could transform her body as they did her reflection.

Her grandmother Martha visited frequently and expressed concern about Kimberly's weight problem and somber attitude. She suggested that Kimberly see a therapist, but Philip bluntly refused. "There is no need to waste my hard-earned money sending her to an expensive shrink!" he yelled. His explosive temper stifled even his mother-in-law, and she decided to keep her opinions to herself.

The situation climaxed the day Kimberly's grades from the fall semester arrived in the mail. When she got home her father erupted, howling, "Why am I paying for your tuition when you're not even in school! You have two incompletes, one D, and two C's!" She stood stock-still as he swatted a dish off the counter and it shattered at her feet.

Waving her report card like a piece of evidence, he threatened that if she didn't lose weight, get better grades, and start looking like a woman instead of a fat little boy she'd be sorry, and kicked out of the house. When he flung her report card in the air and stormed out the back door, Kimberly fled to her room. Plunging face-first into her bed, she wept until her tears ran dry and her eyes burned with redness. "I can't live like this anymore," she bellowed into her pillow. "I can't! I just can't," she cried, punching the mattress, her voice slowly draining of energy, falling to a pathetic whimper.

Late that night, nightmares of her past startled Kimberly awake and she thought of her father screaming at her in the kitchen that day. She hurriedly packed a bag and raced to her grandmother's house. Unable to contain the feelings she had buried for so long, she pounded on the door. "Grandma, open up, it's me! Please open the door!" she wailed.

Startled out of her sleep, Martha slipped on a robe and hurried down the stairs. "Kimberly, is that you?"

"Yes, Grandma, it's me. It's just me," Kimberly said with a desperate sigh. Martha opened the door and Kimberly rushed in, wrapping her arms tightly around her grandmother.

"I need to talk with you, Grandma," she said in a muffled voice, her face buried in her grandmother's chest. "I need to talk with someone I haven't failed."

"What is it, my dear?" Martha asked anxiously. "What happened?"

Kimberly gazed at her grandmother, her eyes wet and jumpy, and said, "I can't live with my feelings anymore and I need someone to help me. No one understands. I need your help.

Do you have any idea what's happened to me? Do you know what he did to me?"

Martha gulped, afraid to say what she feared it might be. Kimberly stood there trembling, her hands flopping, her eyes clenched shut. There was a heavy silence, too burdensome to break. And then, with each word creeping bit by bit from her mouth, Martha asked, "Did he touch you?"

A well of tears emerged and Kimberly cried out, "He raped me, Grandma! My God, why did this happen!" Chills pulsed through Martha's body erupting in a gush of tears streaming from her eyes. She embraced her granddaughter and together they stood weeping desperately in the doorway.

Finally, after losing themselves in furious emotion, Kimberly peered into her grandma's eyes and, with the heartache of someone who had been stripped of her dignity, said, "He hates me, Grandma. I want Daddy to love me, but he hates me."

"W . . . when . . . did he do this to you?"

Kimberly dragged her feet over to the couch, and Martha nervously sat down beside her. "It started when I was eleven and lasted until I was thirteen," Kimberly said, her hands fidgeting in her lap as she spoke. "He warned me not to tell anyone. He told me it was because he loved me, but I knew it was wrong. He used to say I was beautiful. I thought the only way to make him stop was if he thought I was ugly so I ate as much as I could. I had to find a way to protect myself. That's why he hates me now. He said I'm not the same beautiful girl I used to be."

The grief Martha felt as Kimberly related the horrible details was heart wrenching. She was overcome with sadness at what had happened, rage at herself for not noticing the signs, and disdain toward Philip for what he had done to his only child. *What if I hadn't listened to my daughter? What if I'd talked with*

Kimberly about her weight problem and discovered the truth behind it? Why couldn't I see it? The horrid notions swept her mind.

Abruptly, her thoughts were pierced by Kimberly's delicate voice asking, "Grandma, what am I going to do now?" Kimberly was twenty years old, a woman, but at that moment, in that desperate situation, she looked like a defenseless child. Martha stroked the tears from Kimberly's cheeks and said, "You're going to live with me now and we'll get through this together." Then she embraced her granddaughter, trying to wash away the fear and mistrust and make her feel safe and secure for the first time in almost a decade.

Kimberly started seeing a therapist and began the slow, arduous road to emotional and physical recovery. Allison still lives with Philip, too scared to leave, even after learning the truth.

Today Martha showers as much love as she can on her only grandchild. She feels the need to make up for the love Kimberly lost during her teenage years. She pleads with parents and grandparents to talk with their children and grandchildren—to know and understand what they're feeling and possibly rescue them before it's too late. She emphasizes that people cry for help in many ways. Kimberly's weight gain may have been a protection mechanism, but it was also her way of crying for help. "Cries for support come in all forms," she says adamantly. "We just have to listen and be there to help the ones we love in their time of need because, after all, they are our family, and there is no more important bond in all the world."

Kimberly is losing weight and making new friends at school. The sudden outbursts have stopped, but nightmares still invade her sleep. She's thinking about studying psychology, becoming a therapist. Perhaps working with girls and boys who have been sexually abused. She says she doesn't know if she can forgive her father. Maybe someday. She doesn't feel desperate anymore, just cheated. She lost her teenage years but knows that was just one period of her life. She's looking forward now, anxious to make up for lost time. Yearning for those years to vanish from her memory like her reflection in the rippling water.

Inspired by MARTHA HUFFINGTON

How About a Catch?

Every little boy needs a man in his life so they can play catch together. Richie's father had played that role until an unexpected heart attack claimed his life. He was forty-one years old.

It had been a long time, and his throwing arm wasn't what it used to be, but Richie's grandpa Sammy felt it was his responsibility to step up to the plate and fill the role as catcher and pitcher. Early one summer morning he yanked on the frayed string attached to the attic door, unfolded the steps leading to the "hotbox" at the top of his house, and rummaged through a few dusty boxes until he found the one containing his old baseball mitt. Sitting up there with a dim light burning and beads of sweat amassing on his forehead, he blew the dirt off the old glove and slipped it over his left hand. The scent of the well-worn leather rekindled a lot of fond memories. With a sentimental look in his eye, he hoped they could create a few new ones for him and his grandson.

Over the following months, Sammy and Richie could be found on Saturday mornings throwing the ball back and forth across the yard, the dewy grass sticking to their sneakers. In time Sammy took on the role not only of baseball companion, but also of father.

Their catches became a summertime tradition for the next few years, until other commitments and a weak throwing arm took over. Sammy was getting older, and Richie was busy with school. Their times together came less often, but the quality of their conversations and the love they shared was healthier than ever. Sammy was proud of the man his grandson had become. His only wish was that his own son had been there to witness the transformation.

In his first semester at college, Richie got a call telling him that his grandpa had passed away. It wasn't totally unexpected; Sammy had been ailing for some time. Richie returned home for the funeral but had to rush back to school for midterm exams. It wasn't until the Christmas break that Richie had the chance to say the good-bye he felt his grandpa deserved.

On Christmas morning Richie stood alone, reading the engraving on Sammy's headstone as snowflakes sprinkled delicately upon his hair. About ten yards away he noticed a man sobbing at what appeared to be a child's memorial. Richie bent down and at the base of his grandpa's gravestone placed the gloves the two of them had worn many years earlier when playing catch. In each of them lay an old baseball with tattered strings and bruises from connecting with the bat so many times. He cried as he prayed and thanked his grandpa for the times they shared together.

"Was he a ball player?"

Startled, Richie's thoughts were interrupted by the question of the very man he'd seen crying a moment ago. He could still see the tears falling from the man's eyes. Richie looked at him and said, "He was the greatest. He was my grandfather, and when I threw the ball he was always there to catch it and throw it back to me. I could always count on him."

"My son, Terry, and I played catch together," said the man. "Some of my best memories with my son are throwing the ball around on a Saturday morning."

Richie smiled and picked up the two mitts now lightly dusted with snow. He said, "How about a catch?"

"Right here?" replied the man, his hands spread wide at his sides.

"Why not?" declared Richie. "I've got a feeling they'll see us."

So on a nippy Christmas morning, as the snowflakes drifted softly from the sky, Richie enjoyed a game of catch with a stranger. As he caught the ball snugly in his glove and felt the sting in his palm, the vivid memories flooded his mind. He knew his grandpa was watching him. He hoped his dad was, too. And in the distance he could see the man crying and smiling as he snared the ball from the air while standing next to his son's memorial.

Inspired by RICHIE HOFFMAN

It's Never Too Late

*G*randparents are portrayed as affectionate people, pampering their grandchildren with love, milk, and cookies. I wish that could be my story. I tried to deny myself the truth, but no longer have the desire.

I was born to an unwed mother and that misfortune caused my grandma to dispute the fact that I ever existed. Perhaps it was the era in which she grew up, but as a child I did not understand people's intolerance and dogmatic views when it came to certain situations. All I knew was that my grandmother wanted nothing to do with me. She didn't blame me for my mother's mistake; she simply couldn't accept the fact that her grandchild was born out of wedlock.

As a young girl I missed out on the special times granddaughters and grandmothers share, but I learned to occupy myself until the feeling passed. In school other kids prattled on about their grandparents. They spoke of going to the toy store, playing games, and the fun times they had at Grandma and Grandpa's house. I convinced myself that they were lying. Hardening my emotions was the surest way to block out the pain of knowing that I was unwanted for reasons I could not understand.

As I matured, I thought less about not having a grand-mother, persuading myself that I was better off. Fewer family obligations, fewer gifts to buy, that sort of thing. The tactic worked until a stinging realization, as if a bucket of icy water was splashed in my face, awakened me to what I had previously neglected to see. A woman was standing with her granddaughter at the grocery store checkout line in front of me. The little girl, squatting inside the shopping cart, snatched a bag of M&Ms from the rack and struggled to open the wrapper. The woman quickly reacted, making the little girl put the candy back where she found it. Then she vividly illustrated the difference between right and wrong, making sure that her grand-daughter understood that her actions have consequences. I stood there, engrossed, as she educated her granddaughter about stealing and proper values, while at the same time realizing that I had never learned anything from my grandma. It was devastating, feeling cheated out of the love and guidance grandparents bestow upon their grandchildren. *Certainly my grandma had many wonderful stories and lessons she could have shared with me,* I thought.

That afternoon I mailed a letter to her saying that although many years had passed, I felt we could still build a meaningful relationship and that it was something we both deserved. In-cluded was my address and phone number. "Please respond," was scribbled in crayon next to a playful drawing of a little girl holding her grandma's hand.

The phone rang a few days later. The voice on the other end sounded weak and defeated, as if the years had taken their toll. "Holly, I am sorry," were the first words my grandma ever said to me. I was twenty-seven years old.

My mind scrambled for just the right words and although my thoughts fluxed with phrases I could spout, none of them seemed to express my feelings. So instead of thinking about what to say, I just began speaking and found that the right words would not come from my mind but rather, from my heart.

"Hello, Grandma," I uttered.

"My dear, a long time has passed since you were a child and I took that stupid stance," she said. "I was wrong. For years I fought the urge to call you, fearing you would refuse to speak with me."

"There were times, especially when I was a teenager, when I *wouldn't* have spoken with you, but I saw something wonderful the other day, something that made me realize it was both of us and not just me that was missing out on a special part of life. We can choose our friends but not our family, so it's important to nourish those relationships. Years have passed that we can never recapture, but it's not too late for us to begin building a relationship. Rather than contemplating what we lost or should have done differently, I think we should use this moment as a second opportunity to make things right between us. It may be too late for you to rock me in your arms but I'll gladly take a hug. I want to learn about you and learn from you. And I want to tell you about me. We're family, is there anything more important?"

"I used to think that there was," she said in a voice humbled by embarrassment. "I was too caught up with what the neighbors would think and the belief that it was a sin to have children if you weren't married. But no matter what I thought I should have been there for you. I'm so sorry."

"You can be here for me now, Grandma, and I can be there for you. Do you want to give it a try?"

"I can't . . . think of anything I would . . . like more in all the world," she said, her words fragmented by a surge of tears.

As I share this story, Grandma and I have spoken on the phone several times and our relationship has blossomed. We haven't seen each other yet, but arrangements for a first visit have been made. It's on a weekend. I plan on enjoying some milk and cookies. Maybe we'll even visit a toy store. And when I get back, I'll be sure to tell all my friends about the wonderful time I had at Grandma's house.

Inspired by HOLLY NAVARRO

A Measure of Success

For as long as I can remember, I measured success by the size of my stock portfolio, bank account, and other assets. The person with the largest net worth was the most successful. It was calculated and precise.

Most of my friends were business associates. We were all very competitive, which prevented me from sharing personal thoughts and feelings. My business comrades were great to have a power lunch with or hit the links and talk shop, but I wouldn't speak with them about a personal problem. Within my circle of friends, there was only one person I could turn to and share my innermost feelings—that was Charlie.

We sparked a friendship in elementary school, and despite taking vastly different paths over the years, our relationship endured. We didn't understand each other's ambitions, but we respected one another's choices and cherished our time together. With Charlie, I didn't have to worry about keeping my guard up. I could tell him if one of my investments went belly-up or if I was having a bad day. With my business friends, I forfeited my emotions for a callous cutthroat exterior, feeling that displays of vulnerability would turn them against me. I thought it was something we all felt, but none of us ever admitted. Secretly, I suspected that each of us had a "Charlie" in our lives.

Charlie owned a little antiques shop. It was quaint and somewhat off the beaten path, but that's the way he liked it. Together he and his wife ran the place. They didn't get many customers, but the ones they did have were loyal. I don't know much about antiques, but it seems that the items he sold were fairly priced and could be found at almost any antiques shop. What Charlie offered that was unique was a delightful environment. When a customer came through the door, a little bell chimed, signaling Charlie that it was time to offer an enthusiastic welcome. He made all his patrons feel like they were being welcomed home after a long ocean voyage. It was a refreshing change from walking into a store and not getting any acknowledgment at all.

Charlie and I rarely discussed money, and I assumed he was getting by okay. Some days, as I took the elevator to the forty-third floor and marched into my posh office with the panoramic view and my company name, DAVID MCCLINTOCK & ASSOCIATES, engraved on the bronze plaque in the entranceway, I thought of Charlie. Our daily lives couldn't be more diverse. We each had a son, and although we'd hoped they would become friends, they never really hit it off. I wasn't surprised. They grew up in different worlds.

The years passed, and Charlie and I continued to have dinner or go fishing every month or so. In between, my days were booked with board meetings, business lunches, and travel. It seemed like my son was growing up and I was missing it all. I justified it by saying that my connections would open a lot of doors for him and that one day he'd secure a nice inheritance.

Even in my sixties I was still clamoring away at the office, trying to stay on top of my game. Charlie still owned the store, but he worked there only part time. His son was married and Charlie had a new granddaughter whom he just couldn't resist. I thought his life was cute, but somehow felt above all that— like my purpose was a nobler one. Charlie warned me that grandfatherhood would tamper with my priorities. He said I wouldn't have a choice and that the innocence of my grandchild would pull me in; I'd succumb to his or her "baby charms." I sneered and jokingly said, "We'll see." I wouldn't have to wait long before I found out. My son and his wife were expecting their first child.

The birth of my grandson, Jamison, was thrilling, but nothing could induce me to cut back my hectic schedule. I was sixty-six, and my family pleaded with me to slow down and "smell the roses." Their words failed to persuade me. My attitude strained my relationship with my wife and especially with my only son. But it took something more for me to realize the damage I was inflicting.

Charlie and I were the same age. During our midfifties he was diagnosed with a heart murmur. It wasn't serious, just something he needed to monitor closely. At seventy-three the problem caught up with him and Charlie died of a heart attack while preparing lunch for a family picnic.

I loved Charlie, and at his funeral I learned how the world really felt about him. His son spoke of how Charlie had always been there for him. "We never had an abundance of money," he said, "but when my dad was around you could feel the love in the air. His priority was always his family and making sure people felt welcomed when they walked into his store. I think that little antiques shop would have gone under years ago if Dad wasn't such a welcoming soul."

When the funeral ended, I shared a tearful farewell for my dearest friend. As I stood there staring at the picture of Charlie surrounded by a border of exquisite flowers, I realized that he was not only my best friend, he was my one true friend. I could confide in him, feeling safe that he wished me only the best. My son also attended the funeral; he'd always liked and respected Charlie. And as I gazed at Charlie's picture and my eyes brimmed with tears, I heard a voice behind me say, "Why couldn't you have been more like him, Dad? Why couldn't you have been more like him?"

I turned and saw my son standing there weeping, his lower lip quivering. I wanted to feel angry at my son's remarks, but I couldn't. I only felt sorrow, because I knew he was right.

My old life came to a screeching halt that day. I retired from steak lunches with business partners and held my grandson's bottle instead. I no longer put on a suit and tie each morning, but tied a bib around Jamison at dinnertime. I traded in handshakes for hugs. I finally came to know what I'd been missing.

Sometimes I think that Charlie passed on before me because his purpose here was complete. He always knew what was most important in life. People tried to tell me, but I didn't listen. Now I know, and it is wonderful. I have a new purpose—my family and their happiness. It was one Charlie always had, and I've come to understand that his was the nobler one.

Inspired by DAVID MCCLINTOCK

Where All the Roads Lead

*T*wenty-four years had passed since I last saw him, and although I was a pigtailed little schoolgirl when he vanished, I recognized his face instantly, perhaps because it hadn't aged in all those years. He left my mom and me when I was six; said he was going out for groceries, never returned. That night is alive in my mind, like fireworks on the Fourth of July.

My mother was initially concerned: "I wonder where Daddy is? He's been gone a long time." As the hands on the clock ticked by her questions grew more intense, her voice crackling, "I hope nothing happened, my God I hope he's all right."

She called some friends, checking if he had dropped by for a visit. Later, with midnight looming, she phoned the local hospitals and the police department. No one had seen him.

The next morning was Saturday and although there was no school I awoke with the sunrise, eager to greet my father and see the relieved smile on my mother's face. Sunbeams danced on the bedroom's wood floor as my curtain swayed on the windowsill, shielding and then admitting bursts of light. I hopped out of bed and scurried down the hallway to my parents' room. Their bed was made, untouched, so I hurried to the kitchen and saw my mom sitting there, her knees tucked under her chin, her arms wrapped around her shins with a cup of coffee braced in both hands. She was wearing the same clothes, a blue sweater embroidered with a rainbow of flowers on the front and a pair of black stretch pants.

"Mommy, where's Daddy?" I asked. My voice at the time was squeaky, innocent. "Didn't he come home yet?" Looking back, that was possibly the worst moment of my mother's life. Not a day goes by when I don't imagine myself in her shoes, staring at a little girl in frilly pink pajamas, barefoot, pudgy little toes curled up on the cold linoleum floor. How could my mom have answered that question without her heart splintering into a thousand pieces? It was a simple question, but carried with it the weight of the world.

She scampered throughout the house that morning, endlessly peering out the front door. Checking the phone for a dial tone. Watching the cars pass by, hoping my father's would swing into the driveway. Answering the phone with, "Dean, is that you?" whenever it rang. It never was. Every noise was a pinprick, the possibility that it might be him, but it was always something else. Her friend Ruth came over, a welcome distraction as they sat off in the living room, whispering. Investigating from around the corner of the room, I watched silently, rigid as a suspect in a police lineup, and that's exactly how I felt—guilty. Guilty of driving my father away.

Sitting there with Ruth, my mom's hand gestures were hurried and unfinished, as if she didn't know what to say. They leaned toward each other; their fingers laced together, one giving support, the other receiving, and my mother breaking down crying. Reflecting back upon that day, I recall almost nothing except the dread in my mother's eyes as she imagined the worst possible scenario. I know she must have cried alone in her room, throwing pillows, rifling through his clothes in the closet, but in my memory her wails of sadness are silent, as if muted behind thick walls of cotton. I remember her face, her teary eyes, and her mouth taking on sad contortions as the history of the life she and my father shared together spun through the picture frames of her mind.

For a while everyone was confused, unsure if my father would return, but eventually they accepted the harsh truth that he wouldn't be back. My mom tried explaining it to me, saying it was no one's fault, but I couldn't help feeling that my father left because of me.

From that day forward until my teen years, each weekend was spent with my maternal grandparents while my mom worked to earn extra money. That's where I learned the reality that sometimes we lose the people we love most in the world.

"Honey," Grandma said to me one Saturday, "your father loves you very much but sometimes we lose the people we love. Most of the time they join God in heaven, but once in a while they are still here on earth searching for the things that will make them happy."

"But isn't being here with us the thing that makes Daddy the happiest?" I remember debating my grandma's reasoning, desperate to find an answer that would stop the hurt. Of course, there wasn't one.

"Oh yes, dear," she said, "but Daddy felt the need to explore and find other things that might make him happy. Sometimes people feel like they've got a hole, right here"—with her index finger she drew a big circle across my tummy—"and they feel the need to fill that hole. When you're hungry you go to the refrigerator or the cookie jar and grab something to eat. That's because you want to satisfy the empty spot in your tummy. Well, this is kind of the same thing, only what's needed to fill the hole is a lot harder to discover. That's why people leave, to find what they are looking for."

As my grandma shared those words my grandpa held me gently in his arms. I felt helpless, like a bird whose wings were being pinned down. I'd hide in my room scribbling notes to my father, apologizing, begging him to come home. With no place to mail them, I stuffed the letters in my sock drawer. I guess it was good to get my feelings out any way possible.

The worst part of the day was dinnertime with my mom; sadness fell over us like darkness in the forest. I set the table for three, hoping that the door would burst open and my father would spring in wearing a toothy grin. My mother let me keep a place setting for him on the table, and when dinner was over she silently put the plate back in the cupboard and the silverware back in the drawer. The pain of what happened froze inside us like ice overrunning the shelves inside a freezer. The weekends at my grandparents' house were where I thawed out. Their hugs, love, and insights were helping me become a wise young girl, better able to cope with the challenges I was facing.

The years passed and I grew into a teenager. The night my father left became preserved in the tomb of my memory as nothing more than a blur of apocalyptic sadness. I remember sobbing at night sometimes, the guilt I felt gnawing at my heart like a rat nibbling a discarded piece of cheese. By my twenties the pain I felt as a child had healed.

And when I was thirty years old my father suddenly reappeared, a broken man seeking forgiveness. He knocked gently on my front door.

No longer the impressionable child he'd abandoned so many years ago, I was confident with myself, with my place in the world. Standing there in the doorway, he looked helpless, his chin tucked low and his hands buried deep in his pockets, hoping that during his time of need I wouldn't abandon him. I didn't. I remembered my grandmother's words. I remembered the compassion she felt for him. My heart melted and my eyes dripped tears like icicles melting in the sun. I welcomed him into my home. The following morning was Saturday, and although I didn't have to work I awoke with the sun peeking through my window. Stepping into the kitchen wearing a pink robe and making fists with my toes on the cold Mexican ceramic tile I saw my father standing there, staring out the doorway, blinking back the tears. I hugged him, the way my mother hugged me the day he left. And that morning I shared with him the notes I had scribbled and stuffed into my old sock drawer twenty years earlier. The pages were parched with curling edges; the paper crackled in his hands but was soon moist with his tears. Perhaps it was the words I had written, words that can arise only from the innocent, forgiving heart of a child. Perhaps it was the first time he felt loved since the night he left, twenty-four years earlier.

There is a hole in my heart that will never be filled, the child in me that lost her daddy.

But there's the adult part of me that needs a father, too, and so together we're learning about each other and what each of us needs to feel complete. It begins and ends with family.

Inspired by SUSAN WILLIAMSON

The Shortcut

Richard's home life was a dizzying display of drunken outbursts by his father, with his mother cowering in fear. Often she would leave for days, needing to flee the loathsome environment. If there was food in the house Richard made his own lunch, but most days he'd scrounge for half a sandwich from someone at school.

Today Richard skulked as he headed for home. A towering stack of books filled his arms with his report card jutting out from one of them. Two C's, two D's, and one F. He feared the wrath his father would lay upon him that evening and he didn't want to face it.

The path home was just a few blocks, but the rebellious boys always took a shortcut through old man Riley's backyard. Each day Mr. Riley protested as the kids trampled over his flower bed and well-manicured bushes, but he could never catch them—until today.

A few kids coaxed Richard into running through the yard with them. Desperate to get home before his father, he decided to join them and scurry through the backyard. Richard was the only one hauling an armload of books, and as he scampered past the house he tripped over the thick, protruding roots of a weeping willow tree. His books careened through the air, and he hit the ground with a thud. His friends kept on running, jeering as they left him to face old man Riley's vengeance. As Richard lay there, facedown in the grass with his books and papers strewn everywhere and rocks biting into the skin on his palms, he looked up and saw old man Riley looming above him. "You're in trouble now," huffed Mr. Riley.

Richard brushed the grass from his face and shirt and crawled around collecting his books and papers without making a sound. As Mr. Riley watched Richard on his hands and knees, his anger suddenly turned to compassion. Mr. Riley was a retired schoolteacher and knew when a young person was dealing with domestic troubles.

"What's your name?" he asked sternly.

"Richard, sir."

"Well, Richard, I'm Mr. Riley, and I'd like a word with you, so let's have a seat over here."

Mr. Riley pointed to an outdoor furniture set rooted in the grass a few yards away. Richard was bashful, fidgeting with the buttons on his shirt and never looking Mr. Riley in the eye, but Mr. Riley had a way of coaxing young people out of their shells. Forty years as a teacher had taught him a few tricks. He scolded Richard for traipsing through his yard and then made him a surprising offer.

"I saw your report card when it fell on the ground," he said. "It's pretty bad. For someone carrying home so many books it seems like you would have better grades. Don't you study?"

"I guess. Sometimes. It's hard to concentrate at my house, there's too much noise."

"Seems like you could use some extra help with your studies. How about I make a deal with you? I was about to put up a fence to keep those pesky friends of yours from running through my yard. If you convince them not to use my property as a shortcut home, I'll help you with your studies."

Richard was stunned and graciously accepted Mr. Riley's generous offer. More important, he persuaded the kids in his class not to use Mr. Riley's yard as a shortcut, and the flower bed soon returned to its original splendor. In weeks Richard's grades were improving, his self-esteem increased, and he was better able to cope with his precarious home life.

Over the next year, thanks to Mr. Riley's tutelage and encouragement, Richard was getting B's instead of C's, D's, and F's. His confidence soared as he learned to contend with and even heal some of the wounds within his family. During that time Mr. Riley became a sage for Richard, someone whose respect and admiration he desperately wanted to earn.

A few years later, when Richard was seventeen, he and Mr. Riley shared a quiet Sunday morning together—and that's when the truth was revealed about the day they'd met. "Mr. Riley," he said, "do you remember the day I ran through your backyard and ended up facedown in the dirt with my books scattered everywhere?"

"Like it was yesterday," exclaimed Mr. Riley, with a sentimental laugh. "I was angry, but something about you made me feel differently. I could tell you had a lot on your mind."

With a pensive look on his face, Richard confessed, "I was going to commit suicide that day. I was so petrified of what my father would do once he saw my grades that I couldn't think of another way out. I took my books home because I didn't want people going through my locker and feeling sorry for me. Mr. Riley, that day was the first time I ever ran through your yard. I was so scared of my father I just wanted to get home before him so I could take the sleeping pills I had stashed in my room. But when you caught me I knew I wouldn't make it home in time. You offered to help me with my studies that day and no one had ever done that before. That gave me hope that things could change and they have, thanks to you. So now you know, Mr. Riley, you did more than catch me that day; you saved me from ending my life."

Inspired by ALAN H. RILEY

CHAPTER NINE

GIVING OF OURSELVES

Understanding how selfless acts of kindness
can cause our heart to overflow with gratitude and
reacquaint us with all that we have in this world

What do we crave most in this world—attention, love, assurance that we play a significant role in other people's lives? We need all of these things and many more. Examples of sweet-tempered gestures that reveal the magic of contribution can result in opening new doors in people's lives, forever transforming their view of the world. These stories vividly demonstrate that all of us can receive love, attention, and feelings of importance simply by contributing to others, and satisfying their hunger for the same emotions.

A Simple Gesture

*M*ilk, eggs, bread, assorted vegetables, sponge cake, low-fat meat patties, fresh angel-hair pasta, and a box of Twinkies. For years, the supermarket deliveryman brought the same order of groceries to my home each Saturday morning at nine. Lately, however, he had been late, and sometimes it would be three or four in the afternoon before he would knock at my door. My grandson dropped by often as well, always with an armload of goodies, but he'd been traveling for work so I hadn't seen him for a while.

The store was only a few blocks away, but at my age it was much easier for me to get the groceries delivered than take a taxi there and back or bother a neighbor each week. But that afternoon I had no choice. The day had come and gone and the deliveryman was nowhere in sight. I called the store and was told that his truck had broken down and my groceries would arrive first thing the following morning. Well, I couldn't wait until then—my cupboards were bare. My neighbor was gone, so I decided to walk to the store and catch a cab back home.

I don't like to go anywhere without looking presentable, so I put on some blush to make my face look perky, slipped on my red coat, and started on my journey. My block is quiet, but

I had to cross a main thoroughfare. What made it even worse was the McDonald's and gas station located at each corner—the intersection was always busy.

People have become so impatient when they drive, and crossing a busy street always makes me nervous. When I reached the intersection, however, I saw a brawny yet handsome man wearing a blue short-sleeve shirt and a pair of jeans. He was waiting for the light to turn green. I was hesitant at first, but finally relented and asked, "May I take your arm so we can walk across the street together?"

He peeked down at me, smiled, and politely said, "I'd be delighted to walk across the street with you." He extended his arm, I slipped my hand around his big muscle, and when the light turned green, we stepped off the curb and proceeded on our way.

As we neared the other side of the street a car tried to wedge past us, but I felt secure in this man's presence. After we stepped safely onto the curb, I looked up at him and said, "Thank you for being such a kind gentleman and helping an old woman like me across the street."

"You're welcome," he kindly replied. "And thank you for being such a kind lady and helping a blind man like me across the street. Busy intersections like this one always make me nervous."

Inspired by Barbara Elmwood

Graduation Day

The city was slowly coming to life, but I hadn't slept a wink. Newspaper deliverymen were heaving bundles of papers onto street corners and in front of soon-to-be-opened convenience stores and coffee shops. The jerky noises from the sanitation trucks rudely cracked the peaceful morning silence but I was lost in thought, my mind muted from the intrusions of the outside world. I drove down the empty road, splashing through puddles, the blinking yellow traffic lights allowing me to continue my journey uninterrupted. I was heading to my office as I watched my life unfold in my memory, from the opening scenes to the current moment. It was something I always did when a pivotal day had finally arrived for me. When I entered, the stillness of the office building allowed my thoughts to continue like an endless dream, and as I fell into the chair behind my desk I drifted even farther into the depths of my own history.

While I was growing up, my parents had emphasized the importance of education. "It's a first-class ticket for the journey of life. We'll get you on board, by paying your tuition, but you'll have to earn your ride by getting good grades," they said in a tone of voice I didn't question.

"The road to success is paved with books and illuminated by a desktop lamp," my pop said. Neither of my parents had made it through high school. Putting food on the table took precedence over learning algebra and basic chemistry. They valued education because it was something they'd never acquired and having a well-educated son would enable them to feel successful. I vowed never to let them down.

My mom labored in a supermarket and my dad at a trucking company. I was industrious, working hard for good grades while participating in sports and other after-school activities, knowing that scholarships were awarded to the most well-rounded candidates. The rejection letters from all of the scholarships I had applied for were polite but the words *We regret to inform you* singed with pain, as if I was biting down on a piece of tinfoil.

"Don't worry," my parents assured me. "We've been saving money from our paychecks for years, stashing it away in a secret college fund for you. We've got a small fortune in there now. Plus, Ernie has made some contributions. Our job is getting your tuition paid; your job is getting good grades."

"Okay," I said, disappointed that I hadn't gotten a scholarship but grateful that I had loving parents and my grandfather Ernie behind me. I knew that Ernie was helping my parents out with my tuition, although no one ever told me directly. Ever since I was little Ernie worked at a printing company. On Saturdays I would visit him, watching as he mixed colors, set the machines, and magically transformed a blank piece of white poster paper into a glossy advertisement with a rainbow of colors. Sometimes when he did menus for a local restaurant he would drop them off personally, and he'd take me along, knowing that the owner would offer both of us a free meal for the great job Ernie did in creating their menus. One day over a milk shake and hamburger I said, "Grandpa, you have a great job. People are happy with the work you do and they give you free food. What more could you want?" I remember him saying, "I have a good job for never finishing high school, but someday you will have a great job because of your college education. You'll hold a pen in your hand and get ink on the page—not like me," he said with a smile, holding up his hands with splotches of different-colored ink on his fingers.

My parents and Ernie worked hard for many years so I could attend college, and when I arrived for the first day with my trunkload of clothes I was thrilled. The colorful dorm rooms, grand campus buildings, and droves of people streaming in every direction or lounging under elm trees reading and taking naps exhilarated me. Some nights I would purposely escape into the library stacks, reading some obscure novel and getting lost in the adventure on the page. The weeks went fast, too fast, and as Thanksgiving neared and midterms loomed, I got a terrible call.

"Your father had a bad accident at work," my mom said, her voice numb and flat. "But he'll be okay," she added quickly, trying to put a leash on my imagination.

"What happened, Mom?" My heart raced ahead of my breath, ahead of my thoughts.

"He fell off the loading dock and broke his back. One of those terrible things you hear about but never think . . ." She paused slightly. "He has to stay in bed for six months but luckily there was no spinal cord damage so he'll be up and around soon. I hope." I suddenly thought about how tight money was in my family and said, "If Pop can't work, how can we afford the tuition?"

"Well, the nest egg we had been saving for all those years is still there and I'll work a few more hours per week at the market. Ernie has some extra money he'll donate, too. Don't worry about the money. Just study hard."

I visited my parents and Ernie over the holidays. At first my father could barely move, lying rigid as a steel beam. But by the time I left he was getting better. I assured myself they would tell me if money was a problem but took a job in the school library for twelve hours a week anyway, just to help out.

My college years were fleeting, the good times woven into memory before I realized the present had become the past. And before I knew it, the day arrived when I marched down the aisle adorned in cap and gown. From my choice seat among the other proud graduates I saw my parents and my grandfather Ernie standing there waving and smiling. My father running his hand along his jacket lapel and pointing at the award draped around my neck, the one I received for finishing at the top of my class. My success was a reflection of their success and I felt like they should be up there with me, decked out in full regalia. As the ceremony concluded and the graduates crossed the area heading toward their families I took my cap and placed it on my father's head, flipping the tassel over the top. A sign that he had graduated.

"You see, Pop," I said, handing him my diploma, "right there in bold letters is your name."

Blinking back the tears, he chuckled and said, "Well, look at that. I knew making you my namesake would pay off someday.

"Son," he continued, quickly changing the subject, "there is something your mom and I haven't told you. We saved for your tuition but my injury hurt us financially. Ernie took a second job in a fish market at night to help pay for your education. He believes in you the same way your mom and I do, and he wanted more than anything to stand here at your graduation."

My lips quivered and the tears flowed fast as my pop told

me about the sacrifices my grandpa had made. I had thought
about Ernie often as I sat at the big wooden slab tables in the
library, never knowing that he was toiling away, sleeping only a
few hours a night for the past couple of years. I pictured him
standing before a long table, the thick smell of fish lingering in
the air, in his clothes, the scales sticking to his hands and his
eyelids heavy from working so many hours. I recalled the days
when I was little and visited him at the print shop where he was
still working. He'd always said I would graduate from college,
and now my success meant that he had achieved success. I
shook my head, thinking that he had worked so much harder
for this day than I did. While I was studying for exams in a
comfortable library, my grandfather worked two jobs and used
every spare penny to help keep me in school.

My father removed the cap from his head, handing it to me
with a smile. Strolling over, I saw Ernie taking in the sights, his
first graduation ceremony. He'd bought a suit for the occasion,
the first one he'd ever owned. He was sixty-three years old. I
came up behind him, placed the cap squarely on his head, and
embraced him from behind. Whispering in his ear, I said, "Pop
told me about the sacrifices you made for me. All I can say is
thank you. I love you, and I'll always strive to make you proud."

He turned and with his short thick fingers grabbed both my
cheeks, saying, "I am already so proud of you. It will be you
who carries my name into the future." And with that he gave
me a kiss on the cheek and said, "Now, let's celebrate!"

Ring! Ring! The sound blared from the phone in my office,
jarring me back to reality. "Hello?"

"What are you doing?" I heard my wife say on the other end.
"You're running late." My mind blurred, whisking me from the
past back to the present. "I'm on my way," I said, hastily.

My graduation cap sat on the mantel in my office, a reminder of one of the most important things in life—working hard so your children have the opportunity to achieve their dreams. That cap has traveled with me over the years and today, as I hurried out the door, it accompanied me on another journey.

Upon arriving, I saw members of my family milling about while others sat in corners chatting quietly. I wanted more than anything to have a private conversation with Ernie and seized the opportunity when no one else was speaking with him.

"Grandpa, years ago you told me you were proud that I would be the one carrying your name into the future. I hope you're happy with the job I've done so far. I never made a difficult decision without first asking, *What would Ernie do?* Somehow you always seemed to know the way. Perhaps that's because I'm younger than you are; walking in your footsteps, I was unable to see your face when you were confused. The sacrifices you made for me set the course for my life and I have kept the winds at my back. I guess that's the value of an education. All I can say is what I told you the day I graduated: 'Thank you for all you've done for me, and I love you.'"

With those words I tucked the graduation cap under my grandpa's hands as he lay in his coffin. Crying, I whispered in his ear, "Grandpa, I'm so proud that you are the one carrying my name through the gates of heaven."

Inspired by ANTHONY CANSO

A Lost Soul

t was a cold, rainy Saturday in San Francisco, and I was marching briskly through Union Square—an area populated with upscale shops and fine restaurants. The streets were bustling with people bundled up against the rain, which was whipping down in the fierce wind.

I'd just passed through the Macy's Men's Store where expensive colognes were available for testing and, of course, for buying. Fifty dollars a bottle? One hundred dollars? Whatever you desired to make yourself smell a little more tantalizing was available for purchase. Thinking of how fast I could spend my money there, I weaved through the cosmetics counters toward the exit. Struck by the blustery weather, I braced myself against the crisp air and wind gusts as I hiked up the street.

In the midst of all the hustle and bustle, the elegant jewelry shops and fine clothing stores, I spotted a gray-haired woman with chubby pink cheeks squatting in a puddle of water, her body pressed up against a beveled cement planter. Her filthy hands were resting on her lap, exposed to the harsh weather, and her eyes were red and puffy, as if she had just been crying. Her purple jacket and the shabby scarf that covered her neck and mouth were sullied and threadbare. She had on no socks, just a pair of canvas sneakers soiled with street grime. My first thought as I saw her was, *She is somebody's grandmother.* Even in that deplorable situation, I pictured her busily preparing a lavish family feast and wearing an apron she'd gotten from one of her grandchildren with WORLD'S BEST GRANDMA embroidered in bold letters on the front.

Although I was surprised and saddened to see her there, I pressed on. A moment later I passed a brilliant selection of flowers; their beauty and bouquet riveted my attention. I soaked up their aroma and noticed how most people shuffled by, unaware of their captivating scent. Gazing back down the street, I saw people parading by that old woman sitting in the puddle with the same indifference. I felt fortunate having recognized the splendor of the flowers and the despair in that woman's eyes. I bought a flower, one that matched the color of her jacket, and placed it in her lap along with the few dollars I had in my pocket. Her reaction was unhurried. She didn't smile, but I could see a glimmer of thankfulness in her eyes.

This happened more than four years ago. I have passed that flower vendor and cement planter many times since then and have not seen that woman again. I'll never know what happened to her, but I'm almost sure she is somebody's grandmother. Although I wouldn't be surprised if she was still living on the street somewhere, I hope she finally found her way back home.

Inspired by a woman in need

Just a Moment of Your Time

$\mathcal{T}$hank you for taking a few minutes to explain what's wrong with my mom, doctor. I know other people are eager to obtain a bit of your knowledge and bedside manner, but I was hoping for just a moment of your time.

The woman on the other side of this door is not just my mom; she's my children's grandma. They knew I would be speaking with you today so they each wrote you a letter and made me promise to read them. Do you mind? This will take just a second, I promise.

This first one is from my son, Randy. He's five. "Mr. or Mrs. Doctor, I don't know what's wrong with my grandma because I'm only five and am just learning how to tell time but I think my grandma is lucky to have you taking care of her. Since you are a doctor you must be really smart. Doctor, can you please make sure she comes home soon? I miss her a lot. Oh yeah, and one more thing. Can you tell my grandma that I love her very much and that I miss playing cards and games with her? I think that will make her feel better too. Thank you."

I have just one more. This one is from my daughter, Jennifer. She's eight so she has a better understanding of what's happening. "Doctor, I know you are probably busy so thanks for listening to my mom read this letter. I know each patient is important to you but I think if you knew just one special thing about my grandma maybe you would look at her differently. She talks to me about who I can become when I grow up. She tells me that I can become a doctor just like you. I'd like that because I would know how to care for her and I could help other people's grandmas, too. That's what my grandma does, she fills me up with dreams. So doctor, please help her to come home real soon. I need her around to help me become a doctor someday, just like you."

Thanks, doctor. I know my children's letters were simple but they speak volumes of truth. And to be honest, I feel the same way they do. I know you're busy, but if you can, give her just a wink once in a while to reassure her everything will be okay. Maybe you can spend an extra moment with her. She's not lonely, but she is scared, and you can comfort her best now.

I hear the nurse paging you and tomorrow's round of golf is probably in the back of your mind, but please keep my mom, my children's grandma, a top priority for today. It's not that I don't think you will, I guess I'm just overly concerned. We've been the best of friends since I outgrew my teenage years when I thought she was anything but cool. Often we'd go shopping together and "do lunch" while talking about life and the beauty of having dreams. Just like my daughter mentioned.

Doctor, my mother was the first one at this hospital when Jennifer was born. That seems like yesterday, but it was eight years ago. Now she's lying on the other side of this door and my kids need her to be okay. They need more hugs from her, and so do I. If she comes out of everything okay I'm sure she'll give you a hug, too. And doctor, my mom is a great hugger. You'll feel good all day after getting one of her hugs.

I know the day will come when I awake and she won't be

here, but I'm putting my trust in you and God to make sure that today is not that day. I have important responsibilities, but I don't know what it's like to have someone depend on me the way my mom is depending on you. So doctor, for today, please keep my mom in the forefront of your thoughts. I know you have many patients and do the best you can, but I have only one mom and my children have only one grandma.

Your eyes are reassuring; they tell me that you understand. Thank you. I hear the nurse paging you again so I know it's time for you to go. Doctor, thank you for giving me just a moment of your time.

Inspired by GEORGIA LEAHY

Happiness on a String

A single gift that makes another person's eyes twinkle for just a second can replenish our hearts with happiness for an entire day. The truth of that statement revealed itself to me on a day when I needed it most.

It was two days before Christmas, and my class of first-graders was vivaciously anticipating Santa Claus's arrival later that week. The morning commenced with a simple assignment. I had each student write a list of all the things he or she was grateful for that Christmas. It was a project sure to find its way under a watermelon magnet and stuck to the refrigerator.

Like most teachers, I had a pizza and ice cream party for my class that afternoon. I also had a baker's dozen holiday balloons brought in to make the occasion more festive.

The afternoon ticked by, and a bunch of overfed first-graders scurried out the door when the last bell rang. I attended to some last-minute business. It was December twenty-third and I wouldn't be back in class until January fourth. I welcomed the time off, but for me, this Christmas was bittersweet. I'd moved to a new city before the school year began and couldn't afford to fly back and see my family for the holidays. My dad was desperately missing my mom, this being his first Christmas without her, and since he was on a limited budget I didn't want to burden him with my financial dilemmas. I told him I had to work over the Christmas break in preparation for the following semester.

As I flicked the light switch on my way out, I turned to see if I'd forgotten anything—an old habit of mine. That's when I noticed the Christmas balloons tied to a pint-size blue chair near the window. Unsure what to do with them, I grabbed the thirteen ribbons, cinched them together, and, after fighting the wind gusts outside, finally tucked them all into the backseat of my car. Their rainbow of colors buoyed my spirits and gratefully, I didn't feel so alone.

I had the rest of the day free. Since I had already mailed out my Christmas presents and my few friends were either still at work or busy with last-minute holiday preparations, I decided to go for a drive. Most of the area was still foreign to me and I soon found myself winding down an unruffled stretch of road where the trees dawdled overhead and enveloped each other a hundred feet above the double yellow line. The branches reminded me of two friends stretching out to greet each other. It was peaceful, with ribbons of sunlight checkering their way through the dense foliage and creating hints of sunshine and shade on my windshield. It wasn't long, however, before Mother Nature's natural beauty gave way to man-made creations. Turning the corner I noticed a condo complex going up on the right side of the road and what appeared to be a retirement home on my left. I spotted a man decked out in a New York Yankees baseball cap and Hawaiian shirt hunkered in the shade on the porch outside.

Approaching the entrance of the retirement home, I felt compelled to pull in. The balloons crammed in my backseat obstructed my view—and suddenly I knew what to do with them.

Swinging into the parking lot, I lurched into a spot. Opening the back door and grabbing the strings, I unleashed the balloons from the confines of my car and let them float gloriously in the air. It was as if I were holding a rainbow on a string. As I approached the entrance, I waved to the Yankee fan sitting outside. He smiled, raising his hand but keeping his arm glued to the chair.

"Merry Christmas," I said. "Would you like a balloon?"

He grinned. "Sure, I could always use a little color in my life."

I handed him a red one with MERRY CHRISTMAS scrawled in green letters. He tied it to his chair. "What's your name?" I asked.

"People call me Red."

"Just like the balloon?"

"Just like the balloon," he said, sounding a bit like he'd heard plenty of quips about his name.

"Hi, Red. I'm Bonnie. I thought I'd give these balloons out to some of the residents. Will you be here when I get back?"

Red looked at me, opened his hands, and said, "Do I look like I have anywhere to go?"

I entered the doorway with an inkling of trepidation. I only had twelve balloons left and didn't want anyone to feel left out. After speaking with Marcy, the receptionist, I was pleased to learn that the home housed only twenty people, and eight of them were lucky enough to be with their families for Christmas.

"Well, that's wonderful," I proclaimed, "that leaves me with one extra balloon since I already gave one to Red."

Marcy smirked and said, "Don't forget about me. I love balloons, too."

During the next hour Marcy and I made the rounds, elevating the spirits of some people who appeared very downhearted. The place had a feeling not of neglect but forgottenness, and as I went around spreading a little holiday cheer, I couldn't help but think it was one of the best hours I'd spent in a long time. I shared delightful conversations with some of the residents, and met a woman named Beverly Adams who'd grown up near my mom, in North Carolina. I left the balloons tied to the bedposts, gratified to see that each one added an element of zest to an otherwise solemn environment.

Upon leaving that afternoon, I found Red sitting lazily in his chair, looking happier than when I arrived. "Thank you for the balloon," he said, staring up at me.

"You're welcome, Red. Perhaps I'll see you again sometime."

"Perhaps, but probably not," he replied. "Visitors are always welcome, but rarely come."

His words forced me to ponder my plans for later that afternoon. *I'm going home but what will I do when I get there, watch TV?* So I slid over an old white wicker chair with a pale red cushion and plopped down next to Red. For the next two hours we chatted about our lives and traded stories from our pasts. Our conversation flowed as if a gentle breeze was guiding us along. Sitting there, I couldn't help but wonder why I hadn't done this before. Perhaps I'd thought it would be boring or just uncomfortable talking with a stranger in a retirement home. But it wasn't boring, it was enlightening. I had been feeling a little lonely, and so had Red. Together, we shared our loneliness and it blossomed into an unforgettable time that will forever stand out in my mind.

During the next six months, I visited Red often, and we forged a unique and loving friendship. I also became close with some of the other residents there and each one vied for my attention. One day I even took my class of first-graders so they could fill that place with their youthful exuberance.

In June, on the last day of school, after another pizza and ice cream party, I took a baker's dozen balloons to that retirement home. Only this time Red wasn't there. I immediately feared the worst. Marcy handed me a letter Red had written just a few days earlier. Chills coursed through my body and I couldn't suppress the tears. It revealed how he really felt about me.

Dear Bonnie,

Your precious smile and charming way have lightened my heart and cast a smile across my face during the last six months.

Because of you, I have rekindled my relationship with my son, and he invited me to spend the summer at his home in Colorado. Bonnie, it will be the first time I've seen my grandchildren in three years. The level of joy I am feeling right now defies description. My son is picking me up tomorrow, and I asked if we could stop for some balloons before we get to his home. I told him when I lay my eyes upon my grandchildren I want to be holding a rainbow of colors in my hand. When he asked me why, I smiled and said, "I just think that is a wonderful way to begin a loving relationship."

Thank you, Bonnie, for your kindness and for giving me the greatest gift one person can offer another—time.

Love, your friend,

Red

When I finished reading, the page was soaked with my tears. As I pressed the letter against my heart I couldn't keep from trembling. I thought about the things we need most in life and I realized they are simple things. Love, in all its forms; companionship; someone to talk to and someone who will listen to us.

It had been almost a year since I had seen my father, so I asked Marcy if I could borrow her phone. I dialed, and when I heard the gentle-hearted voice of my dad say, "Hello," I uttered the only words I could say: "I love you, Dad, and I'm coming home to see you tomorrow."

Inspired by BONNIE FRANKEL

Breakfast Is Served

Pancakes, sausage, scrambled eggs, wheat toast with strawberry jelly, and fresh-squeezed orange juice. To me, there is nothing better than a hearty breakfast in a bustling diner on a Sunday morning. The weekend I was visiting my grandfather, he suggested that we slip our legs under a table at one of his favorite breakfast haunts—the Pancake Palace.

So bright and early Sunday morning Grandpa tugged open the window shade next to my bed, letting a burst of sunlight flood the room. "I'm hungry. How about you?" he asked, anxious for his first cup of coffee.

With my eyes squinting in the sun I hopped out of bed, signaling that I did indeed have an appetite that needed to be satisfied. After a quick shower I bounded down the stairs, and we were off.

We made small talk as we marched down the street. Then I spotted it—one of those silver diners with the old weather-beaten sign dangling out front. A greasy spoon that served great food where the surly cook in the back labored over a hot griddle and the waitress knew everyone's name and always had a pen stuck behind her ear.

As we grew closer, a few titanic-size men emerged from their trucks and waddled inside—the kind of guys you can find sitting at the counter eating corned-beef hash, drinking leaden coffee, and boisterously laughing about something peculiar.

When we were only a block away, Grandpa ushered me through a dilapidated wooden doorway with a few homeless people sleeping out front. Before I could ask what was happening, he thrust an apron and giant silver spoon into my hand.

"Grandpa," I said, "what are we doing? I thought we were going to breakfast."

"We are," he said. "Only this time we're serving it first. Hey, Chuckie, my grandson is here! Where do you want him?"

From around the corner I heard a deep voice bellow out, "We could use somebody on hash browns!" Before I knew what was happening, my grandfather pushed me toward a giant tray of steaming fried potatoes and a line of hungry people waiting to get served.

So there I was, dishing out fried potatoes to homeless people in a church basement instead of sitting in front of a plate of tasty pancakes. I wasn't happy. Then the unexpected happened. Everyone I served thanked me, and I started to soften. The puss on my face turned to a smile, and I felt like I was doing something special.

I'd woken up wanting to taste buttermilk pancakes but I got a taste for contribution instead. It tasted sweet. It felt good serving others and seeing the appreciation on their faces. By the time ten-thirty rolled around, I had scooped hash browns for close to three hundred famished people. When the work was done I sat down with Grandpa, Chuckie, and the other volunteers and had breakfast. The eggs were dry, the sausages were rubbery, and the coffee was burned, but I didn't mind. I felt good and enjoyed watching my grandfather joke with his friends.

After breakfast I shed my apron, splattered with bacon grease, orange juice, and maple syrup. Chuckie thanked me for coming. I told him I'd like to come back and he said they could always use the help.

On the way home I asked Grandpa why more people don't contribute like that when it feels so good. "Human nature is a funny thing," he said. "People can spend hours watching TV, but when it comes to spending a few hours serving food at a shelter, they don't have the time. It's too bad because they don't realize what they're missing. You didn't realize what you were missing until today, right?"

"Right, Grandpa," I said, aware of the lesson I learned.

"By contributing your time, you receive more than you could ever give."

I went back many times with my grandfather and helped serve breakfast down in that musty church basement. That was a long time ago. Grandpa has passed on, but the memories of those days and the lessons I learned have stuck with me. I've since started volunteering for different organizations, working to help families get back on their feet and offering college scholarships to students with the desire to further their education, but not the means. Together with other volunteers we're making a difference in the lives of people in communities around the country. We've introduced new programs where local schools can get involved in the effort as well. Young students are getting to experience the same feelings of contribution I learned many years ago.

My grandfather liked to joke and say that he was a selfish man, interested in his own happiness. What he taught me, however, was that giving to others enables us to receive more joy and satisfaction than is possible any other way. Perhaps it's okay to be a little selfish, as long as we are giving of ourselves.

Inspired by BART COLUCCI

CHAPTER TEN

ESSENCE AND VITALITY

*Buoying our spirits by discovering the magic
and possibilities in each day we are granted*

We are all familiar with the stories of Hollywood
stars who seem to have it all, yet succumb to a
harmful addiction. In stark contrast, why do some
people who seem to have every reason to be bitter and
angry at the world radiate with joy and optimism for
their future? From talking with these people, I've
learned that they did ask the question *Why me?* It
turns out they simply got a better answer, and that
made all the difference in their world.

The Swimming Lesson

*T*here's a captivating little park overlooking the San Francisco Bay. It's a fantasy-book setting embroidered with a lush grassy knoll and a few park benches. There's even a walkway hugging the brink of the rocky cliff where people can watch the waves collapsing upon the jagged rocks below.

One afternoon, a gentleman recently confined to a wheelchair happened by. He parked his chair along the walkway and gazed out at the glistening emerald water. He remembered with longing the days he used to go swimming, days when his legs were muscular and strong.

He noticed a teenage boy lying on the grass soaking up the sun's rays. He saw the bulging muscles in the boy's arms and chest and assumed he was an athlete. "Do you like to go swimming?" asked the gentleman.

The boy looked up, blocking the sun's rays with his left hand, and said, "Absolutely, swimming is one of my favorite things to do. It's great exercise."

"It must feel good to be so young and strong. If I weren't restricted to this wheelchair I'd be out there propelling myself through the water," the gentleman said.

The boy looked at him and brazenly said, "You could go swimming if you really wanted to. It's just a matter of desire."

The man shook his head and said, "You don't understand. My legs are too weak. My swimming days are over."

Upset by hearing the optimistic words of this robust teenager, the man turned his attention back toward the sea. He studied the waves as they crashed relentlessly upon the rocks and churned violently in the alcoves at the base of the cliff. As the sun moved west across the sky it beat down upon his face and the scent of the ocean beckoned to him.

His mind was adrift when the voice of the young boy saying good-bye pierced his thoughts. Startled for a moment, the man turned to say farewell. That's when he saw the boy being carried back to the car by his grandfather, and he realized this young boy with the muscular arms was paralyzed from the waist down. It had never stopped him from swimming.

Inspired by HENRY SCHUSTER

Purity of Heart

One day Grandma peeked into the TV room and suspiciously asked, "Brian, have you finished all your homework?"

"Sure did!" he answered with assurance. "Grandma, can I ask you a question?"

"Of course, you can ask me anything," she responded, curious as to what would come next.

"Where do babies come from?" asked Brian curiously.

She smiled. "Why, they come from God, my dear."

Brian's inquiry continued. "Grandma, where do people go when they die?"

"If they lived a good life, they go to heaven to be with God. Why do you ask?"

"Well, Grandma, I saw your baby picture, and you look a lot different now than you did then, and I was just wondering how God is going to recognize you."

Grandma laughed uproariously. "Well," she replied, "God knows me because He watched me as I grew up."

"Does that mean God watches me all the time, too?" Brian asked with a stunned expression on his face.

"Yes, I believe so," answered Grandma.

As if he was sitting on a tightly wound coil, Brian sprang up off his seat and scooted upstairs. "Where are you going, my dear?" Grandma asked, puzzled by his swift departure.

From the top step Brian yelled down, "To finish my homework!"

Inspired by Kathy Fitzgerald

A Moment in Time

The doctor said everything was going well. My daughter, Keri, was nearing the end of her third trimester and we eagerly awaited the arrival of the new member to our family.

On October twelfth the moment finally arrived. Everyone scrambled to the hospital, anxious to hear the news. The family was divided—half thought Keri would have a boy and the other half thought a girl would bless our clan. I sensed that she would have a baby girl.

After a few seemingly endless hours, the doctor gave us the glorious news—I had a bouncing baby granddaughter. The family erupted with cheers of joy and laughter and then my son-in-law, Richie, staggered into the lobby, mesmerized. "She's a miracle," he uttered, holding out his empty hands. We all hugged him and asked how Keri was doing. "She's fine," he said, in a trancelike state. "They're both fine and resting comfortably."

The men pulled Richie outside so they could smoke a celebratory cigar and the ladies in the family talked about all the wonderful baby outfits that were available.

Before too long we were escorted down the hall to see the baby resting snugly in her crib. He was right: She was a miracle. Even some of the rugged men in our family couldn't fight back the tears. When I poked fun at them they laughed and turned away. The doctor said Keri would be in the hospital for a couple of days before she and Amy, my new granddaughter, could go home.

The two days flashed by as we prepared for Amy's arrival. The house was decorated in pink and white balloons and ribbons. Our neighbors were bursting with anticipation and kept asking when they were due home. Many of them had seen Keri grow up and now that she was having a child, they felt like they were becoming grandparents, too.

Shortly before it was time to leave, while the whole family gathered at the hospital to accompany Keri and Amy home, the doctor came with some disturbing news. They needed to run some tests. A joyous occasion turned into a frantic need for answers and a hush fell over everyone before they besieged the doctor with questions.

After three tormenting days, the doctor arrived at a devastating conclusion: Amy had severe birth defects. As he dropped the news I felt like collapsing under the weight of his words. My family and I were in utter disbelief. And then I thought of my daughter. *What could she possibly be feeling?* I dashed through the hallway weaving through the gurneys parked along the wall and shelves stacked high with medical supplies. My shoes skidded abruptly as I reached her door. My heart raced in my chest as I cautiously pushed open the door and saw Keri and Richie hugging their little daughter and each other. All three of them were crying.

Keri gazed up at me and said, "I'm scared, Mom."

We met in the middle of the room where I gave her an all-consuming embrace—the kind of hug where I wanted to squeeze out all the fear and pain and leave only the goodness behind. The high-pitched cry of my new granddaughter interrupted us, and Keri went back to hold her baby.

I stood staring at them, feeling numb and helpless. All I wanted was to take the sadness and fear in their hearts, bottle it up, and bury it in the ground forever. But I knew I couldn't do that, so I cried, too. I wrapped my arms around all three of them and buried my head along with theirs.

A moment later I looked up and saw my daughter staring at the cross hanging on the wall above the hospital bed. The tears were trickling down her face but she possessed an aura of peacefulness she didn't have a minute ago.

It's been seven years since that day. As a family, we have experienced many wonderful and painful moments. Amy has grown, but remains dependent on her parents for nearly everything. There were no first words or first steps to celebrate. Instead, we rejoice when she recognizes someone's voice or a musical tune. You see, Amy is completely blind and deaf in one ear, so we work hard helping her distinguish sounds.

My daughter and I don't talk about the day in the hospital too often, but recently, when we escaped for some quiet time together, it came up. I asked about the serenity she exuded as we sat there holding each other that day, so long ago. She took my hand, peered into my eyes, and said, "Mom, on that day at that moment in time, God talked with me. When I looked up at that cross I was removed from everything. I realized God plans things for us that we don't expect or want, but there is a purpose for it. We just have to go on faith. That's the feeling that came over me. A profound faith that God blessed us with Amy because He felt that we could care for her. Special babies like Amy are born every day, and God chose us to be her family. On that day, at that moment in time, I didn't feel sadness, I felt blessed."

Inspired by CLARE TALIA

Eight Ingredients
for a Wonderful Day

*W*hat's taking so long . . . My flight leaves in twenty minutes! . . . Come on already!"

These were just a few of the remarks one man was boisterously making while in line at the Miami International Airport. I was standing two people behind him.

He glanced around as he voiced his feelings, hoping to see others nodding their heads in agreement. The line was long and everyone was anxious to get checked in, but no one said anything. Exasperated, the man said to the gentleman standing in front of me, "Isn't this ridiculous? We've been standing in this line for almost an hour."

The gentleman was chatting with his daughter, but paused for a second, looked at the man, and sarcastically said, "It's terrible, isn't it? They have some nerve actually making us wait."

The man was too absorbed in his own frustration to notice the gentleman's chiding tone and said, "You're absolutely right. I have a good mind to fly a different airline next time."

Ten minutes later the disgruntled man finally got his turn

and approached the ticket counter. The gentleman and his daughter chuckled to each other, and that's when I heard him say, "Sweetie, those bits of advice on attitude my grandfather gave me when I was a kid still come in handy today:

- Smile, because you can't feel anything but happy when you're smiling.
- Offer people compliments whenever you get the chance because it's a nice gesture and you never know how they can help you.
- Always keep one or two jokes handy just in case you need to make someone laugh.
- Look for something beautiful no matter where you are because often the best things in life need to be discovered.
- Shrug off minor inconveniences because if you don't they'll only turn into major ones and you'll have no one to blame but yourself.
- Think of at least one reason why today is special because it will make you appreciate the good days even more and help you get through the bad ones.
- Turn up the radio and sing one of your favorite songs just because it's a lot of fun.
- Judge someone else by looking for only the positive about them because even if you never tell them what you found, you'll feel better about yourself.

"I've always listened to my grandfather's advice, and although it hasn't worked for me every day, looking back so far I can honestly say it has served me well."

With that, the gentleman smiled, strolled up to the clerk at the ticket counter, and made her laugh. An hour later as I boarded my flight I saw that gentleman and his daughter lounging in first class, and I couldn't help but wonder if he'd paid for those seats . . . or if his grandfather's advice had gotten him there.

Inspired by a stranger at the airport

She Had It All

*W*ho's your friend, he's cute," she would say with a playful smile. It was a question she asked often, and I always called my friend over and introduced him to my grandmother. She loved men, especially young ones. Her spunky attitude and candid talk about sex and relationships caught people by surprise. Her dynamic sense of humor made her the life of the party. Everyone wanted to crowd into her spotlight.

At seventy-five she was diagnosed with breast cancer. Despite the ordeal of having her right breast removed, she maintained a superb sense of humor. "I've been trying to lose weight for years and this is the first thing that actually worked," she said gleefully.

"I enjoy the simple things in life," she says. "Hugs, kisses from my grandchildren, and any type of Entenmann's cake. I have a sixth-grade education and spent my working years on my feet. I never traveled or learned to drive a car. My home is special not because of its elegance but for the memories it holds. I've had a good life, married a caring man, and raised a loving family. God has blessed me."

My grandmother's sense of humor is genuine, that I knew for sure, but I couldn't help but wonder if she felt like she'd missed out on a few things. Seeing the world, wearing nicer clothes, being able to afford some of life's luxuries. I got my answer the day I bought a rose and gave it to her while she sat before the mirror, fixing her hair. "I just wanted to let you know I love you," I said. Tears welled up in her eyes. She planted a kiss on my cheek and reached into a white bank envelope on the table and slid out a crisp twenty-dollar bill. "Take this," she said with a grateful look in her eyes.

"But Grandma, I didn't buy you a rose for you to give me money," I said. "I bought you the rose because I love you."

"I know that, honey," she replied, "this is just your tip for bringing me so much happiness."

Inspired by MARY COLUCCI

Kindred Spirits

I will never forget the day Johnny Sugarman came to occupy the vacant bed next to mine in room 314 of North Point Hospital. I had been laid up there for more than a month. My bones ached, even when I rolled over. Getting up to use the bathroom turned into a team effort with the help of a nurse and sometimes an orderly. It was embarrassing, not to mention downright frustrating.

So when a spunky little kid was given the bed next to mine, I had no interest in making friendly conversation. I assumed he was there for a tonsillectomy and would be packing his bags for home the next day.

I was incredibly bored. My only visitors were the doctors or nurses making their rounds, and I spent most days thinking of the past. I'd look at my hands that were once so strong, but were now weak and fragile. Sharing my room with a young boy didn't help. He couldn't have been more than thirteen and had his whole life ahead of him.

His parents visited each day. They seemed like nice people and always said hello to me. I'd nod in their direction, but was uninterested in small talk. Johnny's friends also came by often, but at night, after visiting hours ended, it was just the three of us—Johnny, me, and the uncomfortable silence engulfing us. He tried initiating contact but I wasn't interested. A young kid couldn't fathom what I was experiencing. In a week he'd be gallivanting with friends and I couldn't help feeling envious of what he possessed and what I so desperately desired . . . time.

Johnny was in the hospital about five days when family and friends crammed the room in honor of his birthday. He even attracted the attention of the doctors and nurses. Everyone seemed drawn to this charismatic little boy—everyone except me. As I lay there listening to his animated personality and his witty jokes, I began feeling embarrassed about my behavior. *Here I am alone and he has a cluster of adoring fans hanging on his every word,* I thought. So I started laughing at his jokes, hoping someone would notice and include me in the festivities. Johnny's dad came over and, for the second time, asked if I'd like to indulge in a slice of birthday cake. This time I accepted, admitting it would be a welcome change from the hospital Jell-O. We talked, and I asked when Johnny would be going home. His happy face turned sour, as he whispered that Johnny would never be released and that his son would live out the rest of his days in that hospital bed.

I lay there dumbfounded. I had assumed the boy was in for a simple procedure and couldn't have been more wrong. Johnny had leukemia. Even though he preferred being home, staying at the hospital afforded him a little more time. Johnny felt special memories can be created anywhere and that home was where the family is. Now the hospital was his home.

After an endless procession of hugs and kisses, the party ended, everyone left, and once again we were alone. Johnny was silent. Perhaps he was thinking about the party, knowing it would probably be his last birthday. The envy I once harbored for this boy turned to anger. I was angry with myself for being so wrong, so selfish. At thirteen Johnny knew what I was feeling, but I could never comprehend his situation. During the summer of my thirteenth year I was fishing with my father and playing baseball with the neighborhood kids. I glanced over at Johnny, lying there with his eyes closed, and I realized that in his thirteen years he knew some things about life that I had yet to learn at eighty-seven. I had always regretted never getting married and starting a family, but never more than during those moments of lonely silence in the hospital room that night.

Suddenly I heard a whimper, which opened the gates to uncontrollable sobbing. And then I blurted out something I should have said the first night I met him: "Would you like to talk?" It was something I should have said to many people throughout the years.

His crying stopped, and as he wiped the tears from his face he said, "Really, Mr. Connor?"

"Johnny," I said, "please, call me Larry." So lying in our beds, our eyes staring at the ceiling, we floated through different topics, starting with how we each found the hospital food repulsive to more serious matters like life and better days.

He asked me questions that rekindled thoughts of my early years. I asked him about school and the pretty girls in his class. Over the next few weeks, when the lights were out and stillness filled the air, we enjoyed midnight chat sessions. The youthful spirit of this boy gave me strength. I'd been a bachelor all my life and never experienced the joy of children. Johnny said his grandparents had passed away when he was a baby, and he'd missed out on building a relationship with them.

So that was our routine, lying there in the darkness and talking and laughing until we both drifted to sleep. Lengthy hospital stays consist of routine and more routine. Eventually I came to feel a sense of responsibility for Johnny, and I think he felt one for me. He had the loving support of his family but we were facing the same fate—and that is a powerful factor in uniting two people.

I hoped things would go on like that for a while, but nothing lasts forever. Johnny died in his sleep one morning. At least he died peacefully—his spirit flying up to heaven, remaining forever young and brave. I leaned over to touch his hand—a symbol of good-bye—and there, crumpled in his left hand, was a piece of paper. It eloquently said,

> Please let my family know that I love them and that the memories I shared with them over my thirteen years will be with me always.

I held the note in my hands and wept a sea of tears. His lifeless body was resting comfortably. That's when I noticed a pencil lying on top of his blanket and couldn't help but wonder, *Did he write this note just before he died? Did he decide that it was his time to go?* I guess he was tired of being in this hospital bed and longed to be a normal thirteen-year-old. There is no sickness in heaven, so he headed for his final destination, a place where he can be free to run, jump, and leave his earthly worries and fears behind. I understand, my young friend, and I'll see you soon. I know I'll see you soon.

Inspired by KEVIN CONNOR

CHAPTER ELEVEN

UNDERSTANDING OTHERS

Learning to open our hearts and notice the differences in others with genuine admiration and acceptance

We share the world with people who look different from us in every way. They speak a different language, dress differently, like different foods, and have different ambitions than we do. Is that wrong? The penetrating insights and wide-ranging viewpoints contained in these stories shed light on the similarities common to everyone and enable us to be more accepting of all the people with whom we share the world.

Feelings Unknown

I was thirteen when my grandmother died. To be honest, I wasn't that sad to see her go. I know that sounds cruel, but we didn't have a close relationship. At the time I was a typical thirteen-year-old, self-centered and interested only in spending time with my friends. I felt like my grandma and I were from different worlds. Mine was unfolding and hers was ancient history.

A few days after the funeral, her personal effects were packed in boxes, most of which were stored in the attic of my parents' house. It wasn't long before those boxes and my grandmother herself were a faint memory. I was preparing for high school and battling with an identity crisis—at least that's how I felt at the time. I was invariably thinking about the present or the future—never giving a thought to the past.

Time slipped by and I was about to enter my junior year in college. That summer I came home to do an internship at an advertising agency. I was assisting on a campaign for a product targeting senior citizens. I admitted knowing nothing about seniors, so my boss suggested I talk to my grandparents. I remembered the boxes that I'd helped store in the attic seven years earlier and thought going through them might be the next best thing. It seemed like a lifetime ago.

I found a stack of Grandma's belongings behind a giant box of Christmas ornaments. My last time in the attic was the day I'd helped store those boxes. The distinct attic smell, like a place that time had forgotten, reminded me of that afternoon. Sifting through the boxes, I stumbled upon some old photos and knickknacks no one wanted. And then I unearthed a book titled *Grandma's Diary.* I knew a person's diary was typically off-limits, but I hoped it would give me some insight into what seniors were all about. As it turned out, it exposed me to a world of feelings I never knew existed.

The cover was dusty and frayed and the binding creaked as I carefully folded back the cover, revealing the words:

Written with love for: Mary Ann Bontonovich
By: Henrietta Bontonovich

It was a diary my grandmother had kept about our relationship together. I didn't think we had a relationship, but her writings told a different story. She began the journal the day I was born and described in detail her feelings when she saw me and held me for the first time.

There were at least six babies in the ward that morning, but my eyes gravitated to the angel with the soft gold locks. I knew she was my granddaughter. She was so helpless and yet so beautiful I couldn't stop smiling and had no intention of stopping. When I held her for the first time, my left hand sustaining her fragile head and my right cupping her tender bottom, I was so proud. For me it was a perfect moment in time.

Reading through the diary was like taking a nostalgic stroll through my childhood. Memories that had slipped away from me were written about in vivid detail. Boating at the lake with my father during his only week of vacation. I never knew my grandma watched us from the shoreline and captured her feelings on paper. The words she used to describe our card games demonstrated that for her it was a splendid occasion. I often lost on purpose to end the game so I could go visit my friends. Through her words I saw how much she loved me. Painfully, I came to realize how much I had misjudged her. As I leafed through the last few withered pages I read how she'd wished we had a closer relationship and how much it hurt that I didn't call more often. She'd hoped to tell me about my family history and the grandfather I'd never met. Her final entry chronicled the time my parents went to visit her but, after much pleading, let me visit a friend instead. I can't remember what friend I saw that day, but I certainly disappointed my grandma by not showing up at her home.

I never told anyone about the diary. Somehow I hope that Grandma knows I've got it and it's our little secret. Perhaps I'm just kidding myself, but I like to think somewhere in heaven Grandma knows that I am sorry and that I love her. The diary she kept is a priceless gift I'll always treasure. And someday, if I'm blessed with a granddaughter, I, too, will keep a diary of the relationship we share and hope that after I'm gone she will read it and remember with fondness the times we had together.

The sentiments Mary Ann shared after discovering her grandma's diary were written many years ago. The pages where she captured her thoughts were stuffed inside the cover of a diary she began keeping when her own granddaughter, Sabrina, was born. Today Sabrina has a treasure of memories to enjoy and reflect on for years to come. And someday, many years from now, when Sabrina is blessed with a grandchild, she'll keep a diary, and the cycle of life and love within this family will continue forever.

Inspired by LOUISE BONTONOVICH

Yesterday's Gone

He looks just like me. Can I hold him now? I'm the happiest grandfather in the world because I've got the most beautiful grandchild in the world. I need pictures to send to everyone I know.

I can't believe he's already beginning to walk. I started at a young age, too! I'd like to buy him his first pair of shoes.

When are the two of you going away so your mother and I can watch him for a week or two or three?

Go out to dinner and enjoy yourselves, we'll baby-sit!

So he is showing an interest in baseball—I love it, too!

Grandson, I got us season tickets to the Yankees! How about another hot dog?

Do you need clothes for school? Just let me know. I'll be happy to take you shopping.

That's a wonderful report card. I appreciate you showing me.

Thank you for so proudly introducing me to your classmates at the basketball game. I always wondered about what your friends at school were like.

You're growing into a fine young man. I can't believe you're almost a teenager.

Grandson, I know you're busy with your friends, but I was hoping we could go fishing this weekend. Let me know when you're free, my boy. Anytime is good with me.

Now that you've got your driver's license, how about I take you to lunch? You can drive! Okay, maybe you'll have time next week.

How's college, my boy? I can't believe you're three thousand miles away. I sure do miss you. Are you coming home for the summer? Maybe we can spend a week at the lake? Wow, times sure have changed! I couldn't imagine going to Europe for a summer.

Congratulations on graduating, my boy. Oh, excuse me, I guess *man* is more appropriate now.

Where have the years gone? I can't believe you're getting married. My health hasn't been good but I am determined to join you on that glorious day. I only wish Grandma were here to see it, too.

Grandson, it seems like yesterday when I held you in my arms for the first time. Now you're having a child.

I wish we could have spent more time together.

It's good to hear your voice on the phone, yet it's been a long time since I've seen you.

I was hoping you could come for a visit. You know I can't get around too easily anymore. I understand. Between work and the baby you're very busy. When you find the time, I have a room ready for you.

I've got your picture on my night table. Sometimes seeing a photo of you makes me miss you more. I love you.

Thanks for calling, grandson. I guess your mom told you I was in the hospital. The doctors say I'm doing okay, but I know I'm old, and they can't make me young again, so they just make me comfortable—as comfortable as I can be, anyway. I was hoping you could come for a visit. Oh, I didn't know you had that much work piled up. I understand. I was a young man once, too. I'll talk to you soon I hope. Good-bye.

The following note was found scribbled on a crumpled piece of paper on the old wooden food tray next to Grandpa's bed.

Grandson, for years I asked you for a weekend or even an afternoon. Why did you wait until the day of my funeral to give it to me? The relationship we shared when you were young was precious, and I miss the times we once spent together, terribly. The memories sustained me, but often made it even more painful to accept the fact that what we once had, we lost. Someday you will be a grandpa, and I hope that as your grandchildren grow they will always find time for you. You will not understand this now, my grandson, but for a loving grandpa there is nothing in the world more delightful than the moments spent with his grandson. I pray that someday when we meet again, we can rebuild the relationship we once shared together. Until that day comes, I hope that each day blesses you and your family with health, love, and happiness. Good-bye, my grandson. Please know that you will always have my love.

Inspired by DAVID MCGUIRE

Signs and Sorrows

*S*tephen wept in the hallway, skewered by the pain of what had happened. Leaning up against the beveled mirrored wall, he pressed his hands to his face, consciously avoiding a visual reminder of the hurt consuming him at that moment. "If only I could spin back time, I would do so many things differently," he mumbled to himself. He grabbed his brother by the jacket lapels, asking, "Why did this happen! Why didn't I see it coming!"

Exhausted, he fell into an antique chair nestled in the corner, his head resting in his hands. People milled about like shadows, unnoticed.

"So much lost and nothing gained," he stammered, "nothing but heartache." Stephen's son, Eric, got roaringly drunk the night of his twenty-first birthday and drove his car into a wall at seventy miles per hour. On purpose. He was killed on impact.

Eric's grandfather—Stephen's dad, Sam—awash in feelings of sadness, frustration, and regret, vowed to eulogize his grandson in a way that not only celebrated his short life but also allowed him to speak candidly about death, coping with loss, and sorrow.

"It takes a certain shock to bring us in contact with reality," he said. Pausing, allowing his words to soak into people's thoughts. "We often ignore the things closest to us until trouble descends upon them. We don't give our heart a thought until something alarms us and we rush frantically to the doctor. Often it's the same with those we love. I assumed things were okay with Eric. A few days ago it appeared they were going well and today, all is reversed. I have asked the same questions plaguing you now. *What if? What did I miss? If only.* We will never know the reasons why, but we do know that this was his ultimate wish—to escape from whatever troubles he was feeling. Now, unburdened, he enters his final resting place bathed clean of the fears and feelings that caused him to take his own life. Now it is our turn to grieve, for a time, at least. Sorrow for the death of a loved one is the only wound we consider a duty to keep open, as if that will allow us to stay connected to the person we lost. A cut of our skin, the pain of a breakup, a broken bone, these are wounds we seek to heal.

"People who suffer greatly are like those who know many languages: They have learned to understand and be understood by all. If what we take from Eric's death is a greater understanding of the fears and concerns facing our loved ones, then he has bestowed upon us a gift that can enhance the life of each person here today. Please use it for good."

Sam stepped off to the side, tears slowly leaking from his eyes. The silence at that moment was absolute, as though everyone had vanished.

Suddenly a few hushes were heard among the crowd, and unexpectedly some of the tears turned to smiles. "Look," people said. "Look!" A pure white dove had settled at the head of the casket, perched upon a wreath of red roses.

"It's a sign," said one person.

"Yes," replied another. "A symbol that Eric is in heaven."

Sam stood there crying. *Suddenly everyone is looking for a sign, some glimmer of hope, but what about the signs Eric displayed that went unnoticed?* he thought to himself. His face blinked a sad smile and he said, "I think it's a message for us—to cleanse our hearts of the hurt we feel today and keep our memory of him pure, not casting judgment for the way his life has ended. We don't know what he was feeling so we should not presume to judge him or the challenges he was facing."

People nodded in agreement. For the loved ones standing there with desolate hearts, it would be a long time before their wounds would finally begin to heal. As that dove ascended from the bed of roses, its wings sliding in long graceful strokes, it seemed to brush away some of the sorrow from the hearts of those whom Eric had left behind.

Inspired by IAN SULLIVAN

What's the Difference?

*I*t was around three-fifteen in the afternoon and my grandson, Frankie, came bounding through my front door. "Grandpa, Grandpa," he said, "I just made a new friend at school!"

"Why, congratulations," I replied.

"Yeah, Grandpa, today was his first day, and he sat right next to me. We played games and had lunch together. I like him a lot."

"Well, that's great," I said. And then, as little boys will often do, he quickly changed the subject.

"Can I have some milk and cookies, Grandpa?" he asked, knowing I'm always good for a yes.

"Sure. You grab the cookies and I'll pour two glasses of cold milk for us." As I poured the frothy white liquid I thought about my good fortune. I lived just a few blocks from my son and his family, and my house was only a block away from my Frankie's school. He popped in often, and that always brightened my day.

So perched on a couple of stools while munching on cookies and seeing who could build the better milk mustache, he told me about Jerry, his new friend. Twenty minutes passed, and I knew we'd eaten too many cookies when Frankie picked one up and got that *I'm stuffed* look on his face.

"Uh-oh," I said. "Your mom and dad are going to know I gave you cookies. Let's put these away and hope you're hungry by dinnertime."

As I hugged Frankie good-bye and thanked him for stopping over I said, "Your new friend Jerry is welcome here anytime, so just bring him over. Okay? I've always got milk and cookies and you guys can play video games together."

The following week on one dazzling spring afternoon as I mowed the lawn, Frankie and Jerry came running through the yard. As Frankie eagerly introduced me and I welcomed them inside I couldn't help but think to myself, *Jerry is not what I expected.* Frankie set Jerry up with the video game and helped me get the milk and cookies.

"So what do you think about Jerry?" he asked, seeking my approval.

I leaned down and whispered, "Frankie, I didn't know he was black." Frankie looked up at me with his big blue eyes and said, "What's the difference, Grandpa? He is my good friend and isn't that what counts most of all?"

As Frankie steadily carried the tray of milk and cookies into the den, I stood immobilized, contemplating what my seven-year-old grandson had just said to me. His comment forced me to realize that I had negatively judged a seven-year-old boy by the color of his skin. It never even registered that Jerry had politely said to me, "It's nice to meet you, sir." I was ashamed and questioned how I came to judge people so harshly. I recalled hearing my father talk with his friends. All my life I'd heard that people different from me should be looked upon with a critical eye. I learned that if they're unlike me, they need to prove themselves before they can be trusted.

I thought about my circle of friends. We shared similar backgrounds and beliefs, which only reinforced our prejudice. Deep down, I hoped Frankie would always have an open mind, accepting each person individually. I chuckled sadly, realizing that my grandson, a seven-year-old boy, had shown me the light. Innocence and a pure heart prevailed.

It's been a few months since that day, and my new perspective is enabling me to see the similarities in people who I had thought were so unlike me. Somehow I've learned what I already knew to be true—that we all want the same things in life. To be happy, to love, to laugh often, to prosper, and to be surrounded by family and friends. Those are the most important things and they transcend the differences in people and unite us in the biggest race of all—the human race.

Inspired by EVAN RICHARDSON

Imperfect Beauty

hree young grandmothers were sitting under the dappling shade of a sycamore tree while each of their granddaughters played blissfully in the sandbox nearby. Two of the children were working as a team, building a sand castle together. One girl packed the sand into a plastic red bucket and slid out the mold while the other sculpted it into primitive shapes. They were both beautiful little girls with rolling blond locks, blue eyes like shiny marbles, and adorable smiles. The other child sat off in the corner tossing sand up in the air and occasionally licking it off her fingers. Her grandma kept a close eye on her and hustled over frequently to stroke the sand from her hair and remind her not to put it in her mouth. This routine went on for a little while, and when she sat down again to continue her conversation with the other two ladies, one of them said, "It must be difficult raising a child with so many imperfections." The other woman nodded in agreement.

She gazed at them and said, "Most children her age know better than to put sand in their mouths, but she's learning and will outgrow that soon."

"I guess so," replied the woman, "but I mean it must be challenging, you know, raising a child who acts and looks so different from other children."

She looked out at her granddaughter, who was again licking her sand-coated fingers, before gazing back at the two women and saying, "My granddaughter may have sand in her hair and under her fingernails, but she brings joy to many people, and that makes her beautiful. It takes her longer to learn than most children, but that allows our family to celebrate the little successes that other families may take for granted. When I'm with her, I do have to keep a closer eye—because as you can see, she hasn't realized that there are some things you just shouldn't do. But watching her so closely has allowed me to spot some wonderful expressions that I would have otherwise missed. Occasionally I even catch her staring at me and I chuckle, thinking, *I have to tell her not to lick the sand off her fingers but she learned all by herself how to express love.* The hardest part is thinking of the future, when she realizes that she can't do many of the things other kids can do. And when she comes home crying because of the harsh remarks of another child. Those are the moments I fear, because I don't know what I'll say."

And then the woman looked at the two beautiful little girls playing in the sandbox before turning toward the other ladies, saying, "You said that it must be difficult raising a child with so many imperfections. And you are right, it is difficult. But who among us is perfect?"

Inspired by FRANCINE BYRNES

Beautiful Displays

*I*t was Christmas Eve, and the streets of Manhattan were glistening as a fusion of snow and rain cascaded from the sky. Many people were hustling about, doing their last-minute Christmas shopping. Others stood gazing in awe at the splendor of the Christmas tree at Rockefeller Center.

It certainly felt a lot like Christmas. The Salvation Army volunteers were tolling their bells as the resplendence of Christmas music booming from department stores permeated the air. Best of all, I knew my family was eagerly waiting for Grandpa and me to return from our last-minute shopping. I was in one of those peaceful moods where I felt that all things were right with the world.

Once Grandpa and I completed our shopping, we nibbled on chocolate-dipped biscotti and strolled back toward the car. As we passed the department stores on Fifth Avenue, I gasped in wonder at the magnificent display windows. They were so artistic, so unique. The attention to detail and the passion that had gone into creating those masterpieces were obvious. As I soaked up their charm, however, something else caught my eye.

My grandpa was crouched down offering a cup of hot chocolate and a warm roll to a homeless person squatting on the damp sidewalk. The contrast was piercing. There I was, standing on one of the most exclusive streets in the world, staring at exquisitely designed display windows. With a slight turn of my head I saw an even more beautiful display—my grandpa helping a person in need. I silently watched as he gingerly handed the man the steaming cup and a toasted roll. The man sluggishly raised his chin from the thick layers of soiled clothes and, with a tender smile and a few missing teeth, mumbled, "Thank you. Merry Christmas." My grandpa stood up and gestured to me that it was time to go.

We walked in silence for a few blocks before I was compelled to ask him, "Why did you give that man food, Grandpa? Because it's Christmas?"

"No," he replied. "As you gazed at the display windows I spotted that man sitting on the dank sidewalk with his head buried in his knees. I couldn't see his face, but his hands looked like mine. I'm sure living on the streets will age you, but I figured he was about the same age as me. I thought maybe somewhere he had a granddaughter whom he was thinking about tonight. That's when I glanced back at you and realized how fortunate I am."

Later that night I sipped homemade eggnog and laughed with my family as we sat around a crackling fire. I thought about that homeless man huddled under the beautiful display windows on Fifth Avenue and the thousands of people who stroll past the windows staring in wonder at their charm. I thought of how fortunate I was to see not only those elegant displays but also one human being contributing to another on this, the night before Christmas. I realized that not everything was right with the world, but thanks to my grandpa, things were just a little bit better.

Inspired by LUCILLE DAVIDSON

A Parent's Desire

*S*itting there in the corner were my son's dingy sneakers. A little dry mud was caked on the edges; the shoelace on the left one had snapped but had been tied back together. *I've got a new pair of laces in the closet; I'll replace them later,* I told myself. Next to the sneakers was a pair of my mother's slippers. The terry-cloth fabric matted down hard, they looked dispirited, as if the life had been walked out of them. Next to the slippers was a pair of my shoes. Brown suede two-inch heels that complete the ensemble of my favorite suit—the one I wear on especially important workdays. I stared at the three pairs of shoes, a portrayal of the stages of life, and couldn't help but get teary-eyed.

My mother came to live with my husband, our two children, and me after my dad passed away. Initially we were happy to have her; somehow it helped everyone deal with the loss of my father. As the months passed, though, things grew increasingly tense.

"Here's your dinner, Mom, I hope you like it."

"Oh, but I'm not hungry," she said in a slow drawl, as if she was considering every word before saying it. "The medication

I'm taking ruins my appetite. Didn't I tell you I wasn't going to have dinner?"

"No, Mom, you didn't."

"I'm so sorry. I thought I told you."

"Please try to remember next time. I've got a lot of work to do and the kids are eating at a friend's house so I only made dinner for you."

Her presence drained family time. My husband and I started arguing because he wanted to take the family on a weekend hiking trip and I was afraid to leave my mother alone for that long. I blamed her for the mounting tension in my marriage, and thought to myself that if she weren't living with us we wouldn't feel so trapped. Trips to the doctor were frequent and tedious. Sitting in the waiting room reading outdated magazines, thinking of the meetings I'd postponed, and knowing I had to prepare dinner that night and help the kids with their homework only increased my frustration. It reached a point where having a conversation wasn't worth the effort.

"How are you doing, Mom? How was your day?"

"Mom, how are you doing?"

"Mom," I said, nudging her gently, "how was your day?"

"Fine, dear," she said, oblivious that I had asked her three times. I was mad at myself for getting angry and mad at her for causing me to get angry. My family was young, vibrant. Soccer and baseball games, cookouts, boating—these were the things we liked to do, but caring for my mother made me feel fenced in, like a dog in a cage.

All that changed the night I stood staring at the three pairs of shoes on the floor. The men of the house were at a baseball game, and while preparing dinner I heard my daughter, Victoria, scream, which was followed by a series of thumps, each one amplifying until they suddenly halted. I ran from the kitchen and saw her squatting on the bottom step covered in soap suds. She'd gotten out of the tub and slipped on the top step, bouncing on her little behind all the way down to the floor. Her tender bottom was red as a beet and I couldn't help but laugh a little on the inside. She looked so cute. I helped her towel off, and after pulling on her pajamas, she scurried over with her new coloring book and climbed into her grandma's lap. While cooking dinner I overheard the two of them chatting and couldn't help but eavesdrop on their conversation.

"Who is that picture of, Grandma?"

"That's my mother. This is what your great-grandma looked like in her twenties."

"Do you miss her? I would miss Mommy if I didn't see her every day."

"Oh, I miss my mother very much. She cared for me when I was a little girl just like your mommy cares for you. And the same way I am living here with you now, my mother lived with me. That's what we do for the people we love. There's something I want you to remember, Victoria. You must always remember your past. As you get older and move forward, your mommy and daddy will hold on to the memories they have of you as a little girl, like you are today. Keep that in mind as you grow into a woman. When children do that, their parents are blessed with happy days forever."

I'd heard enough and tiptoed away, the tears streaming down my cheeks. I turned off the stove, called for pizza delivery, and went upstairs and began flipping through old photo albums. I felt so ashamed, so selfish. I had shoved aside the memories and sacrifices my parents made during my childhood to make room for the new, just the way my mother was explaining. While holding photos of my mom and dad when they were younger than I am today I spotted my son's sneakers, my mother's slippers, and my brown suede shoes—a symbol of life's stages.

It was a profound moment. I learned that although my mom and I are at different places in life, she had sacrificed for me— and it is my privilege and duty as her daughter to do the same for her. After all, someday my children will venture out into the world, and I will watch as the distance and pace at which our lives unfold stretch the bond between us. Sitting there, I came to understand the greatest desire of any parent whose children have become adults is to remain a vital part of their children's lives at every stage of life.

Inspired by ANNETTE CARTWRIGHT

People-Watching

Time no longer has the same meaning for me. Mondays don't feel like Mondays anymore, and I don't look forward to Fridays any longer. I enjoy each and every day as it comes. I spend them sitting at a little café on a busy street corner just watching the people go by.

As long as I can remember, I've loved to "people-watch" and wonder about their life stories. When someone catches my eye, I play a little game trying to guess what his interests are; what her name is; what he does for a living. My answers are based solely on what people are wearing, how they walk, and the persona or attitude they exude.

Through the years I have found that there is no shortage of interesting characters. Some people walk by laughing, while others are crying. A few seem angry, while some people gaily run by. Others shuffle like they don't have a care in the world. The people walking alone usually have a serious look on their face—as if they're deep in thought. When I see a person, I ask myself: *What makes her happy? What are his worst fears? What's her greatest accomplishment? Does he like his career? Is she in love?*

Observing the subtle variances that make each person unique has given me a greater appreciation for individuality.

When I was a young man bustling through the chaotic city streets I was too absorbed to notice people's faces. I maneuvered through the crowd as if I was briskly pacing through a labyrinth in a maddening effort to reach my destination.

Now, instead of being in the race, I watch from the sidelines. Perched as an astute observer, I leave prejudice and predetermined judgments behind.

After seeing hundreds of people pass by on any given day, I have come to a conclusion: Despite the differences in dress, hairstyles, and a vast array of other interests and characteristics, we are all very similar.

I see the unflappable businessman with a ruddy complexion toting an attaché case and barking commands into his cell phone. He passes a teenager on a skateboard wearing no shirt and threadbare jeans with a ring in his nose and a cigarette fastened securely behind his right ear. At first impression you would think these two have absolutely nothing in common. But a little contemplation, combined with a fundamental knowledge of human needs, makes it easy to arrive at an unexpected revelation: They are very much alike. Both need to feel loved and appreciated; they just have distinct ways of experiencing those emotions. Both want to succeed, though it's safe to conclude that *success* has different meanings for each of them. Both prefer happiness to sadness. Both battle with feelings of insecurity and revel in the dynamics of feeling self-confident. Both need human contact, and both want to lead fulfilling lives.

From my vigil at the place I like to call the Sideline Café, I have studied the human race and learned to value diversity. I've come to realize that the people I thought were so different from me in fact share many of my traits. While doused in the pandemonium of everyday life I saw the differences between myself and others, and was hasty in my judgments. Now, as I sit and watch an endless parade of people go by, I have come to identify the oneness we all share. I see myself in the people who walk, run, and even shuffle by. Sometimes I like the strengths I see—confidence and charisma. Other times their weaknesses remind me of my own—vulnerability and insecurity. My observations have enabled me to be a more compassionate and understanding human being.

From that little café on a busy street corner, separated by a frail metal barrier, I have stood beyond the human race and peered inward, and that has made all the difference in how I live, and how I view our world.

Inspired by DANIEL BRETT

CHAPTER TWELVE

THE SIMPLE THINGS

*Beholding the splendor in everyday miracles
and ordinary occurrences*

Most of us are consumed with things we have to get done or worry about trivia that will soon be forgotten but, at the moment, appears disturbingly urgent. In the midst of this chaos our attention to the wonders that surround us is muffled. We hear a song and enjoy the beat of the music but never hear the words that may eloquently depict our emotions. Learning to amplify our awareness is essential for absorbing the most out of life. These stories uniquely illustrate how we can heighten our sensitivity to life's hypnotic details.

The Cookie Tower

I was sitting at the table reading the Sunday paper when my grandson, Andy, moseyed through the kitchen door. "Hi, Grandpa," he said, in his childlike voice.

"Hi, Andy," I replied, watching him tread across the kitchen floor. One shoelace was untied, his hair was unkempt, and there was dirt on his face. The dog, Barney, followed closely in tow. I thought to myself, *I love that little kid.*

I meant to go back to reading the paper, but found Andy's behavior much more interesting. I observed as he reached into the cookie jar and stacked chocolate chip cookies one on top of the other on the counter. Then, with both hands, he cupped the bottom of the stack and let the "cookie tower" fall back onto his chest. I guess he didn't mind that his shirt also had dirt on it.

" 'Bye, Grandpa," he said.

" 'Bye, Andy," I said, as he marched out. Barney followed closely in tow. I thought to myself, *I love that little kid.*

I returned to the paper. A moment later I looked at my watch. It was nine thirty-two A.M. I chuckled, thinking of my grandson eating all those cookies. He wouldn't be allowed to eat them if his parents were here. *But I'm a grandparent,* I thought.

Along with loving that little boy, I guess part of my job is to let him eat two handfuls of cookies early in the morning. He's happy. I'm happy. Barney is bound to get some crumbs and he'll be happy, too. Life doesn't get any better than this.

Inspired by STEVEN DEAN

An Old Photograph

*M*emory is a wonderful thing—but it's not perfect. It fades like a pair of jeans that have been tossed in the wash too many times. It chips like old paint, the pieces of special days lost somewhere, swept into the catacombs of our minds.

Luckily there are pictures, especially the old ones with crooked edges and dates from long ago scribbled on the back. Photographs where the haircuts are goofy, the clothes are something we would consider wearing for a Halloween costume, and the faces of family members look young and unfamiliar, almost like strangers. These pictures, pinned down under plastic adhesive in dusty photo albums, help fill in the missing pieces and restore color to the memory of good times and people whose images have begun to fade or chip away.

I held one of those photos in my hand recently. My grandfather Benny, decked from head to toe in white, wearing a painter's cap and carpenter's overalls, was sitting with five of his co-workers in the utility room of Sloan-Kettering Hospital in Manhattan. He was smiling as if he had just thought of a funny joke. The shelves of turpentine and caulking material that filled in the background and the white flecks of paint on his hands reminded me of how hard he worked.

When thinking of Benny, the same memories always pop into my mind. Him taking pictures in the supermarket with his grandchildren. Perhaps it was the embarrassment I felt then and the joy I feel now that causes me to smile. Walking to the movies up the hill past a house that he jokingly said was haunted, I had believed him for years. Come to think of it, with its faded wood planks on the outside, untamed grass crowning the yard, crescent-moon slits carved into the front door, a pack of cats prowling the sagging front porch steps, and rusty cast-iron gate, my adult eyes would find that place spooky, too.

The path to the movies was the same one he trudged each morning before catching the bus on Tremont Avenue that took him to work. I remember him saying it was always dark when he walked to the bus stop and I thought of how brave he was for passing that haunted house before the sun came up.

The photo of Benny sitting there at work was a link in the chain of memories I have of him. It reminded me of the haunted house, the movies we saw, the ice cream he bought us afterward, and how none of us ever knows what moment will define who we are and how we'll be remembered.

What was on his mind when that picture was taken? I wondered.

He liked to whittle slices off a long stick of pepperoni and pop them in his mouth. Maybe he was thinking of relaxing after work with some while watching the Yankee game. I'm sure as he posed for that photo he wasn't thinking, *This is how my oldest grandson will remember me.* I thought of the times at parties when people wanted to take my picture and I said, "No, please, not right now." Maybe I had a mouth full of cake and didn't want that moment caught on film. And maybe I missed an opportunity to be remembered as a fun-loving guy with an insatiable sweet tooth.

Memories fade and chip away, and often the tales of family members who came before us are laid to rest with the people who were around to see those vivid stories unfold. For most of us it's the pictures of old times, good times, family times, that remind us of our history and the people who directly and indirectly influenced our life.

The world's most famous photos were simply one shot on a roll of film when they were snapped. We never know what picture will represent an era, a country, or a person's life. Unique moments captured on film are decided over time and come to define the person, place, or event that keeps the color and pieces of people's memories alive.

Stand before the camera lens often because someday, decades and possibly even centuries from this moment, future members of your family will hold a tattered photo of you in their hands, stare at your strange haircut and funny clothes, and fondly remember you and why you were so special.

Inspired by BART COLUCCI

Home Sweet Home

As an old woman lay dying in the hospital, her granddaughter Jamie came to visit. Feeling helpless, she asked, "Is there anything I can do for you, Grandma?"

"Yes, Jamie," her grandmother said feebly, "I'd like to see my home again. Is there any way you can make that happen for me, my dear?"

"I'll think of something, Grandma," Jamie said. "I'll find a way."

Jamie's grandma passed away a few days later, and Jamie arranged for the funeral procession to pass the home where her grandmother had lived for more than fifty years. Days later, as Jamie helped to clean and organize her grandmother's possessions, she found the following passage scrawled on a crusty piece of yellow paper stuffed in the bottom drawer of an old wooden desk. It was titled "Home Sweet Home."

Home is a place of enchantment that warms the heart and soothes the mind. It is the magic circle where we find peace and shelter from the harsh elements of the weather and the world. When we think of home, thoughts of love and tenderness instantly come to mind. Home has been defined as an oasis in the desert, a place where the fondest memories are created, a place where we are always welcome.

If you ask a child, "What is home?" you'll find that to her it means the world. Home is where she finds the unconditional love of her mother and father. To a child, home is everything that matters. As adults, we remember with tender smiles the magic of the home in which we grew up.

For everyone, home is a place of rest. It is what we seek most at the end of a bustling day. There are many places to find happiness and excitement, but none can match the joy of being home. When we've had enough and need to escape and simply be, home is always our destination.

Home offers stability and peace. It is a familiar place that we have arranged to satisfy our needs for comfort and familiarity. Even after a restful vacation in a beautiful part of the world, as we walk through the front door the words we speak most often are, "There's no place like home." It's where warm greetings await us, whether they are from our spouse and children or the enthusiastic love of our devoted family pet.

Over time, home becomes more than a place to rest the body and mind; it is a haven for memories. For people who have lived in their home many years and raised a family there, the word *home* takes on even greater importance. The scuff marks on the wall are symbols of children playing. The well-faded spot on the floor in front of the stove is a reminder of how many meals were cooked there. The pictures on the walls are examples of how the family has grown and changed. The tiny tree planted in the backyard years ago now towers over the house and is a reminder of how much time has passed.

It's where holidays and birthdays are celebrated. It's where we gather with friends during times of celebration. It's where we choose to be in times of trouble and difficulty. It is a place of solitude and serenity. And while it protects us from the elements of Mother Nature, it showers us with love and blankets us with feelings of security. It is for all these reasons that the old saying speaks so much truth: *Home is where the heart is.*

Inspired by JAMIE FRAZIER

Little Things

Once upon a time, a little boy was eating a peanut-butter-and-jelly sandwich and watching Wile E. Coyote trying miserably to outsmart that feisty Road Runner. After each couple of bites, he took a big gulp from the tall glass of ice-cold milk on the snack table next to him. When reaching for the milk, he noticed his grandmother knitting a sweater nearby.

At first the boy didn't pay much attention, but by the third gulp of milk his curiosity was aroused. "Why are you making a sweater, Grandma, when you can just go out and buy one?" he asked.

"I enjoy making sweaters," she said. "And I pay more attention to detail than most of the big clothing companies who make millions of sweaters."

He looked at the sweater his grandmother was knitting—it was filled with a wide array of vibrant colors and patterns. Then he looked at his own sweater—solid navy blue. "Why are you putting so many colors in your sweater, Grandma?" he inquired.

"Like I said, I pay attention to detail."

"But wouldn't it be faster just to make the sweater one color?"

"Yes, it would, but it's the little things that count," she replied. "Do you know the importance of the little things?"

"No, Grandma. I usually like things big," he confessed. "Like cookies and bowls of ice cream."

"Well, let me teach you about the 'little things.' My grandma taught me this lesson when I was little and it has made all the difference in my life."

Taking his hand gently in hers, she said, "The greatest joys in life are made up of little things—a kind word passed from one person to another, a friendly wish, a courtesy, a compliment. These are the *little* things that make a vast difference.

"Your great-great-grandma told me many years ago that moments are the golden sands of time. She said, 'Every day is a little lifetime, and if we seize each day we are given, the effects can be life changing.'

"Mountain springs are small, but they are the source of raging streams. The helm of a ship is tiny, but it keeps the massive ocean liners on course. Nails and screws are small enough to fit in your hand, but they hold large buildings and bridges together. A word, a smile, or a frown are little things, but they can alter someone's mood and the course of his entire day. You see, it's the little things in life that make a big difference.

"Remember, even the biggest things are just an abundance of little things combined. The ocean is made of water droplets. Grains of sand join to make giant rock formations. Little acorns scattered on the ground are the beginning of immense oak trees. The person running a marathon must do it step by step. The person writing a book must do it one word at a time. And the little boy eating a peanut-butter-and-jelly sandwich must eat it one bite at a time—no matter how large that bite might be!

"Many people think details are so small that if they are overlooked, no one will notice. They couldn't be more wrong. The smallest leak may sink a ship. A tiny preference toward bad behavior can lead to a life of crime. A willingness to tell a white lie makes it easier to one day tell bigger lies.

"Noticing the little things has resulted in some of the greatest discoveries and creations. Michelangelo, the legendary artist, was explaining to a visitor what he had been working on since their last meeting. 'I have retouched this part, softened this feature, and brought out that muscle,' he said proudly. The visitor replied, 'But these details are unimportant.' Michelangelo responded, 'It is in the details where one finds perfection.'"

Grandma continued, saying, "You are smart not because you know one giant piece of information, but because you know thousands of little facts. You may think many of these facts have little or no use, but you'll find that they all serve a purpose and will come in handy during the most unexpected times. People will ask, 'How did you know that?' and with an impish grin, you can respond, 'I just pay attention to the little things.'"

More than two decades have passed since my grandmother shared her thoughts with me about the "little things." Over the years I've heeded her advice, learning to pay attention to the details. From the lines in the petal of a flower to the nooks and crannies hidden in the crevices of the Grand Canyon, I look for the little things and am pleasantly surprised by what I find. One day, when I am fortunate enough to have a grandchild and she is ready to learn, I will be there to teach her about life's little things and how they make all the difference.

Inspired by MARY COLUCCI

Hot Dogs and Little Hands

houghts of you, grandson, as I hold your hand. The softness of your skin reminds me of how young you really are. It reminds me of your innocence and your naive view of the world. It is a thing of beauty. Your supple little hand tells me that you have no prejudice or hostility toward anyone. You offer only unconditional love.

As your little hand pushes down on my knee and you thrust yourself onto my lap I notice how fragile your hands are. The nails are tiny. As I look at them I see the evidence that would find you guilty of playing in the dirt. That's not a crime, of course, at your age; it's to be expected.

I look closely at your right hand as you use it to grab my shirt and situate yourself comfortably on my left knee. The gentle tug on my shirt feels unusually good. Often I shake hands with grown men or get a pat on the back from someone whose hand is adult size. The kindhearted grip you have on me feels much more pleasant. It feels like love.

I extend my hand and offer to shake yours. Maybe it's only the second or third time you've shaken hands. I think maybe it's your first, but you give a good shake, so I know you've had some handshaking experience. The handshake is my way of saying that I think you're a man. At least, that's what I want you to think. Little boys like you always want to be treated like a man. The thing is, I like you just the way you are.

In the midst of our conversation, your left hand goes up and with four fingers, excluding the thumb, you scratch an itch on your nose. One finger would have done the trick but I guess you wanted to make sure you got that itch. Maybe it was a big itch and you figured one little finger wouldn't do the job. I noticed that all four fingers seemed to have worked. You didn't scratch again.

Your grandmother brings us each a hot dog with mustard. I'm glad to see you don't like ketchup on your hot dog; I never understood why people put ketchup on a hot dog. I easily hold the bun in one hand and a napkin in the other to wipe my mouth. I notice you have a solid two-handed grip in the middle of your bun—no chance of that hot dog sliding out the rear and onto the floor. Your dog, Patches, is disappointed. He looks hungry. The napkin Grandma gave you is on the table. No need for that when you've got a perfectly good shirt to catch the mustard droplets, right?

I finish my hot dog in a few bites; you take about ten. Thanks for taking your time. I enjoyed watching you. As you lick the mustard off your fingers I realize I forgot to tell you to wash your hands. But I guess the dirt under your fingernails wasn't any worse than eating a hot dog. Who knows what they put in those things, anyway?

Here comes a friend of yours. With your little hand, you pull on my shirt collar, lowering me down to your height. You plant a kiss on my cheek and say, "Thanks, Grandpa." And with that, you're gone—not far, probably into the backyard.

I look over and there's the napkin Grandma gave you. Still untouched. I guess it's more fun to use your shirt. I take the napkin and date it. The caption: HOT DOGS AND LITTLE HANDS. Suddenly it's priceless. Thanks for the memory, grandson.

Inspired by BART COLUCCI

A Perfect Fit

*I*t was a Friday night, just a couple of weeks into the New Year, and I was at Macy's, sifting through the cubbyholes where they keep the Levi's 560s, relaxed cut. With the chances of finding my size dwindling, I was thrilled to come across a pair I thought would fit. Tugging them from the pile crammed into the small red-and-blue cube, I hurried to the fitting room to try them on.

Standing there in that tiny closet, my old pants crumpled in a ball on the corner seat and my potential new ones hanging on the hook, I did what most people do—became a fitting room model. Taking a good look at myself—up and down, back to front, my neck craning over my left shoulder to get a glimpse of what people see when they're walking behind me—I thought, *Not bad, used to be better, could be worse. Room for improvement? Are you kidding?*

Grabbing the pants from the hook, I slipped them on. It was like squeezing a Butterball Turkey into a Ziploc pouch. I left the pants behind, atop a pile of clothes that previous fitting room models rejected probably for the same reason—none of us was quite ready for the fashion runway.

Standing back among racks of shirts and surrounded by

posters noting how stellar I could look in one of Calvin Klein's sweaters, I spotted three generations of men engaged in very dangerous behavior—shopping without the guidance of a woman. A grandfather, father, and son, asking each other for advice, all looking a little perplexed and the boy, about twelve, wondering what he'd done to deserve such punishment. The father, a round jolly-looking man with jowls for cheeks, pulled a pair of pants off a rack and, hugging them against his waist, bellowed, "Son, what do you think of these?"

The man's rumbling voice reverberated throughout the store, causing heads to turn even over in the jacket section, about fifteen feet away.

"Daaad," chimed the boy, mortified that his tubby father was drawing attention to their little huddle among the khakis.

"Well, I'm going to try them on, see if I can pinch myself into them," he said with a hearty chuckle, and disappeared around the corner.

"Steven," said the grandfather quietly, "don't be so ashamed of your dad. He's a good man."

"Yeah, but he's embarrassing, Grandpa. Can't you see that?"

"He doesn't do it on purpose. Part of your embarrassment comes with your age. Twelve-year-olds are always ashamed of their parents. What if I gave you a big sloppy hug right here?" The boy cringed in disgust, as if someone told him the roast beef he was chewing was actually cow's tongue.

Laughing, Grandpa said, "Your dad's feelings erupt when he sees you. Ever since he and your mom separated, he misses you terribly. He loves you, so make his feelings a top priority. Okay? Plus, no one is immune; we all have embarrassing moments, even parents with their kids. One day your grandson may be embarrassed to be seen with you. I know; hard to believe since you're so cool, but it could happen. When your dad comes out, tell him the pants look sharp on him. It will make his day."

A moment later the father emerged from the fitting room, without the new pants. "Dad, where are your pants?" said the boy. "They looked sharp on you."

"Hanging in the dressing room," he said with a smile. "That mirror tells no lies. I'll come back in a month or two, give them another try. But thanks for the compliment; that means a lot to me. Where's Grandpa?"

"You know him, checking out the Armani ties," said the boy. "He told us to meet him over there."

"My dad, he's always in style," said the father. "Come on, let's go."

Standing behind a rack of discounted shirts I watched them amble away, leaving me with a tender heart and my thoughts prying into the past, searching for times when I'd felt embarrassed or ashamed to be seen with someone who cared about me. I couldn't help but wonder why many of us risk hurting the feelings of the people who love us most just so we can appear more favorable in the minds of people we'll probably never see again.

I came there that night hoping to get a pair of pants and couldn't find a size that fit. Instead I walked out with something priceless that didn't cost me a dime. That's the thing about wisdom: Someone always pays a price to acquire it, and there are plenty of people eager to give theirs away for free; all we have to do is listen. Unlike a pair of pants that we can't squeeze into, when it comes to knowledge and the wisdom of understanding others, it's always a perfect fit.

Inspired by three strangers at Macy's

CHAPTER THIRTEEN

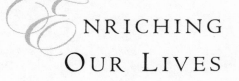

ENRICHING
OUR LIVES

*Revealing unlikely avenues that lead
to emotional highs and the best
things life has to offer*

Opportunities for happiness are always within our
grasp. When speaking with people who consciously
pursue ways to improve their lives, it becomes obvious
through their words and actions that they seize every
chance to invigorate their friendships, offer a kind
word to a stranger, and dedicate their time to what
they truly love. This results in a level of joy that few
people ever behold. They don't just look forward to a
special occasion that is far away; they live in the

moment, making sure each day is uniquely memorable. Through their wisdom and the delightful parables they share, each of us can learn to do the same.

You've Got Twenty-Four Hours . . . What Would You Do?

*H*ow would you spend your time if you had only twenty-four hours left to live? That was the question Judy McFarland, a fourth-grade teacher, delicately posed to her class of twenty-eight students. It was a lesson about values, and helping each student recognize what is most important in his or her young life.

As the students busily worked on their assignment, Judy sat grading papers behind her large pinewood desk at the head of the class. Every few minutes she looked up, her eyes sweeping over the innocent little souls that filled her classroom. Most of the students were busy scribbling down ideas in their notebooks; a few were looking up, their eyes rolled back, intently thinking about what to write next. That evening, while relaxing on the lounge chair in her backyard, Judy read the assignments, and was pleasantly surprised by what she discovered.

"My family is the most important thing in my life," stated Joshua, a boy with curly blond hair from the third row. "Maybe that's because I'm only nine and don't know anybody else yet, but even if I did I think my family would still be the most important. So if I only had one more day I would spend it with my family on a picnic where we would eat pizza and ice cream—my two favorite foods. The really special thing I would do is spend a little time with each person in my family and tell them why I love them. I fight with my brother and sister sometimes, but that would not be a day for fighting. It would be a day for love. I would spend time alone with my mommy and daddy, and my grandmas and grandpas, too, because they love me very much, and I love them."

Sammy, the class clown and occupant of the first seat in the second row—where he could be watched closely—said: "I would spend the morning doing what I do every Saturday with my big sister, Linda. We go to the children's hospital near our house and visit the boys and girls who live there. I bring comic books and a different movie each week, but on this Saturday I would bring all my movies and books and give them away because I wouldn't need them anymore. I would spend the rest of the day with my family and my pet hamster, Joey."

Sabrina, a bashful little girl with brown pigtails tied with pink ribbons who sat in the back of the fifth row, said: "I would share my day with the two people who are most nice to me. First, my grandma, who I live with and who treats me better than anyone else in the whole wide world. She hugs me and loves me and makes me feel warm and safe. The other person I would share time with that day is you, Ms. McFarland. You spend time helping me to learn more and become a smarter person. You are helping me build a future for myself and I would want to thank you because you're doing such a great job. I know because my last report card had a gold star on top."

Judy sat there, her eyes prickling with tears as she thought of the kids in her class. She pictured the setting—her standing at the front of the room, a rainbow of construction-paper cutouts stapled to the walls, a piece of white chalk in her right hand, and each student sitting attentively in his or her seat. *Sometimes I wonder about the effect I'm having on my students,* she thought to herself. After reading those assignments she smiled, knowing that her influence was positive and profound. *I've got them for seven hours a day,* she thought. *I am a teacher, and I see the strength of the future sitting in my classroom. I am a teacher, and am helping to shape the world.*

And then Judy asked herself, *What would I do with my last twenty-four hours?* She beamed as the answer quickly revealed itself. As it turns out, she would spend a portion of that day doing exactly what she loves. Teaching.

Inspired by KIM HUNTINGTON

Children Laughing

*M*y wife, Beverly, and I loved to roam through the park near our home. We'd sit hushed on a bench near the edge of the pond and listen to the water slap gently against the rocks. We'd watch the ducks and the funny way their feet looked as they paddled through the water. Of course, we'd bring some crusty old Italian bread with us. Usually it was left over from the Sunday dinner we'd had with our family the night before. The ducks would jostle for it as soon as it hit the surface of the water. Those were wonderful times.

Beverly died a few years ago, and Tommy, my son-in-law, got a job offer that was too good to pass up, in a town more than one thousand miles away. In no time I was the only one left at the Sunday family dinner, and the Monday-morning strolls with Beverly had become a memory. Life got very lonely, very quickly.

I still meandered through the park each Monday morning and, although I was alone, I could feel Beverly's spirit near me. Plus, it was the one time each week that I could hear that glorious sound of youth.

An orphanage was nearby, and each morning around ten o'clock the kids were let out to play. They thundered out the doorway and, for the next twenty minutes, ran impulsively, played games, and had a marvelous time. In a world filled with anger, prejudice, and crime, hearing the virtuous laughter of those children was something I anticipated all week. Then I asked myself, *Why wait all week?* So I started going most mornings to feed the ducks and listen to the children play.

After a while the children and the staff got used to me being there. When the ball accidentally flew over the fence, I'd hustle over and toss it back to their side. A chorus of "Thanks, mister" sounded, and I felt like a part of their game.

Then winter came, and the pond and playground became an arctic wasteland. I still took the occasional stroll through the park, but it wasn't the same. I didn't have Italian bread with me and I didn't have to retrieve a ball that was kicked too far. It was lifeless, and I longed for the springtime.

Finally it came—the sun burst forth, the flowers bloomed, and the pond and playground experienced a reawakening. The ducks and the children were back, and so was I. The kids remembered me and so did the faculty. One of the teachers, Ms. Santorini, asked if I'd like to volunteer at the orphanage and keep an eye on the children during recess and lunch period. "I would be delighted," I said, with unabashed enthusiasm.

As we experience life, some doors close forever, remaining memories of our past, and new doors open, ready to provide us with fresh adventures that hopefully enrich our lives even further. And so a new chapter in my life began. After fifty years of being away, I stepped back into a classroom. The aroma of crayons and Play-Doh, the construction-paper cutouts adorning the walls, and the chalk dust rekindled the wonderful memories of my childhood.

As the children returned from playing outside I heard a few

of them whisper, "That's the man who gets our ball back for us. What's he doing here?"

"Class, we have a new volunteer who's going to join you during playtime," said Ms. Santorini. "I'm sure many of you have seen him when you play outside."

"Do you like kickball?" a little boy blurted out.

"Sure," I said with a smile. "I love kickball."

"Are you going to be here every day?" asked another boy.

"As long as that's okay with Ms. Santorini," I said, smiling.

"What do we call you?" asked another child.

One little girl with blond pigtails tied in frilly pink bows shouted out, "Can we call you Grandpa? We don't have any grandmas or grandpas."

And the kids in unison shouted, "Yeah! Can we, can we?"

My heart thumped in my chest as a surge of emotions swept through my body and my eyes bubbled with tears. I said, "Please. That would be perfect."

And suddenly a new stage of my life revealed itself. Along with being a grandpa to my daughter's children, I became a surrogate grandpa to more than thirty kids at the Lakeside Orphanage.

Inspired by DOMINIC TOWNSEND

The Wishbone

My grandma Rachel and I had just enjoyed a delicious lemon-herb chicken dinner complete with fat-free potato salad and a couple of diet cream sodas. I couldn't eat another bite, but Rachel had a hearty appetite and picked a few pieces of white meat off the bones.

Laughing on the couch next to her, I smiled when she swiveled toward me holding a wishbone in her hands. I reached up and grabbed my side. A second later, *snap!* and we both hastily looked to see who got the wish.

"Oh no," Rachel said, staring at her piece with the bony lump on top and then over at mine, a frail twig. "I didn't make a wish because I was hoping you would get it."

"Rachel," I said, "I didn't make a wish either because I wanted you to get it." We stared at each other, basking in the sentiment of the moment, each holding the greasy bones in our hands. Then Rachel hugged me, her eyes moist with tears.

"I guess that means we both want the best for each other," she said with a tender smile.

"It sure does, Rachel," I replied, and with the snapping of that one wishbone, both our wishes came true.

Inspired by IRINA USHAKOVA

Odd Moments

*S*tumbling into the house, I looked ragged and tired, and felt even worse. After kicking off my shoes, I groped for the remote control and found it stuffed deep in the cushions of the couch along with some spare change and stale popcorn. Clicking the power button, I drifted off into a mindless television trance.

My afternoon stupor was cut short, however, when my grandfather Jimmy shuffled in wearing a dapper white tennis outfit and acting more enthusiastic than when he pops a few Viagra and sneaks off with my grandmother. I had accidentally found the bottle of pills a few weeks earlier in the cushions of the couch while looking for the TV remote.

"Dennis, what's the matter with you?" he exclaimed.

"I'm just killing some time before my afternoon classes," I said, defending my laziness.

"Come on, you're young. Where's your energy?"

"I'm on empty and just want to chill for a few minutes before it's time to go."

I couldn't shake him that easily. "Look at me," he said. "There's something important I want you to understand. Do you know how many minutes people waste each day while they're waiting for something—the bus, a taxi, a phone call, a ride, their next class?"

Waiting for the Viagra to kick in, I wanted to say, but I refrained. I heard it works pretty fast, anyway.

"If you tallied up all those minutes, there are probably four or five hours a week you could put to good use," he said. "And I'm only talking about the time you spend waiting around or just 'chilling,' as you put it.

"I'll make you a deal. Give me whatever time you have before your next class and I bet you'll be convinced that killing time is hazardous to the health of your future. What do you say?"

"What are we betting?" I said jokingly.

"Okay, wise guy," he said. "Fifty bucks. And since you're a poverty-stricken college student I'll let you pay me in installments, ten dollars a week."

"Okay, Grandpa," I said. "You're on."

"I'm going to tell you a story about a man who lived more than a century ago. His name was Elihu Burritt. Mr. Burritt learned to speak over a dozen languages using only a thirst for knowledge and the spare moments scattered throughout his day. People proclaimed him a genius, but he shunned the label, saying his success was attributed to carefully employing his 'odd moments.' Time that most of us use to catch a few minutes of television.

"Elihu Burritt was a blacksmith—certainly not a member of society's upper crust—but he applied his time wisely. He said, 'All I have accomplished or hope to accomplish is by plodding, persistence, and perseverance. The same way ants build up their hill—one particle at a time. If I was blessed with any ambition it was to prove that people could learn a great deal about the world and master different subjects simply by using the odd moments they come across each day. Sewage dumps often repulse people but if each of us could see the amount of time we waste piled up into a giant heap, we'd certainly change our ways.'

"Take a tip from Mr. Burritt: Killing time is a horrible waste. Choose a pursuit, something you would like to master, and learn it in your odd moments. Within a year you will have conquered that subject and your friends will declare you brilliant. You can share the same wisdom with them that I shared with you today. Don't say anything. Time will tell if I've convinced you, but I suspect you'll owe me fifty bucks."

Grandpa slapped me gently on the knee and, with a spring in his step, trotted out for a game of tennis. I sat in quiet contemplation. I hadn't expected anything he said to affect me, but I was intrigued. What skills could I possess six months from now if I put my time to better use? I certainly wouldn't remember catching fifteen minutes of TV reruns. So I grabbed the remote control and clicked the power button. As the screen faded to black, I thought to myself, *I've seen that episode anyway.*

It's been a while since my grandfather shared his wisdom with me and almost as long since I paid him the fifty bucks. At first I didn't think he'd accept the money, but he took it, gladly. Probably used it to buy some more Viagra. I've heeded his advice and made good use of my odd moments. That day I decided to start reading about computer science, a subject that fascinated me but which I knew little about. Since then I've become an expert in computer software and started my own firm. These days I have very few spare moments, but thanks to my grandpa and the wisdom he shared with me, my future is in creating new technologies that will help change the way the world works and plays. At fifty bucks, it was a lesson well worth the price.

Inspired by DENNIS SILVERMAN

That Could Be You

When you get stuck driving behind an old person who's moving slow, remember, someday that could be you.

When you're talking with your grandma and you have to repeat the same thing a couple of times before she understands, remember, someday that could be you.

When you're standing in line at the checkout counter and the frail old woman seems to take forever making out her check, remember, it only takes her a few seconds extra, and someday that could be you.

When you help your grandfather out of the car and you're in a rush to get inside, remember to be patient, because someday that could be you.

When you see old people using walkers to get around, don't pity them—they're determined to get where they're going. And remember, someday that could be you.

When you see a grandparent playing with grandchildren, smile and remember, someday that could be you.

When you hear that a seventy-five-year-old man went skydiving for the first time, remember that, with the right attitude, someday that could be you.

When you hear a Harley-Davidson roar up and you notice

that Grandma and Grandpa are out for a joyride, remember, someday that could be you.

When you see old people, look beyond the gray hair and wrinkles and think of the lives they've touched, the stories they can tell, and the extraordinary experiences they've had, and remember, someday that could be you.

Inspired by WALTER BURNS

The Shineologist

*T*he circular black-and-yellow tins were stacked four and five high under an old chair supported by stainless-steel legs and overlaid in cheap burgundy leather, parched and splitting from so many years in service. The brushes were blotted with black fingerprints and the bristles sullied with dark polish. A few dingy rags folded neatly into squares were stacked, ready to be used when called upon. The dull metal footrest extended beyond the seat of the chair, waiting for the next person in need of a shine to sidle up.

It was nine A.M. and I was seated at gate twelve of the Oakland International Airport. It was two days before Thanksgiving and the place was bustling. Absorbed in a Stephen King novel and hoping my flight would depart on time, I spotted a mountain of a man lumbering toward me, his upper body jolting on his long, sturdy legs. Sporting black pants, a blue shirt, and a crisp green apron, his Brillo-like hair was combed back tightly against his head with ribbons of gray coursing through it. Toting a pitted metal toolbox with sturdy silver latches, he carted the tools of his trade.

My judgments dashed to the forefront, branding him an uneducated man who must have made some bad choices in his youth, thus relegating him to a menial job shining shoes at the airport. Within ten minutes, however, I would know his name, a portion of his life story, and come to the realization that my observations couldn't have been more wrong.

My nose was submerged in my book when I spied a short potbellied gentleman who appeared to have swallowed a chubby pumpkin waddle up to the chair as the shoeshine man stacked tins of brown polish underneath. Gazing down at his shoes, his meaty hands held out like an opera singer's, the man had the look of a child who'd gotten caught misbehaving. Wondering if there was any hope for his shabby pair of boat shoes, he asked, "How much for a shine?"

The shoeshine man had his back turned but briskly swiveled around on his rubber heels and said, "Three dollars for shoes and four dollars for boots, and the main thing is your satisfaction—step on up."

His comment seized my attention, forcing me to withdraw from my book and watch as something wonderful and unexpected transpired. The shoeshine man flicked the top off a new tin of brown polish, smeared a healthy wad on his thumb, and, while humming a jolly tune and swaying his spacious hips, began kneading the polish around the tops of the man's shoes and along the sides. His hands were like girders, dwarfing his customer's feet as he made rapid, circular motions with his thumb. Using a tiny brush he buffed up the edge of the soles, paying strict attention to every detail. Within moments the weather-beaten pair of boat shoes that had seemed good only for mowing the lawn or cleaning the garage took on a rich luxurious sheen, like the luster of Godiva chocolates in an elegant display case. The shoeshine man snatched a folded rag from the pile, and briskly snapped it over the tops of the man's shoes, buffing them to a splendid gloss. He even retied the laces before giving the man a gentle slap as if to say, *Now you can walk proudly.* And with that the man climbed down from the chair, paid up, and buoyantly rambled away, staring at his shoes with amazement.

As the shoeshine man vigorously scrubbed his hands on a towel, another man approached requesting a shine. The same attention to detail was given and three minutes later, sliding off the chair, the customer replied, "You do a great job."

"It's important to take pride in your work, no matter what you do. I aim to give a ten-dollar shine for three dollars."

As his customers approached I realized that everything about the shoeshine man aimed at increasing self-confidence. His patrons climbed into a throne seated a few feet above the rest of the crowd as he worked his magic at their feet. They came feeling dissatisfied about their appearance and hoping he could enhance their presentation. His hands pulsating on their tired feet were relaxing, and his animated personality buoyed their spirits. As they climbed down from the chair and marched away, a lively bounce in their step, I realized that the shoeshine man was in the self-improvement business, and his impact was boundless. The shoes he shines travel thousands of miles by plane, foot, and car. Their owners tread through snow, ice, and rain, and the grime from the unforgiving city streets takes a toll. His job seemed almost trivial at first, until I saw the businessman getting a quick shine before hopping a flight to New York for an important meeting. And the nervous young man who may have been going to visit his girlfriend's family for the first time. The young boy who shimmied up on the chair was perhaps going to visit Grandma and Grandpa and hoping to make a grand entrance. And then I peered curiously down at my own pair of shoes—black, dull, neglected. The shoeshine man was enjoying a cup of coffee when I approached.

"Can I trouble you for a shine?"

"No trouble at all," he said, "after all, that's how I earn my living."

I ascended into the same throne where thousands of satisfied customers had sat before me, the roughness of the cracked leather skidding over my pants. Propping my feet on the footrest, the shoeshine man grabbed my ankles, which felt like twigs in his powerful hands, as he positioned my feet at the best angle for him to do his job. Flipping the top off a lid of black polish, he ran his thumb along the rim and amassed a healthy gob on his finger, which he then began massaging vigorously into the tops of my shoes.

"I guess you meet a lot of interesting people in this profession," I asked, hoping he would be interested in conversation.

"Oh, I could tell you some stories," he said, and began humming a tune.

"How long have you worked here?"

"Fifteen years. I planned on only a few weeks but . . ."

"Are you from around here?"

"Nooo . . . My port of entry into this world was eastern Arkansas. I grew up there chasing southern ladies," he said with a mischievous smile. "I'm a shineologist by trade. Got my cobbler's license over forty years ago. I've cobbled shoes in Alaska, Austria, New Jersey, and the Bronx. Been married six times, too."

"Sounds like you could write a book," I said, realizing there was more behind the man than anything I had expected.

"Oh, I've thought about it. I've got a few ideas scribbled down but they're stuffed in the drawer of an old rolltop desk I've got at home. Most of my story is still in my head. Maybe I'll write it someday, when it's more complete. I'm just getting started. I learned to read only five years ago; I was forty-nine

years old. My granddaughter was learning to read in school
and since I wanted to spend as much time with her as possible,
we studied together. These days I'm wearing out my library
card, can't get enough of books."

"Have any recommendations?"

"Sure do," he said, jerking open the clapboard drawer beneath my seat to reveal an immense volume titled *The Science of
Mind.* It was a book I'd read years earlier; one I never suspected
would be housed in the drawer of a man who earned his living
shining shoes.

"*As a Man Thinketh* by James Allen is a great book, too; you
should read it," he declared.

Shocked, I agreed that it was a fantastic book—perhaps the
most insightful book on the power of thought ever written.

"I'm just trying to be a superb human being," he said. "I
enjoy shining shoes and meeting people but I'm studying to be
a deacon. I've shined thousands of shoes over the years and
now I'd like to shine some hearts. Too many people in the
world forget what's really important. They just need a little
buff and polish, help them see things more clearly. You know,
it's our shoes that tell our story. After forty years I can look at
a pair of shoes and guess what the owner does for a living, his
attitude about the world, what kind of house he lives in, and if
he pays attention to detail. It's been said that the eyes are the
mirrors to the soul; well, I like to work from the bottom up,
and I think that shoes are, too. 'Shine on,' is what I say. Everything always looks better with a 'shine on.' "

He slapped the tops of my shoes, signifying another job
well done. I gazed down and saw a forlorn twosome of black
leathers transformed into a sparkling pair I was proud to display. "What's your name?" I asked, hopping down from the
lofty perch.

"Chester, and thank you for the hospitality, sir."

"You're welcome, Chester, it's been my pleasure," I said, aware that another gentleman was patiently waiting for a shine and perhaps a subtle boost of self-confidence. Taking a seat, I watched Chester work his magic with a few more customers before he retreated down the hallway, out of sight.

Arriving in Atlanta five hours later, my shoes were still gleaming. Marching toward the baggage claim, I passed a shoeshine man buffing up a pair of black cowboy boots. *Four dollars?* I wondered. I didn't know the price, but I'm sure when that cowboy dropped his wooden heels to the floor and his boots sparkled beneath his Wrangler jeans, he swaggered away with more confidence than he'd come with.

How clearly do we see things, circumstances, situations, other people, our world? Perhaps Chester was so wise because it's easier to see things when they shine. Maybe too many of us view the world through clouds of preconceived ideas and opinions we accept as true. As I hoisted my bag off the carousel, I couldn't help but wonder, *What would happen if we all "shined on" and saw the world sparkling before our eyes?*

P.S. Chester, since you read so much, I hope that one day this book is resting in your hands and you discover the impact you had on me. And by the way, it's been over a month and I just gazed at my shoes—and they still look great. Thanks for the shine.

Inspired by CHESTER,
last name unknown

CHAPTER FOURTEEN

Warmth and Wisdom

*Uncovering the morsels of timeless wisdom
that warm our hearts and nurture our spirits*

Foresight. It's the ability to anticipate the future so we
can make better decisions in the present. From
renowned business leaders to bashful children
beginning their first day of kindergarten, everyone is
eager to learn and none of us can advance without the
insight we receive from those who came before us.
The people who know the most about life—its
possibilities, its heartaches, and everything in
between—share their wisdom and show, by example,
how each of us can better prepare for our future.

The End of Innocence

I'm ashamed to admit it, but I was one of the kids in school people loved to hate. My friends and I were part of the "in crowd," with a warped sense of self-importance, making us feel that the normal rules of decorum did not apply. Most kids were friendly to us, preferring to stay on our good side, but I can't say the reverse was true: There were always one or two whom we targeted for insults, mocking them for our own entertainment.

One of our victims was Walter—we called him Wally. I can see him now as if I were looking right at him, an awkward model in an art class I was told to sketch. The gawky curves of his face studded with pimples, the bulbous nose with the flared nostrils, the ears that looked like lapels, and the tangled locks of hair that he always brushed away from his eyes. While everyone else nonchalantly carried one or two books, Wally lugged a stack in his hands or strapped them in a sack slung over his shoulders. He teetered when he walked, the weight of those books rocking him from side to side.

My friend Vinnie fingered Wally the first day of school, putting gum inside the combination scrambler on his locker and knocking books from his hands. We'd laugh and watch as

Wally ran up the stairs into the boy's bathroom, trying to fight back the tears.

He sat in the last seat of the last row, behind everyone else, where roaming eyes couldn't gaze upon him. He wore the same clothes to school each day: a ragged brown pair of Hush Puppy shoes, a white button-down shirt with a dingy collar, and a pair of matted brown corduroy pants with horizontal creases every few inches from waist to cuff. The pants looked as if they'd been crammed into an old steamer trunk for twenty years and finally removed when he slipped them on without throwing them in the wash.

He delivered newspapers on Wednesday afternoons and Sunday mornings. I'd see him sometimes when he stopped in front of my house. It was always an awkward moment, pretending we didn't see each other although we were aware of each other's presence. I felt like a jerk during those encounters, laughing at him during school and watching from the corner of my eye as he stuffed a newspaper into my parents' mailbox that afternoon. He tried to hurry away, pedaling furiously but never getting far. The rusty old bike he rode—with a missing rear fender and a chain that unfastened every few minutes—made a quick getaway impossible. The papers he delivered always had a few black smudges from the grease he got on his hands while looping the chain over the teeth of the bike crank.

Staring at him as he pedaled away, his upper body leaning over the handlebars, standing instead of sitting, his dirty white shirt flapping in the breeze over his bony torso, I thought about the firecrackers my friends and I sometimes hurled at him during school—those stinging words about the clothes he wore and his homely appearance. But one day Wally didn't come to school and a new kid delivered the paper that afternoon. *What happened to Walter?* I wondered. Suddenly I was using his real name and realized I didn't even know his last name. And I couldn't help but feel regret for the harsh words my friends and I had launched in his direction.

Years later, long after I'd lost touch with my pals from high school and Walter had faded from memory, I moved to a new neighborhood with my family. It was a difficult transition, especially for my son, Hank, who was beginning his sophomore year in a new high school. He came home the first day and barricaded himself in his room. Things went on like that for a while before he finally opened up, telling me about the kids at school and how they were mocking him—the new kid with the braces and ugly haircut. My stomach churned as the memories of my youth came spinning toward me. I remembered the guys I'd hung around with and Walter, the kid we taunted mercilessly. Now my son had been cast in that dreadful role.

The things other kids mocked my son about—his braces and haircut—I never even noticed. All I saw when I looked at him was a young man whom I was proud to call my son. I couldn't help but think that Walter's dad must have felt the same way, so many years ago. The teasing continued even after Hank's braces came off and I got him an expensive haircut instead of taking him to my nine-dollar barber. It seemed the taunting even got worse after that, for a little while. Hank had tried to change his image and was being punished for it. The other kids had pinned him in a cage, refusing to let him out.

I never told Hank, but I went to see his teacher, Mr. Simmons, asking if there was anything that could be done.

"Mr. Fitch," he said, "when parents come to see me they only want to know if their son or daughter is working diligently. Many of them forgot how hard it is growing up. The algebra test I'll give next week, most of the kids will forget how to do those equations by next year. What they'll remember, what will stay with them throughout their lives, is how they were treated by their classmates, and not all kids will have pleasant memories. Hank is a good student and a good boy and although I discipline the kids in my class I cannot monitor everything they say. I've been teaching for a long time and believe that the most important thing for young people to learn is to believe in themselves. That's where you come in."

"But what these kids are saying is destroying Hank's self-esteem! I can see it. He's not the same boy he used to be," I said.

"My son was the same way in high school," replied Mr. Simmons. "The other kids rode him, looking for any excuse to tease him. My wife was sick at the time and we didn't have money to buy new clothes so my son was forced to wear the same outfit to school each day. The other kids ridiculed him, tearing down his self-confidence, so at night, when he came home, I helped build him back up again. He got a job and studied hard in school. I told him he could do anything with his life and those other kids, one day they would be a distant memory. I've got a grandson now, about Hank's age, and I'm helping build walls of confidence for him, too."

"I'll do my best to build up Hank's confidence at home but he's the one who has to attend school each day and bear the brunt of those remarks." Standing there I couldn't help but think, *Why can't everyone see the goodness in him that I see? I introduce him to people I meet and state with pride, "This is my boy."* "Thank you," I said, and turned to leave.

"I understand how you feel," said Mr. Simmons. "Allow me to introduce my son to you. Here's his picture. He faced the same challenges as a boy that Hank is facing now. Feeling out of place, the target of jokes and harsh words from fellow students. But today he's a respected doctor, a proud husband and father, my best friend. Stand by your son the way I stood by mine, Mr. Fitch, and build those walls together."

I took the photo, grasping the frame in both hands. Staring hard at the picture, I saw a confident-looking man. But then, after a moment, I slowly began to see the awkward curves of his face, minus the pimples. The bulbous nose with the flared nostrils, the ears that looked like lapels, and—although not as long as they used to be—the tangled locks of hair he always brushed away from his eyes. I was staring at Walter. His name embroidered on the white jacket he was wearing said it all: WALTER PATRICK SIMMONS, M.D. I clenched my mouth shut, fighting desperately not to say, *Mr. Simmons, I was one of the boys who teased your son in high school.* Instead, I thanked Mr. Simmons for his time, thrust the photo back into his hands, and rushed out of the classroom, tripping over the leg of a desk along the way. Across the hall I shoved open the door to the boys' bathroom and cried. I cried for the way I was as a boy: Too weak to stand on my own, I hid in the crowd. I cried for Walter and Mr. Simmons and the nights he had stood talking to a locked bedroom door trying to console his son, the same way I was trying to help Hank today. And I cried because the kid I mocked as a boy, the one whom I thought wouldn't amount to anything, had suddenly become a source of inspiration for me, and the type of person that I hoped my son would one day become.

Inspired by HANK FITCH

Reflections on the Passage of Time

*T*was clamoring away at the computer keyboard when I felt your hand laid gently upon my shoulder. You leaned down and whispered in my ear, "Edward, I love you. It's great seeing you this week."

I stopped my tapping to say, "I love you, too." I let you know that it was great seeing you, and with that, you idly turned away and paced back to your room.

Looking at you, I could see that you didn't have to lean over much to whisper in my ear. You've gotten a little shorter from the last time I saw you. You always joked that you were shrinking, and now I see it's true. You're a little more hunched over than you were a few years ago. And your steps are more a slide than a walk. Maybe the arthritis in your knees prevents you from picking up your feet. But all the signs of age don't change the way I feel about you, Grandma. I just love you more each day.

If I said that you'd aged gracefully, you'd scoff at me and laugh. I'd explain that it's your attitude that has enabled you to age gracefully. You maintain the same sense of humor you had twenty years ago. I bet you've got the same need to tell jokes now at eighty that you had when you were twenty. That's why you've aged like a fine wine.

You've said that you've lived a simple life, but a good one. You fell in love with a wonderful man and were married to him for forty-two years before he died. Earlier, when we enjoyed a quiet lunch together, you told me that it wouldn't be long now. I knew what you meant, but I didn't want to hear it. I brushed off your comment and said, "Grandma, you've got another twenty years."

You giggled and said, "In twenty years you'll have to carry me around."

Our laughter was followed by a moment of silence. You gazed outside at the wind blowing through the trees and my attention was caught by the sound of the TV—it was turned to CNBC, and the talk was of the stock market. "The Dow was down fifty-three . . ."

I looked back and saw you enjoying the view. The breakneck pace of Wall Street and the stress of the traders on the floor were in stark contrast to you sitting peacefully on the sundeck. The traders anticipate what will happen by the closing bell at four o'clock, but for you the hours on the clock no longer matter—time has a more profound meaning.

You glanced back at me and said, "There are some things I would have liked to do with my life, but my life had other plans for me." I softly nodded my head, letting you know I understood. Daily commitments prevented you from pursuing a dream. I sensed a slight amount of disappointment in your voice. I guess every life has a few regrets.

As you sat there, Grandma, I learned a lot from you. Even when you weren't saying anything, I learned things just by studying your face and your eyes. I couldn't do that with someone who hadn't lived as many years as you. We don't see each other often, so I see the changes in you. I joke that you've got another twenty years, but I know it's not true. Part of me feels that I should move closer to you, but I've built a life for myself and just can't pick up and move, so I visit as often as I can.

I'm in my thirties now, Grandma, and love you more than when I was a little boy. Often it seems that as children grow up and their grandparents slow down, the relationship starts to wane. That didn't happen to us. I'm thankful, because a strong relationship with you has truly enriched my life. I love you, Grandma.

I saw you getting up and asked if there was anything I could get you. You said thank you, but no. As long as you can do things yourself you will do them. I watched you walk away— your body hunched over and your feet sliding along the floor. I laughed to myself and thought, *Luckily, she has linoleum.*

As if you knew I was watching, you turned and gave me a wink. It was your way of saying *I may not win any races, but I'll get there and I'm doing just fine.* As you cautiously turned the corner, I said to myself, *I love you, Grandma. I really do love you.*

Inspired by MARY COLUCCI

Travel Companions

*S*peech! Speech!" It was my grandfather Raymond Whistler's ninetieth birthday party. We were in the midst of a blowout bash celebrating a wonderful man and the remarkable life he had lived. The ninety candles on the cake looked like a bonfire burning, but with the enthusiastic help of his grandchildren and great-grandchildren, the flames were snuffed out and only hints of smoke emanating from the blackened wicks remained. It was an appropriate setting. The smoldering candles that had burned luminously a moment ago reminded me of my grandfather. He still had fire in his eyes but the light was slowly extinguishing.

The crowd of friends and family chanted for him to make a speech. Ray, as everyone called him, always had a few witty things to share, and everyone hoped to glean a little wisdom from this exceptional man. "Speech! Speech!" they demanded. Ray slowly raised his hand and a hush fell over everyone's lips. He smiled and began . . .

"Many hands are involved in the creation of a life. Each one of you has touched and molded me in some way, and I am grateful. I could not have reached this milestone if it weren't for the support and love I received from family and friends over the years.

"My mother and father traveled to this country when I was a baby. The hurdles they overcame on their journey have allowed me to stand here before you. They guided me as a child; as an adult I sought their advice. I keep the memory of them close to my heart. When the roads diverged before me and I was unsure of which route to travel I always asked, *What would Mom and Dad do?* After that, my decision was easy.

"You, me, each of us, we are never alone. We go through life with 'travel companions.' These are the people with whom we share time and who have helped shape us into the individuals we have become. There are also the guardian angels who look over us. I feel the presence of my mom and dad watching over me and hear their words whispering in my mind. Life is a journey, and it's one we cannot travel alone.

"Scanning the room, I see many faces that don't look like they've been around as long as mine. I guess that makes me the oldest one here. It also means I've made more mistakes than anyone in the room. Perhaps that's why people always ask me so many questions. They figure I've been around so long I've probably made every mistake there is, so based on the process of elimination I must have all the right answers.

"The fact is, I have come to a point in my life where I know that I don't know very much. At twenty, I thought I knew everything. Now, at ninety, I know that I know very little. You might want to jot that down; it's sure to be the smartest thing I'll say this evening.

"I have been blessed with a loving family and great friends and remind myself of that fact during times when I feel desperate and alone. I hope you do the same. We will all stand under the sunshine of success and the rain of failure during our tenure here on earth. Success is sweeter when we have people to share it with and failure is easier to overcome when we have people to lean on. Recognize your travel companions: They are the ones who stick with you through the seasons of life. We owe them a debt of gratitude, for without their support our lives would be stripped of the things we treasure the most—love, camaraderie, and happiness. They are the ones who make life worth living and help us become better people than we ever could be on our own."

A small fan club waited to give Ray a hug and wish him a happy birthday as he finished his speech. *He's traveled farther than the rest of us,* I thought, and the way some people look at a child, innocent and unknowing, is perhaps the way he sees most of the people in this room. Ray has already been the age that I am now, and therefore knows some of what lies ahead for me. I see my wife, Sarah, talking with a friend and I wonder what Ray thinks of when he sees us together. *Opportunities to grasp, struggles yet to face, heartache to endure.* Sarah has been my travel companion for a few years now, just a short span of time. So I smile and blow a kiss her way as I step in line, the last person waiting to speak with Ray this evening. I want to wish him a happy birthday, but I've also got a lot of questions and don't want anyone standing behind me. Ray is a travel companion of mine who has already journeyed down many of the roads I have yet to take. I know there will be plenty of things I'll have to figure out on my own, but the same way Ray reflects upon his parents for advice, in the years to come it will be his voice I hear during the times when I feel lost and alone.

Inspired by PETER WHISTLER

Midnight at the Diner

*M*y life is like a junk drawer. A bunch of odds and ends, nothing complete, nothing useful on its own. Just pieces that haven't been thrown away yet because maybe someday, with a little luck, they'll be put to good use, somehow, somewhere."

It was late, past midnight, when I got a call from my friend Kelly asking me to meet her and she shared those feelings with me. While sitting in the back booth at a Waffle House and emptying four cups of coffee, I listened. Her mother had recently passed away, her dad had been laid off from work, and the few relationships she did have were like musty clothes hanging in a closet that no longer fit. They just filled her life with clutter.

Kelly was abused as a child. Not severely enough that people had noticed, but enough to damage her on the inside, emotionally. An uncle who had moved away and lost touch with the family was the source of her emotional anguish. She saw a couple of different therapists as an adult but always stopped treatment, although she never said why, just that she wasn't getting anything out of it, so why waste the money?

I've always felt that one of the best ways to heal painful old memories is to begin creating happy new ones. That may seem obvious and perhaps even naive, but if we don't create happy memories for ourselves then what are we left with, except the ones we'd rather forget?

Pointing to a crumpled pile of blue Equal packets, a couple of stained napkins, and a bunch of empty creamer containers, she sighed, confessing, "This is what I feel like sometimes."

"Would you like another cup, honey?" the waitress asked.

"Number five, why not. Thank you, Bernice," I said, having already noticed her crooked name tag. I smiled at her, aware that she'd heard portions of our conversation over the past two hours when returning to fill my bottomless cup. She appeared to be about fifty, but working nights in a diner could age you, I thought, so she may have even been younger. She filled the mug about an inch from the top and fished a couple of creamers from the pocket in her grease-splattered brown apron. Slid them over to me with a smile. Strands of lifeless brown hair were slipping out from the bun she tied on top of her head, and her black shoes looked as if they'd made a few thousand trips from the counter to the tables. I noticed her fingers, red around the tips from years of hard work, but her nails were painted a soothing shade of pink. A sign that there was another part of Bernice peeking out from behind the dingy uniform and plates of waffles and grits she served to her customers.

"Do you like working nights?" I asked her.

"I don't mind," she said. "My daughter is a single mom. She works full time and goes to school, so working nights means I can take care of Kylie, my granddaughter, during the day." Her tired brown eyes suddenly sparkled.

Swiveling around and heading toward the counter, she abruptly turned back, placing the hot pot of coffee down on the table. "You mind if I say something?" she said. "I never went to college and I may be just a waitress on the graveyard shift but working here has taught me a lot about people. What makes them happy, sad, and how they end up feeling one way or the other. You'd be amazed at what people admit to when sitting alone in a place like this at three in the morning. I guess they feel safe. The rest of the world is asleep, a lot of them have been driving and thinking, and when they get here they're in need of some conversation so they open up, telling me their most private thoughts and feelings. I've seen people come here after a night out and they're hungry, laughing, and having a great time. At another booth some lonely guy is staring at his reflection in a spoon, watching his nose grow and shrink depending on what side of the spoon he's gazing into. One night a guy locked himself in the bathroom. Threatened suicide. The only people here were the cook and me, and he doesn't speak much English. I dialed nine-one-one but ended up talking the guy out of there before the police showed up. He was eating a waffle, on the house, when the cops arrived and carted him away.

"Honey," she said, turning to Kelly, "have you ever seen one of those bird feeders that hang off a tree and the birds fly over and peck at it when they're hungry? That's probably how you feel, like you're being used and pieces of you are missing. When we give to others and don't get anything in return, that's what happens. There are selfish people in the world and, like those birds, they'll nip away at whatever you have to give—love, money, your time—but they won't give back. You've got to cut those people off and give to the ones who appreciate you. By doing that not only will you feel complete, you'll expand. Sift through that junk drawer of yours," she said with a wink, "and throw out the stuff you don't need and put to good use the things you do. Now go home and get some sleep, you've got a big day coming up."

"What do you mean?" Kelly asked. "What big day?"

"The first day of spring is a couple of days away. That means you've got to throw out all the old stuff you don't want and buff up the things you want to keep. Strengthen the relationships in your life that are most important, like family and friends. Like this guy here."

She pointed at me.

Kelly smiled. It was the first one I'd seen in a long time and I couldn't help but chuckle to myself that it was a night waitress at the Waffle House who helped her through that storm. I knew she had other issues to face, but Bernice gave her a boost. A running start.

On the way out I held the door for a rumpled man who looked like he had been driving all night. It had begun to drizzle and a light mist silvered the parking lot. Sliding behind the wheel of my car, I watched the man take a seat at the counter while Bernice poured him a cup of coffee. At that moment she seemed much more than a waitress. In the hazy solitude of the night, with the diner's yellow neon sign flickering in the mist— a halo?—she seemed like a guardian, soothing the spirits of lonely travelers while the rest of the world slept. Starting my car, I shrugged off that thought, saying, "Come on, I'm just getting caught up in the mystery of the moment. The stark silence of the night."

Then Kelly appeared, clicking her ring on my passenger's-side window, a smile stretched across her face like a rubber band. As the window slid down she reached her hands out to me and said, "Thank you. This is the best I have felt in a long time. I know it sounds crazy but I'm going for a drive. For the first time in a long while I actually feel like being alone with my thoughts. Maybe straighten out that junk drawer in my head."

She blew me a kiss, hopped into her car, and sped off. I sat watching the rain cluster on my windshield, Bernice a blurry vision behind those cascading droplets. When I flicked the handle the wipers swiped the rain, clearing the scene. She saw me sitting in the car and raised her hand. I waved back and drove out of the parking lot recalling a phrase I've heard many times before: *God works in mysterious ways.* With a half smile I thought to myself, *Perhaps Bernice is one of His employees.*

Inspired by BERNICE,
last name unknown

Guess Who?

I always laugh when I call my grandmother. She'll pick up the phone by the third ring, but it takes a few seconds before she raises the receiver to her ear and says, "Hello."

"Hi, Gram!" I enthusiastically blurt out.

"Who is this?" she asks with a baffled tone in her voice. "Brian, is that you?"

"No, Gram, it's Eddie."

"Oh, Edwood [that's the way she pronounces my name]. I get all you boys mixed up. Brian, George, Michael, Pete, Tom . . . I don't know who's who anymore."

Gram likes to joke about how mixed up she always gets, so she tosses a few extra names into the mix. I have only two brothers, Mike and Brian. I don't know who George, Pete, and Tom are—perhaps older gentlemen in the neighborhood who have the hots for my grandmother.

Grandmas come in all shapes and sizes, but there's one thing they have in common—grandchildren. Grandmas are also notoriously loving individuals. There are three things you can count on when you stroll into Grandma's house.

One: The delight in her face as she greets you at the door. Who else is ever that happy to see you? But that's how grandmas are made.

When you need a little unconditional love, Grandma is always there for you.

Two: The furniture and decor of her home probably haven't changed since you were young. That's part of her charm. The Christmas gift you gave her when you were five still sits proudly on display, and the smell and look of the house rekindle fond memories of years past.

Three: Whether you're hungry or not, you're going to eat. Grandma always has something tucked away in the fridge for special visitors. And if she doesn't, she'll whip up a tasty dish within a few minutes.

Shannon, a little girl in the second grade, described grandmas best. The class was having a discussion about religion and the teacher asked, "Why didn't God put angels on earth?" Shannon raised her hand and said, "He did, we just call them grandmas."

Inspired by MARY COLUCCI

The Life of a Grandchild

As a Baby Grandchild

Who are these people who look at me with delight in their eyes? I'm just lying here, and they seem captivated by me. They even like changing my diaper; something must be wrong with them. Other babies seem to have these strange people hovering over them, too.

Oh! Now I get it. These giddy people who can't stop smiling are grandparents. I hear all they do is brag about their grandchildren to anyone who will listen. Well, as long as they feed me, that's fine with me. I think I'm going to like my grandparents.

As a Young Grandchild

I've known my grandparents for a few years now and I've got their purpose figured out. They're like representatives for Santa Claus. Since he only comes once a year and brings gifts for everybody, grandparents come around regularly and attend to only a few children—their grandchildren.

Mom, when are we going to Grandma and Grandpa's house? They're the best. They let me eat as much ice cream as I want. How come you're not like them? Don't you want to make me happy? You do? Well, then, why can't I have ice cream before dinner? But it says ALL NATURAL right here on the box. It's just like vegetables, only it tastes a lot better.

As a Teenage Grandchild

Can I bring a friend to Grandma and Grandpa's house? Sometimes I get bored over there. They're not as much fun as they used to be. Mom, when are we going to leave? We've been at Grandma and Grandpa's all day. Don't you know I've got more important things to do?

As a Young-Adult Grandchild

Sorry, Grandma and Grandpa, I won't be home when you come over. I've made plans with some friends to go away for the weekend. I'll see you next time. I'd like to attend the family gathering, but I've got other commitments. You understand. Sure, Mom, you know I love Grandma and Grandpa, but I'm busy. They can't expect me to just slow down.

Yes, Mom, I've been meaning to call them, but you know how things go. I've got final exams coming up. Thanks for coming to my graduation, Grandma and Grandpa. Sorry we didn't have more time to talk but I'm heading to a party with some friends. 'Bye.

As an Adult Grandchild with a Family and a Career

I know Grandma isn't doing well, but what can I say? I'm twelve hundred miles away and busy with work, not to mention the kids. I'll give her a call.

How are you feeling, Grandma? I know it's been tough since Grandpa passed away. I hope to see you soon.

No, I can't get away this weekend. The kids have Little League and I've got a dinner party on Saturday. I'm sure you'll be out of the hospital and home soon, Grandma.

I have to reschedule the meeting for next week. My grandmother just passed away and I've got to attend the wake and funeral.

As a Retired Grandchild

It feels great to have the pressures of work behind me. Now I can spend time with my grandchildren. Hello, son, I was hoping you'd like to bring my grandkids over for the weekend. We can have a barbecue. Oh, you're busy with work and the kids have swimming practice . . . well, maybe in a couple of weeks when your schedules clear, okay?

It's good to see you, son. Where are my grandchildren? Didn't they come with you? Oh, they wanted to go over a friend's house instead? Do I understand?

Yes, for the first time I do.

Inspired by LEONARD GIBNEY

ALSO AVAILABLE FROM WARNER BOOKS

THE GRANDPARENTS' TREASURE CHEST
A Journal of Memories to Share with Your Grandchildren

The times we spend with our grandchildren are among the most precious of our lives. So are the memories we share. This unique, beautifully designed journal gives grandparents a special way to celebrate the lives they've shared with their grandchildren in their own words. And as grandparents record their grandchildren's achievements and family stories, they will pass on important lessons and create a priceless gift of love that can be treasured for generations.

A PARTING GIFT
by Ben Erickson

When his eldest son was about to graduate from high school, Ben Erickson, an award-winning furniture maker, decided that he wanted to give him something unique, something that would last him the rest of his life. And so he wrote his son a story. This is a powerful, poignant novel of a troubled teenager who is drawn into the world of a reclusive widower and comes to realize that his future is one of new wonders and endless possibilities. A moving tale of love and loss, friendship and wisdom, *A Parting Gift* is for everyone who has ever pondered the mystery of life.

"A touching story in the tradition of *Tuesdays with Morrie*."
—*Birmingham News*

more . . .

WHAT OUR CHILDREN TEACH US
Lessons in Joy, Love, and Awareness
by Piero Ferrucci

Children can turn our lives upside down and try our patience. But they also have the power to teach us the greatest lessons we'll ever learn. Through sometimes hilarious, often moving, and always insightful anecdotes, Piero Ferrucci eloquently shows how each moment of parenting holds hidden surprises and opportunities for change. With their honest hearts and open minds, children can help us to reconnect with our own innocence and lead us to a place where we are more in touch with our true essence . . . and the many blessings in our lives.